D1294510

Sapphistries

Sapphistries

A Global History of Love between Women

Leila J. Rupp

NEW YORK UNIVERSITY PRESS

New York and London

ITHACA COLLEGE LIBRARY

WITHDRAWN

HQ
75.5
.R87
2009

4/94831
$25.46

NEW YORK UNIVERSITY PRESS
New York and London
www.nyupress.org

© 2009 by New York University
All rights reserved

Library of Congress Cataloging-in-Publication Data

Rupp, Leila J., 1950–
Sapphistries : a global history of love between women / Leila J. Rupp.
p. cm. —
(Intersections: transdisciplinary perspectives on genders and sexualities)
Includes bibliographical references and index.
ISBN-13: 978–0–8147–7592–9 (cl : alk. paper)
ISBN-10: 0–8147–7592–6 (cl : alk. paper)
1. Lesbianism—History. 2. Lesbians—History. I. Title.
HQ75.5.R87   2009
306.76'6309—dc22   2009024580

New York University Press books are printed on acid-free paper,
and their binding materials are chosen for strength and durability.
We strive to use environmentally responsible suppliers and materials
to the greatest extent possible in publishing our books.

Manufactured in the United States of America

10 9 8 7 6 5 4 3 2 1

To Verta, again

Contents

Preface

WHEN I HAVE told people, over the past couple of years, that I was writing a short, accessible, synthetic global history of love between women from the beginning of time to the present, they often laughed or rolled their eyes. I understand why—it is an insanely ambitious project. So I am especially grateful for the confidence of Michael Kimmel and Suzanna Walters, editors of the Intersections series, and Ilene Kalish, executive editor at New York University Press, that I could pull this off.

The idea for this book emerged from a course called "Sapphistries" that I developed at the University of California, Santa Barbara—or maybe it was the other way around. Having returned to my original academic home in women's studies, I decided to shift my focus from a comparative angle on male and female same-sex sexuality to a concentration on desire, love, and sex between women. It has been an adventure, and I am grateful for the students in my "Sapphistries" classes for their enthusiasm for the subject, their perceptive questions, and helping me to think about things in new ways. I am also thankful for the work of my colleagues in the Department of Feminist Studies—Jacqueline Bobo, Eileen Boris, Grace Chang, Barbara Herr Harthorn, Ellie Hernández, Mireille Miller-Young, Laury Oaks, and Barbara Tomlinson—all of whom, in vastly different ways, have opened my eyes to new ways of looking at teaching and scholarship. My chair and friend, Eileen Boris, has been particularly supportive. And I could not have gone on without the wonderful work of our Feminist Studies staff, Lou Anne Lockwood, Christina Toy, and Blanca Nuila. Lou Anne, in particular, has shared lunches, coffees, heart-to-heart talks, and dog-sitting for Phoebe.

Of course this book could not have been written without the amazing scholarship—far more than I thought when I set out to write—of so many fine scholars. The notes and references track their contributions, but I want to name a few here whose work I have used especially extensively: Evelyn Blackwood, Bernadette Brooten, Rudolf Dekker and Lotte van de Pol, Lillian Faderman, Marti Lybeck, Jacqueline Murray, Gregory

Pflugfelder, Tze-lan Sang, Valerie Traub, Ruth Vanita, Martha Vicinus, and Saskia Wieringa. Thank you for making this book possible. It goes without saying that the mistakes—and how could there not be many in a project of this scope—are mine alone.

I would also like to thank a number of scholars, students, and friends who suggested books or articles, sent me unpublished or newly published work, answered frantic queries, or just provided reassurance that I was not entirely overlooking something important. These include Ken Andrien, April Bible, Kerstin Bronner, Elise Chenier, Laura Doan, Cameron Duder, Stephanie Gilmore, Carrie Hamilton, Danielle Hidalgo, Marti Lybeck, Mark McLelland, José Ramos-Rebollo, Erika Rappaport, Jens Rydström, Birgitte Søland, Zeb Tortorici, Valerie Traub, and Martha Vicinus. Lachelle Hannickel and Suzanne Braswell translated the caption for figure 14, for which I am very grateful.

In the midst of writing this book, I was heartened by the reception of my talk at the Women's History Workshop at Ohio State, my former home. The enthusiasm and support of my former colleagues—and not only my dear friends and women's historians Susan Hartmann and Birgitte Søland—meant so much. I doubt that I ever would have attempted to write a global history without having been part of the world history group at Ohio State, so I thank them as well. I am also grateful for the comments of Tom Laqueur and audience members at the session where I talked about this project at the American Historical Association conference in 2009. Having finished the book, I had the pleasure of speaking at the University of Connecticut, where I benefited from the questions and comments of colleagues from history and sociology.

At New York University Press, Aiden Amos provided valuable advice on the illustrations. Despina Papazoglou Gimbel managed the production process efficiently, and Andrew Katz did a careful job of copyediting. My friend Kate Weigand, a scholar in her own right, produced a beautiful index.

I could not have completed this project without the financial support of the UC Santa Barbara Academic Senate and the Division of Social Sciences and the incredible resources of the University of California libraries, especially the interlibrary loan department. Melvin Oliver, Dean of Social Sciences, provided research support, a job as Associate Dean to occupy my free time, and the kind of encouragement, friendship, and laughter that one does not always associate with the title "dean." Lisa Leitz has been the most astonishingly creative research assistant, working magic on a regular basis. I don't know how she does it, but I could not have survived without her help.

I am also indebted to Lisa Duggan and Arlene Stein (the formerly anonymous reviewers of the book proposal), Ruth Vanita and a still-anonymous reviewer of the manuscript, and other anonymous readers who provided both criticism and support in the process of my final career review in the endlessly bureaucratic University of California system. John D'Emilio, Estelle Freedman, Joanne Meyerowitz, and Joan W. Scott read parts of the manuscript and wrote letters in support of a fellowship proposal, for which I am very grateful, even though I didn't get the fellowship. Later, Joanne, Birgitte Søland, and Verta Taylor read the whole thing solely out of friendship (and more, in Verta's case). All the comments and suggestions from these generous colleagues proved challenging and helped greatly to improve the manuscript. There were many moments when I wondered why I had taken on such a foolhardy project, and Birgitte especially buoyed me when I needed it most.

Phoebe was with me through almost every minute of work on this book. She didn't help at all, but her devotion goes a long way.

And then there is Verta, to whom I dedicate this book. For thirty years, she has worked and played with me, inspired me with her brilliance, and loved me through good times and bad. When we first met, we used to joke about being sure to leave behind evidence of our relationship so no future historian could say we were just good friends. In a way, that is what set me on the path of writing *Sapphistries*. Verta, I can't imagine my life without you.

1

Introduction

Sap·phis·tries \'saf-əs-trēs\ *n* : Histories and stories of female same-sex desire, love, and sexuality, after Sappho, sixth century BCE poet of Lesbos.

THE LESBIAN POET Sappho, whatever her erotic history, bequeathed both her name and her place of residence to the phenomenon of desire, love, and sex between women. Her iconic image as a lover of women has transcended the boundaries of history and geography, bestowing on women who desire women the labels *Sapphic* and *lesbian*. Because the term *Sapphic* has a longer and more widespread history than *lesbian*, I have named this book *Sapphistries*, an invented word, although not an entirely original one, to embrace all the diverse manifestations of women and "social males" with women's bodies who desired, loved, made love to, formed relationships with, and married other women.[1] *Sapphism* is a name that stuck through the centuries, and not only in the European tradition. An eleventh-century poet in Muslim Spain earned the moniker "the Arab Sappho."[2] A Japanese loan word, *saffuo*, coined in the 1900s, refers to female same-sex sexuality.[3] A Chinese critic in 1925 translated one of Sappho's fragments into Chinese, pointing out that women's same-sex love is called "sapphism."[4] A conference in Melbourne, Australia, in 1995, organized by lesbians from minority ethnic and racial backgrounds, took the title "Sappho Was a Wog Grrrl."[5] How impossible it is to disassociate Sappho from her legacy is suggested by the fact that, in 2008, a Greek court dismissed the request of three residents of Lesbos for a ban on the use of the word *lesbian* for anyone other than inhabitants of the Aegean isle.[6]

The only term that has a broader historical reach, if not the same poetics, is *tribadism*, from the Greek and Latin words meaning "to rub," in its numerous linguistic variations. The Arabic terms *sahq, sihâq,* and *musâhaqa* are all derived from the verbal root *s-h-q*, meaning "to pound, bruise, efface, or render something soft," sometimes translated as "rubbing."[7] In Hebrew, the term for women who have sex with other women is *měsallelet*, meaning "to rub."[8] Female same-sex behavior in Chinese is called *mojingzi*, "rubbing mirrors" or "mirror-grinding."[9] The word in Swahili for a lesbian is *msagaji*, which means "a grinder."[10] In Urdu and related languages, the terms for female same-sex sexual activity—*Chapat, Chapti*, and *chapatbazi*—are all related to flatness or flattening.[11] *Tortilleras* is the term used to refer to lesbians in Cuba and elsewhere in Latin America.[12] A French dictionary from 1690 defined a *tribade* as "a shameless woman enamored of one of her own sex" and finished off the definition with the simple statement "Sappho was a tribade."[13] An English pamphlet from 1734 blamed Sappho for introducing "a new Sort of Sin, call'd the *Flats*."[14] So I suppose my title might have more global reach if it were called "Tribadie" or "Rubbing through Time," but both lack, in my opinion, the elegance of "Sapphistries." In the interest of elegance, too, my subtitle (and sometimes text) intends "love" to cover desire and sex as well, and "women" to include those with female bodies who might not have identified as women.

It is, I must admit, an audacious undertaking to tackle desire, love, and sexuality across such vast expanses of time and space. On the one hand, the enormous variety of ways that women have come together in societies ranging from ancient China, India, and the Mediterranean world to contemporary Thailand, Mexico, and South Africa can only support the social constructionist perspective on sexuality that insists on the impact of societal structures and concepts in shaping the ways that people experience desire, have sex, form relationships, and think about themselves. On the other hand, the very act of putting between two covers such a wide range of ways that women have loved one another raises the danger that we think of them all in one large category.

Some scholars, for political reasons, insist on that category being called *lesbian*, even if that was not a term or concept embraced by a particular society.[15] Adrienne Rich in 1981 famously introduced the concepts of *lesbian existence* and the *lesbian continuum* to embrace a wide range of woman-bonding behaviors characterized primarily by resistance to male domination.[16] Since then, debates have raged on about what qualifies a woman as a lesbian throughout history and across cultures.[17] Taking off from Rich and following her emphasis on autonomy from male control, medieval historian Judith Bennett argues for the term *lesbian-like*, which she uses to describe a range of medieval European women. She tells, for example, of two different convents that housed women who fit her concept. One was founded by a widow in Ferrara who put together her dowry with contributions from other women to buy property and establish a community that she managed to keep out from under male Church authority for almost twenty years. She and her companions lived together, devoting themselves to religion and good works, and when she died, she named another woman her heir, with the obligation to maintain the community in the same form. With the language of piety, she created a life independent of the control of men, whether husbands or Church authorities. The other convent was in Monpellier and housed former prostitutes who were old, repentant, or moving away from prostitution to marriage. They were not cloistered and had only minor religious duties. In neither case is there any evidence of same-sex desire or sexual behavior, but that is precisely Bennett's point: that, in the first case, the desire for independence from men is "lesbian-like" and that, in the second, the long historical connection between prostitution and same-sex love is suggestive.[18]

I understand the appeal both of boldly claiming visibility where it barely exists by embracing the term *lesbian* and of keeping the association while recognizing the differences between contemporary lesbians and what Bennett would call "lesbian-like" women of the past. But I have chosen a different path. Too broad use of the term *lesbian*, I think, downplays the differences among women, especially when the concept and identity of lesbian is available and women choose not to embrace it, as occurs in many parts of the world today where a transnationally available lesbian identity is known but women who desire women have different ways to think about themselves. So I choose to use a term that does not apply to women themselves but to their histories and stories. And, unlike Bennett, I am not willing to consider women who sought independence from men and women who sought the privileges of men, if they did not also give some hint of desire or love for women, as part of sapphistries.

The question of whether sex matters in determining who is part of "lesbian" or "lesbian-like" history has been much debated. This issue came to the fore particularly in the context of romantic friendships, the passionate and socially acceptable ties between women in the nineteenth century that first came to attention in Carroll Smith-Rosenberg's classic article "The Female World of Love and Ritual."[19] Then Lillian Faderman, in her pioneering book *Surpassing the Love of Men*, connected romantic friendship to contemporary lesbian feminism while arguing that most romantic friends "probably did not have sexual relationships."[20] Whether or not romantic friends—or other women who expressed passionate love for each other—engaged in sexual acts is a question that increasingly aroused fierce debate in the context of the feminist "sex wars," a struggle born in the 1980s over emphasizing the pleasure as opposed to the danger of sexuality. The most recent studies of romantic friendship, by Martha Vicinus and Sharon Marcus, leave no doubt about the erotic and sexual aspects of at least some of these relationships.[21] In the ongoing debate about how much sex matters, I come down firmly on the side of the centrality of sexual desire, erotic love, and/or sexual behavior in thinking about which women in the past and present are part of this story.

But of course the difficult question is, what counts as desire, love, and sex? Are expressions that sound to our modern ears like desire actually that? Can we tell erotic love from nonerotic friendship? Is genital activity necessary to a sexual act? Is genital activity always a sexual act? These latter questions are especially difficult. Having read about the caressing of breasts between two African American women in the mid-nineteenth century and European and U.S. romantic friends kissing and hugging and lying with heads in laps, my students in one class, having been asked what counts as sex, thought they knew where to draw the line: what they called "tongue action" in kissing and "below the waist action" in caressing counts as sex; anything else does not. But such a definition, though clearly making sense to twenty-first-century U.S. college students, cannot stand up to the girls and women in Lesotho who French kiss, rub one another's labias to stretch and beautify them, and even engage in cunnilingus but who insist that it is not sexual because there is no penis. Nor can it stand up to !Kung San girls, who likewise engage in sexual play but are not sure what it means, asking, "Can two vaginas screw?"[22] So what looks very much like sexual activity to us may not be understood that way, and what may not seem to cross whatever line we imagine divides foreplay from sex may in fact very much count as sex to the women involved. And all the same uncertainty applies to what counts as desire and what counts as erotic love.

Then there is the problem of evidence. Given the long history at play here and the extremely limited literacy of women, testimony from the mouths or pens of women is very rare until modern times. So most of the evidence we have through the centuries comes from men: their prohibitions, their reports, their literature, their art, their imaginings, their pornography, their court cases. Here and there the views of women themselves can be gleaned, and I have tried mightily to make use of the creative research of scholars who have listened and heard the voices of women, even if we need to acknowledge that the context and filtering of such voices mean that they are in reality representations rather than some fundamental truth about experience. We also have to assume that the representations, both textual and visual, created by men tell us something about the possibilities of love and sex between women in different societies.

But I recognize that any decision about where to draw the lines—who is in and who is out in a history of love between women—is tricky. Perhaps most problematic is my inclusion of female-bodied individuals who did not or do not consider themselves women, even if they did not or do not consider themselves men. Judith Halberstam develops the concept of "perverse presentism" to suggest that "what we do not know for sure today about the relationship between masculinity and lesbianism, we cannot know for sure about historical relations between same-sex desire and female masculinities."[23] Because we often do not know what such individuals themselves thought about their gender and sexuality, and because the act of female bodies having sex together was often what the authorities saw as most important, I include them here, being careful not to assume either that they were transgendered in a contemporary sense or that they were like female-gendered women who desired or had sex with other female-gendered women.

Although most of my sources are conventional historical ones, I am also taking liberties by using some literary texts not as historical sources but as ways to help us imagine answers to questions that cannot be addressed with existing evidence. These are texts that reflect their own time and place while portraying another. So, for example, I use Erica Jong's *Sappho's Leap: A Novel*, which reflects contemporary thinking about the fluidity of sexual identities, to engage with the historical Sappho's sexuality; a short story by Sara Maitland, "The Burning Times," to think about the possibilities of witchcraft accusations and love between women; and, in the riskiest historical move of all, Jackie Kay's *Trumpet*, a novel about a contemporary British biracial transgendered musician, to imagine what the wives of women who secretly crossed the gender line through past centuries might have thought. I am aware of the conceptual risks posed by such a strategy, but I believe that the advantages outweigh the danger of contributing to a vision of transhistorical sameness.[24] And I am inspired by Monique Wittig, who wrote in *Les Guérillères*, "Make an effort to remember. Or failing that, invent."[25] These literary texts, as imaginative interpretations, remind us that historical scholarship, too, although based on evidence, is also an act of interpretation.

Sapphistries not only brings together extremely scattered and disconnected research on a wide range of phenomena but also, I hope, contributes to ongoing discussions about the nature of sexuality across time and place. Certainly the range of ways that women have come together makes clear that how women act on their desires, what kinds of acts they engage in and with whom, what kinds of meanings they attribute to those desires and acts, how they think about the relationship between love and sexuality, whether they think of sexuality as having meaning for identities, whether they form communities with people with like desires—all of these are shaped by the societies in which they live.

At the same time, however, we must confront the persistence of certain patterns in the history of female same-sex sexuality, particularly the role of female masculinity and the eroticization of friendship. That is, we find very different societies shaping erotic relationships between women in quite similar ways. Here it is useful to remember that anthropologist Carole Vance, in a classic article on social constructionism, pointed out that recognizing ways that societies construct sexuality differently does not mean that there are never similarities.[26] Making a similar point, literary scholar Valerie Traub confronts the question of why certain ways that women loved women in the past seem so familiar despite very different social contexts. She proposes a new way of thinking about the sense of "uncanny familiarity" that strikes us so often in thinking about women's relationships with women in different times and places. To simplify a complex argument, she suggests that there are certain overarching ways that desire, sex, and love between women have been understood and enacted across time and that those understandings and definitions appear, disappear, and reappear at different points.[27] What she calls "cycles of salience" account for our sense that, for example, medieval nuns in love are like nineteenth-century romantic friends. It is Traub's hope that such a perspective will make possible "a transnational history of lesbianism" across time; it is my hope that *Sapphistries* makes a start in that direction, even though that is not the description I would use.[28]

The ways that love between women has been understood, I suggest, include the following: that a woman who desires other women is *masculine*, that her *body marks her as different from other women*, that she is *wanton*, that she is *deprived of access to men*, and that she *hates men*. These understandings emerge in different conceptions across history and cultures, as we shall see in encountering manly women, female husbands, butches, and Thai *toms*, all embodying masculinity; hermaphrodites and women with enlarged clitorises, whose bodies mark them; wanton women, including those from Lesbos, witches, prostitutes, and aristocratic tribades;

secluded women, nuns, and schoolgirls, all presumably deprived of men; and man haters such as Amazons and lesbian feminists. At some points in time, in some places, one or another conception holds sway. That is why we can make transhistorical comparisons without assuming some essentialist "lesbian" that can be found everywhere.

But these are just the ways that women who love women have been understood from the outside. What about their own conceptions, their own understandings of who they are? This is where the two persistent forms of relationships come into play: masculine-feminine attraction, in which gender difference is eroticized, and eroticized friendship, in which sameness shapes desire. As we move throughout time and around the globe, we find these two patterns appearing and reappearing.

The existing works that have tried to encompass a global history of same-sex sexuality, based mostly on the history of men, have constructed three or four basic categories of relationships: those differentiated by age, those differentiated by gender, sometimes those differentiated by class or race, and those not differentiated in any of these ways. That last category tends to be the most rare and the most modern.[29] These categories have less resonance in the history of female same-sex sexuality. Cross-generational relationships, though not entirely missing, are not as central, and the eroticization of racial/ethnic and class difference that has been identified for men has little counterpart among women. Nondifferentiated relationships seem to be much more common.

David Halperin, in his provocative book *How to Do the History of Homosexuality*, suggests that it may be, because of male dominance and female subordination, that "the history of lesbianism exists in a different relation to time . . . from the history of male homosexuality."[30] Much of the history of male same-sex sexuality is shaped by elite men's privilege to penetrate social inferiors, including boys, women, slaves, servants, and lower-class men, as long as they also fulfilled their familial responsibilities to marry and beget heirs. We need to ask, how has women's relative lack of privilege and lack of access to public space shaped an entirely different story? Likewise, the part men play in sexual acts, as inserters or what I like to call enclosers, plays a central role in how they are perceived, with those who wielded their penises privileged over those who enclosed those penises. The story for women is different: whereas masculine women who penetrated their lovers with penislike objects tended to arouse particular horror in some places, sexual role is less important, as the persistent image of mutual rubbing attests. And the emphasis on transformation when elite men could no longer penetrate any of their social inferiors without consequences for their normality and masculinity has no counterpart in the history of women. I hope to show, then, how the different trajectories of female as compared to male same-sex love and desire transform our understanding of the history of sexualities.

Another major goal of this book is to undermine a Western-dominated narrative of progress and to join the voices of scholars who have argued for a complex understanding of the ways that local and global identities interact in the contemporary world.[31] The historical sources are much more numerous for Europe and the United States and for modern history, so there is no way to provide a balanced account with regard to coverage. But I have worked hard to locate scholarship on every part of the world and, more important, to avoid a narrative of triumphal progress based on the Western tradition. This is not to deny how much the successes of lesbian, gay, bisexual, transgender, and queer movements, where they have flourished, have changed the world for the better. But a global view makes clear, for example, that emergence into public, so important in the story of same-sex sexuality in the Western world, is not everywhere significant; that desire and love between women can flourish within heterosexual social arrangements; and that the emergence of a lesbian identity—the focus of so much of the scholarship on the history of female same-sex sexuality—is a minor part of the story of sapphistries. A global view also reveals the persistent inclination to blame others—people from other countries or class or racial others within a society—for sexual desires and behaviors denounced as deviant.

Beginning with an imagined prehistory and moving around the globe, this book provides a uniquely sweeping and global view of female same-sex love and sexuality.[32] Chapter 2 deals with mythical prehistories of woman-only societies and theories of the origins of human societies, as well as creation stories and myths from diverse cultural contexts that engage with the possibilities of female same-sex love. Chapter 3 ranges across Egyptian, Chinese, Indian, Inca, and Aztec civilizations, providing context for the better-known histories of Greek and Roman cultures, including Sappho of Lesbos. Then, in chapter 4, I move across a long stretch of time, considering the traditions of the great world religions and then exploring women's relationships in sex-segregated spaces such as monasteries and polygynous households, women mystics and witches, and women caught in the act of having sex with other women. Chapter 5 turns to institutionalized cross-gender or third-gender phenomena in

Native American, Indian, and Balkan societies; "female husbands" who, as social males, married women in some African societies; and women who secretly crossed the gender line and married women in early modern European societies and later in the United States, Australia, and New Zealand. Chapter 6 explores the emergence of nascent communities: the beginnings of urban groups of women (the "roaring girls" of London, the "randy women" of Amsterdam, women in brothels and prisons), aristocratic European women accused of tribadism, marriage resistance movements in China, portrayals of love between women in Urdu poetry, and the emergence of romantic friendship among women across Europe and the United States. In chapter 7, I explore, in the context of different words applied to women who had sex with other women, the emergence of the concept of the *lesbian*, its spread from the European sexologists to China and Japan, and the complicated responses of women around the world, who sometimes acknowledged and sometimes rejected and sometimes ignored a potential new identity. Chapter 8 treats cultures and communities of women who, sometimes deliberately and sometimes not, made love between women public. Beginning with communities of schoolgirls in Europe, the United States, China, and Japan, I turn to feminist communities; the private-yet-public world of the Paris salon of Natalie Barney; the lesbian commercial establishments that emerged in New York, Paris, and Berlin in the 1920s and in other places in the 1950s; and the growth and spread of lesbian publications and organizations from the 1920s on. Chapter 9 considers the wide range of ways that women in the contemporary world have continued to love women, from finding one another in sex-segregated spaces to falling in love with co-wives to marrying one another legally to crossing the gender line to embracing masculine-feminine pairings to falling in love with their friends—in fact, every way that women in the past found to express their desire and love. The conclusion reviews this sprawling history and returns to the question of how a consideration of sapphistries revises our understanding of the global history of same-sex sexuality.

So *Sapphistries* is the story of goddesses and Amazons, Sappho and the Arab Sappho, nuns and witches, manly women and female husbands, roaring girls and aristocratic tribades, sworn sisters and sweet *doganas*, schoolgirls in love and Parisian salonnières, German girlfriends and butches and fems, mummies and babies, *toms* and *dees*, *tombois* and *mati*. But let us begin at the beginning by wondering whether sex between women might have existed in the earliest human societies.

2

In the Beginning

(40,000–1200 BCE)

HERE IS ONE imagined beginning, not of the world but of human society:

In the beginning of time, there were only women, bearers of two unbroken X chromosomes. They reproduced through parthenogenesis, a process that occurs elsewhere in the natural world, in which females give birth without contact with males. And human—that is, female—society was a wonder to behold. Then some disease or bombardment of radiation from the sun damaged one healthy X chromosome, chopping off the right lower leg and creating a mutant, man. This was the beginning of the end for a glorious lost civilization in which women were at first the only and then the superior and dominant sex. For the mutation that brought men into the world began a long process that culminated in the triumph of a men's revolution—and the beginning of recorded history. The revolution was so complete that it wiped out almost all memory of the earlier great civilization. But hints remain: myths of Atlantis and other lost worlds, the complexity of ancient languages compared to modern ones, ancient maps that depict parts of the world with inexplicable accuracy, and the earliest origin stories in which the world is created by a goddess. The peaceful, matriarchal, utopian world of the women—"the first sex"—gave way to the brutality of the mutants, as women, who chose their sexual partners, turned to meat-eating men, whose dietary habits increased both their overall body size and the heft of their organs of reproduction. Thus, the fall of woman came through the pull of a metaphorical, not literal, snake.

This is the tale spun by Elizabeth Gould Davis in a provocative—dare I say outrageous?—book first published in 1971, in the context of the resurgence of U.S. feminism.[1] It is a counternarrative to the biblical tale of Adam and Eve, offering man-created-through-a-genetic-mutation-from-woman as an alternative to woman-created-from-the-rib-of-man. Davis says nary a word about sex between women, but her tale opens up the

10

possibility of a sort of 1970s-style lesbian commune lost in the mists of time.

That possibility is taken up with gusto in another imaginative and equally provocative account of the origins of human society. In *Lesbian Origins*, lesbian feminist sociologist Susan Cavin boldly proclaims that, since we cannot ever know what the earliest society was like, her theory is as good any other foisted on us by what she calls "patriscientists" (defined in her glossary as "scientists who are apologists for patriarchy").[2] Based loosely on primate behavior, creation myths, and (in truth) wishful thinking, Cavin depicts a "gynosociety" composed of women and their children, with males after adolescence fewer in number and consigned to some unspecified place outside society proper. Sex between women is a central part of gynosociety since it fosters cooperation, says Cavin. Heterosexuality is not unknown, so women do have sex with the extrasocietal males, but it is neither exclusive nor preferred. Because of sex segregation and the predominance of women, asexuality and what Cavin calls "bisex" and "homosex" are prevalent.

What happens to this world? The patriarchal revolution that Davis envisages resulting from women's poor selection of mates comes for Cavin when the first woman relents and lets her son remain inside once he is grown and then takes him as a lover, incest taboos not being in force in this world. With that first misstep, the utopian world of gynosociety starts to come tumbling down, with men eventually taking charge of women's sexuality and reproductive abilities and creating the world that we know all too well. Cavin thus reverses the judgment associated with nineteenth-century evolutionary theories that posited woman-dominated societies and unrestricted sexual encounters at the beginning of human society and then triumphal progress toward a patriarchal social structure.[3] Her tale has echoes in the Chicana feminist reinterpretation of the Aztec myth of Coyolxauhqui, the moon goddess. Coyolxauhqui tries to kill her mother, who is pregnant with Huitzilopotchli, the war god, but he bursts from his mother's womb, dismembers his sister, and flings her head into the sky, where it becomes the moon. In the feminist telling, Coyolxauhqui is not a murderous daughter but, rather, is making a valiant attempt to save the world from war, slavery, and imperialism—from the consequences of male domination.[4]

The newest addition to the genre of alternative creation myths comes from novelist and Nobel Prize winner Doris Lessing, who tells a tale prompted, she says, by a "scientific article" arguing that "the basic and primal human stock was probably female," with males "a kind of cosmic afterthought."[5] The story is framed by the ruminations of a male historian in ancient Rome, who tells us, "In Rome now, a sect—the Christians—insist that the first female was brought forth from the body of a male. Very suspect stuff, I think. Some male invented that—the exact opposite of the truth."[6]

In Lessing's imagined world, the first humans were the Clefts, females who reproduced without males, "impregnated by a fertilizing wind, or a wave that carried fertility in its substance."[7] As in Davis's tale, there is no sex between women here. They mutilate, kill, or abandon the occasional malformed offspring, known as a Monster, born with a "clutch of protruding flesh there in front where they had smooth flesh, a neat slit, fringed with soft hair."[8] But the abandoned Squirts, as they come to be called, do not die, but are rescued by eagles and raised elsewhere. And in Lessing's tale, the Clefts and the Squirts find one another, as they seemingly are destined to do. The Squirts, who lack the knack of giving life, are "tormented by the demands of their maleness" and "driven by powerful instincts," until they find Clefts who, seeing their hunger, have sex with them (and clean their huts to boot).[9] In Lessing's telling, heterosexuality is inevitable. Eventually the Clefts can no longer reproduce without encountering the Squirts' "tubes," and the old ways die out. Again, the rest we know.

Admittedly this is all rather far-fetched, but why not imagine an alternative to heterosexual origins? Why not parthenogenesis or homosex? Since we do not know anything about sexual behavior at the beginning of human society, why should we assume that same-sex sexuality was taboo? Are there any hints that sex between women may have existed in the beginning?

The problem is, of course, that creation myths and other stories that explain the way the world is mirror the societies of their creators, just as the tales I have just described are spun within particular political contexts. So it is not surprising that most of them take a heterosexual shape, as in the Adam and Eve version, with a god or some gods and a man and a woman and eventually a child. Still, the fact that it is women who give birth to children, and that the role of men and sexual intercourse in paternity was not always understood, means that some stories give a starring role to a female figure.

Take, for example, creation stories that feature a goddess in the beginning. There are scholars who argue that originally goddesses created and ruled the world and that the emergence of god-centered religions represented a kind of heavenly male revolution mirroring what went on in the material world. Thus, feminist scholar Merlin Stone, in her 1976 book *When God Was a Woman*, unearths goddess religions of the ancient Mediterranean world and argues that the Bible represents a conspiracy to rewrite history and slander the goddess, resulting as well in the increasing societal subordination of women.[10] All that talk of honoring no other gods referred, Stone argues, to the goddess, whose primary symbol, the serpent, comes to play such a diabolical role in the biblical version of the fall of man and woman.

More dispassionate scholars agree that the stature of goddesses declined over time, perhaps as men began to conquer rather than stand in awe of the forces of nature. So what can we make of the history of goddess worship? At a time when the link between heterosexual intercourse and the birth of children was unknown, it would not be surprising for women to have been viewed as the creators of life. Mothers would also have the only evident connection to the children they bore. In such societies, both goddess worship and matrilineal descent would make sense. Whether such representations mean anything about the status of women, much less the possibilities of female same-sex sexuality, is another question altogether. Marija Gimbutas, an archaeologist who has written extensively about goddess worship, argues that the civilization of the goddess was peaceful and egalitarian—in short, the kind of paradise that both Elizabeth Gould Davis and Susan Cavin depict.[11] Needless to say, such a conclusion is controversial.[12]

Even advocates of the goddess as a victim of a patriarchal revolution most often point to her heterosexuality, for she tends to take a young male god, sometimes her son, as lover or husband, and that male figure (shades of Susan Cavin's account) takes over to become the primary deity. Still, it is worth noting that myths do not all feature a heterosexual version of creation. In a Kamia (Native American) origin tale, White Woman bears many children not conceived by a man.[13] Another Native American creation myth, from the Hopi, describes nothing but water and two goddesses, both named Huruing Wuhti, in the beginning of the world. They lived in the ocean, one in the east and one in the west, and they created land between the seas. When the sun called attention to the fact that there were no living things on the new land, they made a bird to fly over and view the land, then all sorts of animals, and finally a woman (first) and then a man.[14]

Ancient Indian texts also include stories of births unconnected to heterosexuality. A common tale, according to scholars Ruth Vanita and Saleem Kidwai, involves a deity providing some kind of magic food or drink

Figure 1. An image of the "dual feminine." Devika-puram (city of the Goddess), Tamil Nadu, fifth to seventh centuries CE. From Gita Thadani, *Sakhiyani: Lesbian Desire in Ancient and Modern India* (London: Cassell, 1996).

that results in birth. In one case, King Saudyumni drank the water intended for his wife and gave birth from his thigh. In another, two women split what was meant for one and gave birth to half a child each. Taking a different form, a story about Aruna, god of dawn, has him assuming the form of a woman to attend an all-female celebration where women danced naked. In his female body, he sleeps with two women and gives birth to a child by each.[15] In a manner reminiscent of Merlin Stone, Indian feminist scholar Gita Thadani reads the classic Sanskrit texts to argue that the existence of an older matriarchal society has been covered up, although hints can be discerned of "dual feminine" deities in the *Rig Ved* (4000–1500 BCE). (See figure 1 for an example of this kind of representation.)

In contrast to the emphasis on gods and goddesses as consorts, dual feminine deities could be lovers, mothers, or sisters. Images such as the following suggest the possibility of same-sex eroticism: "from the bosom of the mountain, desirous and content, two mares, like two bright cows as mothers licking, caressing and kissing."[16] In a Japanese tale, Ama no Uzume (the Alarming Heavenly Female) makes sunlight return to the Earth by coaxing the Sun Goddess Amaterasu out of her cave by revealing her breasts and lifting her skirt to just below her genitals.[17] What if such stories reflect the existence of fluid sexualities? What if goddess-worshipping societies facilitated women's love for other women? Can we glean any hints of such a possibility?

One imaginative tale is spun by novelist Anita Diamant, who creates from the Old Testament story of Dinah, daughter of Jacob, in the Book of Genesis, a fascinating tale of love and lust. In Diamant's novel *The Red Tent*, she seems to suggest a connection between goddess worship and indifference to men, if nothing more.[18] Jacob, who worships the god who demands that all others be put aside, takes four sisters as wives. Zilpah, who is devoted to the Queen of Heaven and sees herself as "the keeper of the mysteries of the red tent," where women gather once a month to bleed, is the only one uninterested in sex with Jacob.[19] She turns white when she learns that she is to be given to him. She puts off going to his bed and tells her niece Dinah that she considers it a duty and that she never expects to enjoy it. She bears twin sons and never sleeps with Jacob again.

The story embroiders the argument of Merlin Stone, for the women defend the old ways and "the great mother, who goes by many names, but who is in danger of being forgotten."[20] In the red tent, women not only bleed together at the time of the new moon; they also initiate girls in menstruating for the first time by opening their wombs with an image of the goddess. The wives of Jacob contrast their ritual, which ensures that a girl's first blood "goes back to the womb of Inanna, to the dust that formed the first man and the first woman," to the fate of women who worship the jealous god, who "have set aside the Opening, which is the sacred business of women, and permit men to display their daughters' bloody sheets."[21] It is only a story, of course.

Cavin sets great store in tales of all-female societies in different places around the world. There are, of course, most famous of all, the Amazons. They come down to us as a nation of women warriors, described by Aeschylus as "the warring Amazons, men-haters" who lived in the vicinity of the Black Sea in what is now Turkey.[22] What fascinated the Greeks about them was their military prowess and the fact that they lived without men, reportedly seeking out males in neighboring societies once a year in order to conceive children. If the Amazons bore sons, they either gave them to the men who fathered them or, shades of the Clefts, mutilated or killed them. Greek sources suggest that the Amazons thrived during the Bronze Age (3000–1200 BCE). Homer, in the first text to report on them, calls them "the equal of men."[23] Later texts mention a lost epic recounting the story of the Amazon queen Penthesilea fighting with Achilles, who kills her and then falls in love with (or in some versions has sex with) her corpse. Hesiod describes Hercules defeating the Amazons, and Diodorus of Sicily, writing in the first century BCE, has Hercules slaughtering almost all the Amazons and then raping their commander, Melanippe, and giving Antiope, a princess, to Theseus as a reward. Theseus took Antiope back to Athens as his concubine, and when the remnants of the Amazon nation attacked Athens to rescue her, Antiope fought against them. Diodorus also tells of an Amazon named Thalestris, who approached Alexander the Great with a proposal that they together conceive a girl child. They made love and hunted lions for thirteen days, but Thalestris died without giving birth to the superchild sure to emerge from such a union.

From the late seventh century BCE, the Amazons appear in Athenian art (for an example of a Greek statue, see figure 2), and then Herodotus, writing in the fifth century BCE, tells the most extensive tale about them. According to Herodotus, the Greeks defeated the Amazons in battle and sailed away with them as slaves. Somewhere in the Black Sea, the Amazons staged a successful revolt but, not knowing how to sail, ran the ships aground. On land once again, the Amazons found horses, tamed them, and began to fight the local population of Scythian men. The Scythians, amazed to find that their enemies were women, decided to court rather than battle them, and in this they succeeded.[24] The Amazons settled down with the Scythian men but clung to their traditions of riding, hunting, and fighting.

Later in the fifth century BCE, Pseudo-Hippocrates reported that the Amazons cauterized the right breast of girls in infancy so that they would be better archers and dislocated the joints of male children "so that the male race might not conspire against the female race."[25] The Amazons rode and fought and did not have sex until they had killed three enemies. A slightly different story comes from the pen of a writer in the late third century CE, called Justin, who has the Amazons settling near the Black Sea with their husbands, who were then killed off in battle. The women began to seek out men for the sole purpose of conceiving, murdered their sons, and burned off the right breasts of their daughters. Under their queens Marpesia and Lampedo, they conquered much of Europe and Asia.

Figure 2. Greek statue of an Amazon. From
Dietrich von Bothmer, *Amazons in Greek Art*
(Oxford: Oxford University Press, 1957).

Stories about Amazons, according to Cavin, can be found from northern Africa to eastern Europe to central Asia to India, China, and Mongo-
lia.²⁶ Diodorus of Sicily claimed that, prior to the Amazons living around
the Black Sea, there were warlike North African women who were "greatly
admired for their manly vigor."²⁷ A society of women who burned off their
breasts and remained virgins while they fought and took on male roles
lived on an island and conquered the surrounding peoples. Under their
queen, Myrina, they founded cities, including Mitylene on Lesbos. These
are the women known as the "Libyan" or "Black" Amazons. One recent
study cites a slew of reports from around the world: Ibrahim Ibn Jaqûb,
an Arab writer in the tenth century CE, reported on a city of Amazons in

central Europe; an Indian historian in the twelfth century told of an eighth-century king encountering an Amazon society; Chinese chronicles located Amazons near Tibet and on the east side of the Caspian Sea; and Marco Polo spun tales of an island of women in the Indian Ocean, between India and East Africa.[28] European explorers in the sixteenth century and beyond reported Amazons in Latin America and Africa, which suggests to Cavin that female-dominated societies survived for a long time in some places. A sixteenth-century Spanish text describes "an island called California, very close to the Earthly Paradise, inhabited by Black women without a single man among them."[29] A 1967 book tellingly titled *Our Primitive Contemporaries* describes "the far-famed Dahomean 'Amazons'" as "the shock troops of the army, the best disciplined and most redoubtable warriors."[30] The British explorer Richard Burton witnessed the women soldiers of Dahomey, who fought against the French in the colonial wars at the end of the nineteenth century.[31] The Amazon warriors were reportedly not allowed to marry or have children but had courtesans available for sexual purposes.[32]

Stories reminiscent of those about the Amazons emerge in Tamil folk tales still popular in rural India.[33] Societies of women flourish in *Alliyarasanimalai*, a woman-centered ballad about the "kingdom of Alli," the heroine of the tale. Although the story says nothing about sex between women in this all-female land, it does make clear that women were strong, able to fight, and uninterested in men. Arjuna, a prince and hero in other tales, in this story falls hopelessly in love with Alli and sets out to force her to marry him. She is, however, determined never to marry and is guarded by women warriors and surrounded by women who administer the city, advise her, and serve as priests, executioners, hunters, and friends. Even her elephants are all female. Although Arjuna uses devious and magical powers to rape, impregnate, capture, and finally marry Alli, she eventually returns to her kingdom, where she teaches the son that she bears to take revenge on his father. Sanskrit texts, too, refer to an Amazonian kingdom known as *Strirajya*, a matriarchal country where, according to the *Kamasutra*, "dildos are much employed."[34]

Note that in all these stories, stretched across centuries, the most important characteristic of the Amazons is their military prowess, which links them to masculinity, a theme we shall encounter again and again. But what about sexuality? Most of the tales emphasize the Amazons' virginity in combination with their control of their own sexuality and their refusal to stick with one man: when they want to reproduce, they seek out men and for the most part do not settle down with them. It is also worth noting that "virginity" can be assumed to refer to lack of sexual interaction with men. Fear of female-controlled and unrestrained sexuality is the not-very-sub subtext, and the conquering or taming of the Amazons reassures the men relating and absorbing the tales that all will be right in the end.

Is there evidence that Amazons, whether in history or myth, were lovers of women? The ancient sources seem to be silent on this question, despite the knowledge of such possibilities. A strange little book published in 1972 that purports to pull together all the ancient sources on the Amazons in order to create a narrative of the rise and fall of the Libyan Amazons, followed by the fuller story of the Amazons of Asia Minor, speculates about their sexual practices. If, the author asserts, they did without men most of the time, "we must confront as our sum an erotic practice rarely if ever associated with them." He goes on: "Since purity and celibacy are hardly to be credited to women so vitally conscious of their bodies, female homosexuality must be the explanation for the gratification of their impulses and for the success of their military operations."[35] He has no evidence but cannot picture successful warriors going without sex. So he imagines: "Away from combat their concern would be with the suppleness of their muscles and the shape of the legs of the companion with whom they would bed that night."[36]

Others, less focused on Amazonian appreciation of a beautiful leg, offer bits and pieces of evidence. A German author who argues, Cavin-like, that Amazon societies were the remnants of original matriarchal societies trying their best to survive in an increasingly patriarchal world refers to the existence of vulva-shaped monuments in likely Amazon locations.[37] According to Cavin, a passage from a sixteenth-century explorer who traveled down the Amazon River observed, "There are some Indian women who determined to remain chaste; these have no commerce with men in any manner, nor would they consent to it even if refusal meant death . . . ; each has a woman to serve her, to whom she says she is married and they treat each other and speak with each other as man and wife."[38] Such an account connects with the phenomenon of gender crossing that we shall encounter later in Native American and other societies and ties it to same-sex sexuality. The only other reference I have found comes from Richard Burton, who says that the Amazons in Dahomey in the nineteenth century preferred "the peculiarities of the Tenth Muse," a reference to Sappho and her assumed proclivities.[39] Why, then, have Amazons come to have such an association with female same-sex love? Is it their sexual freedom and independence from men?

For a moment, let us turn to the wonderfully imaginative portrayal of ancient Amazon society in novelist Erica Jong's *Sappho's Leap*.[40] Sappho, about whom more later, meets up with the Amazons on the island of Crete, one of the places associated with goddess worship and the prominence of women. Sappho, her loyal slave Praxinoa, and her trusted friend Aesop (of the fables) begin to explore the island, only to look up at the sound of horses' hooves to see a one-breasted girl on horseback, wearing silver chain mail. She is Penthesilea, named after the great queen, and she and her companion warriors take the three prisoner. Aesop becomes their stud—Penthesilea explains that they rescue female infants exposed on hilltops from throughout the Greek world but also capture men to give them babies and that they have ways of giving birth only to girl babies. Sounding like Elizabeth Gould Davis, or a 1970s lesbian feminist tract, Penthesilea announces that men are a different species and that the Amazons have no need for them. Praxinoa, who as a baby had herself been abandoned and taken into slavery and who loved and had sex with Sappho, is enchanted with the Amazons and chooses to stay among them.

When the Amazons discover Sappho's identity, they rejoice, for their goddess had promised that the great poet and singer would come to them. Antiope, the Amazon queen, welcomes Sappho with a feast and announces that the goddess had brought them together so that the singer from Lesbos could write a history of the Amazons that would counter all the slanders that had been told about them. Sappho is distraught, not knowing how to write on command and disgusted by the relentlessly rosy history the Amazons begin to recount to her. While she struggles to write what the queen has commanded, she finds that the young Amazons have discovered the sailors from her ship and are experiencing forbidden love and lust. When the maidens are taken prisoner by Antiope and sentenced to death, Sappho forges ahead with her epic of goodness and beauty in order to save the erring Amazon maidens.

Eventually Sappho succeeds in convincing the queen to let them all go, and, saying a sad farewell to Praxinoa and setting to sea once again, she learns from the refugee Amazons that their world was not all it seemed. In reality, the Amazons kill or abandon male infants, just as other Greek societies do away with girl babies. Sappho wonders if anywhere "peace and justice could exist between the sexes." She worries that everywhere "men dominate women or women get even by dominating men" and that "two sexes seem to be a recipe for grief and warfare." Her Amazon informant, infatuated at the moment with an Egyptian sailor, replies, "Then we should invent *more* sexes—just to confuse everyone! That will solve the problem! . . . Let's have men with breasts and women with phalli!"[41] In this way, Jong makes the story of the Amazons reverberate with contemporary queer worlds of gender and sexual fluidity. Later, when Sappho pays a visit to Hades, she encounters the Amazon queen Antiope, who accuses her of corrupting the Amazons with her ideas of justice. "Now they nurse their boys instead of throwing them to the wolves. They suckle their own doom!" she says, sounding very much like Susan Cavin. "It will come to no good. Their own sons will overthrow them!"[42]

Sappho's Leap takes the ancient tales about the Amazons as a starting point, and what Jong creates from a twenty-first-century perspective is a world in which sexuality is fluid. The Amazons are lovers of women, but the young maidens who run off with Sappho's crew also delight in men. In that sense, her depiction accords with what we know about the sensibilities of the ancient Mediterranean world. That the Amazons lived (mostly) without men evoked images of independent sexuality and female power, something that, as we shall see, did not sit well with Athenian men. Scholars have treated the Amazon stories alternatively as fact, as a reflection of the older goddess-worshipping societies, and as a psychological projection of men's need to separate from their mothers.[43] Although there is no historical evidence that the Amazons as an independent female society existed, despite graves of women buried with their weapons, the stories about them and the power of their image for women who loved women throughout the centuries tell us something important about conceptions of women and women's sexuality.

This history of Amazon tales and creation stories from around the world suggests that, notwithstanding the relative silence on the subject, female same-sex love could have existed from the beginning. Think of the possibilities of the Talmudic tale of Lilith, Adam's first wife, a figure rehabilitated by Jewish feminists.[44] A female demon of the night who poses a threat to uncircumsized male infants and men sleeping alone in houses, the figure of Lilith came into Hebrew tradition from Mesopotamia. Lilith refused to lie beneath Adam during sex, insisting that they were equals because both had been created by God from dust. Resisting Adam's attempts to overpower her, Lilith speaks the name of God and flies out of the Garden and through the air to the Red Sea, a place populated by lascivious demons. Although Lilith's promiscuity there results in the birth of demons, and she later comes back to seduce Adam, what if that was not the only sexual misconduct in which she engaged?

A less speculative possibility for the existence of female same-sex love in ancient tales can be found in Plato's telling of a myth that he attributed to Aristophanes in *The Symposium*.[45] According to Aristophanes via Plato, human beings originally had four arms, four legs, two faces, and two sets of genitals: they were like two people glued back to back. Some were male, some were female, and some were mixed, both male and female. At some point they annoyed Zeus, so he cut them in two to punish them. At first they clung to their lost halves, paying no attention to eating, and when one half died, they sought out another of the same sex as the dead half. So Zeus took pity and invented sexual intercourse to assuage their longings. As a result, men feel desire for either a lost male or a lost female half, and likewise some women are attracted to men, some to other women. Here, at last, is a tale that places love between women at the beginning.

But of course by the time Plato told this story, we are well into recorded history, and, as we shall see, the world in which he lived was well aware of love between women as well as love between men. The goddesses of Greek mythology are not traditional wives and mothers—Hera alone, the wife of Zeus, is married, and she is hardly a model of contented domesticity.[46] Artemis, the goddess worshipped by the Amazons, is a solitary hunter who shuns contact with men. She is a virgin in the Amazonian sense of owning her sexuality, for stories about her reveal her erotic attachments to the nymphs who were her companions in the forest. Kallisto, a beautiful nymph who was Artemis's favorite, caught the eye of Zeus, who knew she would not be interested in a man. So he disguised himself as Artemis, and Kallisto responded to his advances until he gave himself away and had his way with her. But that Kallisto had welcomed Artemis as a lover is telling.[47] Aphrodite, too, the goddess of love (and of Sappho), celebrates lovemaking of whatever kind, as long as it brings mutual pleasure. So we can see in Greek mythology the reflection of a society knowledgeable about and open to diverse kinds of sexual desires.

But these are all stories: is there any evidence of how women might have lived and loved before recorded history? One possibility comes from Bronze Age frescoes preserved by a volcanic eruption in 1625 BCE in a settlement called Akrotiri on an island in the Aegean Sea. Like other representations from Minoan Crete, long known for the prominence of women, the wall paintings give centrality to female figures, depicting them in different age groups marked by size and costume and hairstyle. Women are also associated in the paintings with the cultivation and use of saffron, which has important medicinal qualities, particularly for eye-sight. The markings of the eyes seem to suggest that females and the youngest boy child had clear eyesight, whereas the other male figures did not. One scholar interprets these frescoes in a highly speculative way as depicting a homosocial world in which women had high status, attended to their bodies and those of the children, and engaged in initiatory prac-tices that may have involved homoeroticism, although there is no depic-tion of anything we would call sexual.[48] It is a vision of a world in which women's connection to plants and healing and their centrality in the com-munity meant that they were valued rather than dominated, and in which their communal rituals may have involved erotic elements so common in initiations.

A final way to think about the earliest societies is to look at societies with subsistence economies, social structures based on kinship, and no formal state structure, assuming that there may be some relationship be-tween the form of such societies and attitudes about sexuality. What can we learn about love between women in kinship-structured societies? Not much, as it turns out. We know a great deal about male same-sex behavior but precious little about that of females.

Anthropologist Evelyn Blackwood argues that sexual relations between women in societies based on kinship groups are shaped by women's eco-nomic contributions and social status. Among the Azande in Africa, for example, wives controlled the produce from plots of land they received from their husbands and sometimes after fulfilling their wifely respon-sibilities formed sexual relationships with other women, often co-wives. They may even have partaken in a ritual that formed a permanent bond, with domestic and trade consequences for the community as a whole. A ritual practice known as *bagburu* marked intimate ties between married women and could be followed by lovemaking.[49] Relationships among co-wives may have existed in other polygynous African societies, including the Nupe, the Haussa, and the Nyakyusa.[50]

In other kinship-based societies, childhood and adolescent same-sex sexuality was acceptable, sometimes as part of initiation rituals. In !Kung San society in southern Africa, girls took part in sexual play with one an-other.[51] In central Australia, Aranda girl cross-cousins who would, by the customs of kinship, later become sisters-in-law had sex using an artificial penis, and even when grown they might have sex by "tickling the clitoris with the finger" and then engaging in tribadism.[52] Initiation schools for ad-olescent girls in Dahomey taught exercises to thicken the genitals, which might lead to sexual activities that did not earn reproach.[53] Where sexuality is valued, rather than repressed, sex play among children, whether heterosexual or same-sex, does not seem to be a problem.

What this scanty evidence suggests (aside from the fact that male anthropologists have tended not to be interested in or have access to women) is that there is no good reason to assume that the earliest human societies would have forbidden or even had negative ideas about sex between women.

We can never know what really happened in the beginning, but what all these stories—myths from early civilizations as well as contemporary imaginings—tell us is that thinking about sexuality at the origins of human society is profoundly shaped by the social and political context of the spinner of the tale. We shall see that goddesses and Amazons, like Sappho, thread their way through the centuries of sapphistries, suggesting how important imagined beginnings have been.

And why not imagine alternatives to what Adrienne Rich called "compulsory heterosexuality?"[54] Here is a fanciful origin tale:

In the beginning, the great goddesses gave birth to everything living, all of the flowers and trees and plants, all of the fish and birds and insects, all of the animals that swim or fly or crawl or walk. To some they gave their most precious gift, the ability to give birth to beings like themselves. To others they gave a supporting role. Each being they created had a special part to play in the world, and none was meant to rule over all others. Among all the richness of the world, they created people. Although they differed a bit from one another in color and hair texture and size, and they came with various configurations of body parts, their differences were less important than their similarities. They lived on land and breathed air, they took a long time to reproduce and become self-sufficient, and they had a great capacity for sexual pleasure, a gift the goddesses had bestowed on them. They found what they needed to eat to sustain themselves in the world that the goddesses had created, and they honored the goddesses by creating beautiful things and inventing fanciful tales and making pleasure in diverse ways with their bodies. And every time they created beauty or understanding or pleasure, of whatever kind, the goddesses smiled.

And that is where this myth will end, because we know too well what happened, even if we do not know why. Why should sex between women not have existed in the beginning? That is the question we need to ask, even if we can never find evidence that it did. For asking opens up the possibility of viewing differently what we do know about the past.

3

In Ancient Worlds

(3500 BCE–800 CE)

. . . If I meet
you suddenly, I can't

speak—my tongue is broken;
a thin flame runs under
my skin; seeing nothing,

hearing only my own ears
drumming, I drip with sweat;
trembling shakes my body

and I turn paler than
dry grass. At such times
death isn't far from me[1]

SO WROTE SAPPHO, in the sixth century BCE, to an unnamed re-
cipient whose "enticing / laughter . . . makes my own / heart beat fast."
It certainly sounds like an expression of desire for someone whose voice
is a "sweet murmur." It is without doubt, I would argue, an expression of
desire for a woman.

It is from ancient worlds—from Sappho—that women who love
women have gotten our most persistent label. Why did Sappho's legacy
have such lasting power? Why does she stand out so strikingly in our history? To attempt to answer those questions, we must turn to evidence
that has come down to us from the first civilizations that recorded their
histories. By "civilizations," I mean the earliest societies that accumulated
surplus resources, created state structures, and left some kind of written

or artistic record. These societies emerged in Mesopotamia around 3500 BCE; in Egypt and along the Indus River in northwest India by 3000 BCE; on the island of Crete, along the Huanghe or Yellow River in China, and in Mesoamerica (the Olmec civilization) in the mid-second millennium BCE. Between 1000 and 500 BCE, around the Mediterranean and in Asia, the growth of empires and innovations in religion, philosophy, and culture resulted in the rise of what we have come to call "classical civilizations." In the early civilizations and even in classical times, written records, not surprisingly, tend to be silent about sexuality in general, much less about female sexuality, much less still about female same-sex sexuality. But there is fragmentary evidence—laws, visual representations, and cultural productions, almost entirely from the minds of men—that suggests that love between women was not unknown.

The legal codes of Mesopotamia, for example, have some references to male same-sex sexuality, but they say nothing about women having sex with other women. Likewise, the Hebrew Bible does not mention female same-sex sexuality, although it does condemn male same-sex anal intercourse.[2] European missionaries in the sixteenth century reported that the Mayans allowed sex between young men.[3] In all these cases, women are nowhere to be found.

What evidence we do have of female same-sex sexuality in diverse ancient societies is fragmentary. Pottery depicting same-sex sexual acts, including between women, from the Mochica (100–800s CE) and Chimu (1100–1400s CE) civilizations that flourished before the advent of Inca rule in what is now Peru suggests at least knowledge, and perhaps acceptance, of such relations. The document known as the Florentine Codex—written in Nahuatl, the indigenous language of the Aztecs, shortly after the Spanish conquest—suggests that preconquest Aztec attitudes toward both male and female same-sex sexuality were not as harsh as those of the conquistadors. For both men and women, it is the violation of gender expectations that is noted: "She is a woman who has a foreskin, she has a penis. She is a possessor of arrows; an owner of darts . . . she has a manly body . . . she often speaks in the fashion of a man, she often plays the role of a man. She possesses facial hair." But it is not just gender transgression that marks the *patlācheh*. "She is a possessor of companions, one who pairs off with women. . . . She has sexual relations with women, she makes friends with women. She never wishes to be married."[4] The tone is one of disapproval, but there is no call for punishment.

On the other side of the globe, ancient Chinese texts referred to *tui-shih*, "eating each other," to denote oral sex between women. A writer in the second century CE, Ying Shao, commented, "When palace ladies act towards each other as man and wife, it is called *tui-shih*."[5] Women married to the same man and living in the same household had the opportunity to have sexual relationships with one another, and such bonds could in fact make for harmonious living. An ancient sex handbook described a complicated position in which a man could have sex with two women at the same time while the women could also enjoy genital contact. The term *mojingzi* ("rubbing mirrors") described the possibility of tribadism.[6] But in general, ancient Chinese literature paid little attention to same-sex sexual encounters, because what was important was the exchange of essence between men and women. Women in polygynous households having sex with one another did not really matter as long as they gave their *yin* essence to the men who kept them.[7]

We know a bit more about female same-sex love in ancient India (ca. 1500 BCE to the eighth century CE). Medical, grammatical, and religious texts recognized a "third sex" and acknowledged male, female, and third-sex desire as possibilities for anyone, regardless of the construction of their physical bodies.[8] A classic Sanskrit medical text described women having sex: "When two women erotically aroused, getting pleasure in intercourse, exchange the *shukra* [white fluid], a boneless foetus is formed."[9] A commentary noted a condition in which a woman who, because her mother was on top during intercourse when she was conceived, "although feminine in form . . . mounts the woman like a man and rubs her own vulva against that of the other."[10] Another commentary calls to mind the Amazons in describing women who have sex with women as "man-hating" and "breastless."[11] Legal penalties existed for sex between women, but they were less than those for sex between men, and both fines were low, indicating that these were minor offenses.[12] And the famous *Kamasutra*, a text written in the fourth century CE and based on earlier erotic writings, describes women engaging in manual stimulation, using dildos, and enjoying oral sex. Sex between women may occur occasionally or be preferred by some, and it may be between equals or between those differentiated by age or status. The text is not judgmental about the possibilities of pleasure.

These scattered references indicate that female same-sex sexuality was not unknown in a variety of ancient worlds. But the preponderance of information about love and sex between women comes from the ancient Greek world, so that is where we shall dwell for a moment.

We have already seen that the ancient Greeks told stories about goddesses and Amazons living in the distant past, what we call the Bronze Age (3000–1200 BCE). It was not until the Archaic period of Greek history (800–500 BCE) that we begin to have written documents, including the poetry of Sappho. What did the ancient Greeks have to say about their own worlds? What can we learn about love between women?

The slim evidence comes from three different areas of the Greek world: Sparta, Athens, and Lesbos. These societies developed very different social structures and cultures that had a profoundly different impact on women's lives in general and the possibilities of love between women in particular. In the seventh century BCE, Sparta developed a militaristic regime that valued men as warriors and women as the bearers of warriors. Citizen women, freed from traditional women's work by the labor of slaves and lower-class women, kept their bodies physically fit in order to bear healthy children, and sexuality was not rigidly confined to marriage because what was most important was that women bore children. The Spartans lived communally but segregated by sex for the first three decades of life. Men lived with their fellow warriors until the age of thirty, although they married at eighteen, and sex between men was common. In fact, when couples married, the brides dressed in men's clothing and cut their hair in the male style, presumably to lessen the unfamiliarity of the experience for the husbands. From the Athenian perspective (and most of what we know about Sparta comes from the hostile Athenians), Spartan women enjoyed incredible freedom. According to Plutarch, the best Spartan women loved girls.[13] A philosopher reported that Spartan women had intercourse with girls in an initiation rite before their marriage.[14] The Spartan male poet Alcman, writing in the seventh century BCE, composed a maiden song, a hymn intended to be sung by unmarried girls, that names and praises the girls in the choir. They sing that their leader, an older woman, "exhausts me," which one scholar has argued could refer to an emotional and sexual attachment.[15]

Athens, in both the Archaic and Classical periods (500–323 BCE), was an entirely different story. Adult citizen women lived in a sex-segregated (but unlike Sparta, private rather than communal) world, in the women's quarters of their husband's house. Religious festivals offered the main opportunity for citizen women's public participation, although lower-class and slave women went out in public in other contexts. Citizen women married young, around fourteen, to men of around thirty. Men had access to other men and to prostitutes or slaves for sex, and of course Athenian culture celebrated homoerotic and sexual relations between older and younger men.

And what about love and sex between women? In contexts where women lived apart from men, as did upper-class women in ancient Athens and elsewhere, sexual relations between women may have flourished away from male eyes. Certainly the later Orientalist and salacious tales of sex in the harems of the Middle East suggest that, when men stopped to think about it at all, the possibility worried them. A few Athenian vase paintings depict women with dildos and female prostitutes seemingly engaged in sexual acts with one another, but all these tell us for certain is that Athenian men (the creators and probably audience for the vase paintings) knew that women could pleasure themselves or one another.[16] (See figure 3 for one of the existing examples of two women in a sexual pose.) Other vase painting, some on items designed for use by women, show women in domestic scenes, preparing brides for their weddings, singing and dancing, and bathing in ways that suggest homoeroticism.[17]

We know nothing at all about love between women from the perspective of women themselves, only from the writings (or artistic productions) of men. Aristophanes, author of the play Lysistrata, produced in 411 BCE in the midst of the endless war between Athens and Sparta, portrays as lustful the women who agree to try to end the war by staging a sex strike against their husbands, but they never think to turn to one another. Plato, as we have seen, attributing the story to Aristophanes, imagined the origins of women who love and desire women. But the female beings searching for their lost halves are not in Plato's eyes the equals of the male beings searching for their lost halves, and in his later work, Plato calls all same-sex love unnatural.[18] A writer in the third century BCE called on Aphrodite to turn against two women who were engaged in "not beautiful" sexual relations, and an ancient commentator explained that he was accusing them of being "tribades," signifying a masculine or hypersexual woman and seemingly suggesting penetration, either by an artificial penis or a naturally enlarged clitoris.[19]

What else can we say about love between women in Athenian society? Lucian of Samosata, writing several centuries after Plato in the second century CE, in his Dialogues of Courtesans depicts two prostitutes, Clonarium and Leaena, talking about Leaena's lover, Megilla, a rich woman from, tellingly enough, Lesbos. Megilla, revealing a shaved head underneath her wig, seduces Leaena after a banquet, showing her that she could satisfy her as well as a man and offering her gifts. Leaena is ashamed because Megilla is "frightfully masculine" and loves her unnaturally, "like a man."[20] Two things are significant in this depiction: the connection of an aggressive woman from Lesbos with masculinity and the portrayal of the seduced as a prostitute. Both masculinity and prostitution, as we shall see, have a long history of association with female same-sex love. A lyric poem by Anacreon, a lover of boys who was born about 570 BCE, tells of a girl from Lesbos who, at a banquet, spurns him and instead lusts after another woman, suggesting that the courtesans and dancers who would have attended and been enveloped in the erotic atmosphere of a banquet

Figure 3. Athenian vase painting. From K. J. Dover, *Greek Homosexuality* (New York: Vintage Books, 1978).

Figure 4. Sappho. Alinari/
Art Resource, NY. From
Jane McIntosh Snyder,
Sappho (New York: Chel-
sea House, 1995).

(where men may have been engaging in sexual acts and respectable citizen
women would not have been present) may have turned to one another.[21]
Again, we see the association of prostitutes with same-sex sexuality, a connection reinforced by the fact that the term *hetairistria*, which is related to
hetaira, meaning "courtesan," was sometimes used to refer to women who
had sex with women.[22]

Given these sparse depictions, it is with relief that we turn from Athens
to Lesbos. Sappho was born in Mytilene on the island of Lesbos around
612 BCE. She was a poet and singer and seems to have been the head of a
kind of community of or school for girls who, before they married, learned
to sing and play instruments and dance, to become beautiful and graceful
and sensual, and to love.[23] (See figure 4 for a Greek statue of Sappho as a
singer.)

Sappho's lyrics, like those that begin this chapter, speak of love and desire: "Love shook my heart like a wind falling on oaks on a mountain."
"Once again limb-loosening Love makes me tremble, the bitter-sweet, irre-
sistible creature."[24] Sappho's relations with the girls about whom she wrote

has led some scholars to see her not as a lover of women but as a teacher of sensuality, one who prepared girls for marriage.[25] Of course, marriage was the goal for women, even on Lesbos. But in the Greek world—and perhaps especially in the world of Lesbos, known for its passionate sexuality—sexual desire did not confine itself to one sex or another. Athenian comedies used the words *lesbiazein* and *lesbizein*, meaning "to play the Lesbian," to refer to all sorts of loose sexual behavior.[26] Women from Lesbos gained their sexual reputation particularly from their reputed proclivity for (heterosexual) oral sex.[27]

Part of the mystery surrounding Sappho comes from the fact that we have only fragments of her songs. Yet, despite attempts in later centuries to deny the erotic elements of Sappho's lyrics, their portrayal of love for women shines through. For example, in her only complete song, preserved for posterity in the hand of a later writer, Sappho addresses Aphrodite, the goddess of love, asking for her help in winning the love of a woman. Aphrodite flies to her rescue, asking who has done her injustice and promising to change the heart of Sappho's beloved: "For if indeed she flees, soon will she pursue, / and though she receives not your gifts, she will give them, / and if she loves not now, soon she will love / even against her will."[28]

One fragment of Sappho's lyrics takes up the question of what is the most beautiful thing on earth. Some people, Sappho tells us, say it is an army of horsemen, but for her it is "what one loves." To illustrate, she tells of Helen of Troy, "who surpassed all mortals in beauty" but under the influence of Aphrodite left her husband and child and parents out of love for Paris. (Here Sappho is negating Homer's tale of Helen's being abducted by the Trojan prince Paris.) This reminds Sappho of Anaktoria, "who is not here. / Her lovely walk and the bright sparkle of her face / I would rather look upon than / all the Lydian chariots / and full-armed infantry." Yet another fragmentary song tells of a woman who has left Lesbos and thinks back with desire of Atthis: "But she, roaming about far and wide, / remembers gentle Atthis with desire." This and other fragments suggest that erotic relationships may have formed not only between Sappho and the young women in her community but also among her students, although of course we cannot assume that the songs are autobiographical.[29] And finally, a very fragmentary song tells of a woman weeping because she must leave Sappho. In response, Sappho reminds her of the "beautiful things that happened to us," including (and these are all the words that have come down to us in this stanza) "And on a soft bed / . . . tender . . . / you satisfied your desire."[30]

Perhaps Sappho's songs are also about actual sexual encounters. Is it possible that the following fragment is about the clitoris and men's ignorance of its possibilities, as one scholar has argued? Sappho wrote, "like the sweet-apple / that has reddened / at the top of a tree, / at the tip of the topmost bough, / and the applepickers / missed it there—not, not missed, so much / as could not touch." Could such lines as "The groom who'll enter / is as big as Ares" depict the penetration of heterosexual intercourse in comparison to tender and gentle love between women, as in "May you sleep then / on some tender / girl friend's breast?"[31] Or, more subtly, could it be that the song about the "beautiful things that happened to us" describes movement on the body from the head to the neck and on down to end in satisfied desire? From a different translation of the fragments: "With many garlands of violets and roses . . . together, and . . . you put around yourself, at my side, and flowers wreathed around your soft neck with rising fragrance, and . . . you stroked the oil distilled from royal cherry blossoms and on tender bedding you reached the end of longing."[32]

It is because of the power of Sappho's songs—not to mention her lonely voice in the record of women desiring women in ancient worlds—that she has played such a central part in the story of love between women. Despite all the later attempts to destroy or reinterpret her work—as being addressed to men instead of women or designed to introduce young women to heterosexual love or describing an anxiety attack rather than desire—Sappho has come down to us as the emblematic lover of women, the model for the possibility of same-sex desire and love. She had a Hellenistic imitator by the name of Nossis, who wrote epigrams in the third century BCE acknowledging Sappho as her model and Aphrodite as her goddess of choice. Although none of Nossis's surviving words are directly erotic, her connection to Sappho and her praise of desire and love are important because the voices of women are so rare:

> Nothing is sweeter than desire. All other delights are second.
> From my mouth I spit even honey.
> Nossis says this. Whom Aphrodite does not love,
> Knows not her flowers, what roses they are.[33]

Was Sappho a "lesbian" in any sense other than coming from Lesbos? That is a more complicated question. The earliest reference to Sappho as a lover of women comes from a papyrus written in the late second or early third century CE that is based on a lost text about Sappho from the fourth century BCE. "She has been accused by some people of being licentious in her lifestyle and a woman lover," the author notes, neither confirming nor denying the accusation.[34] The question is one taken up in Erica Jong's joyous portrayal of Sappho, which suggests some possible answers. Jong, it should be said, catapulted into the world of contemporary literature with her erotic heterosexual romp *Fear of Flying*, which gave the world the term "zipless fuck" to describe the ideal of a sex act so perfect and instantaneous that zippers need not be unzipped.[35] So it is from a kind of contemporary sexual-liberation perspective that she writes about the past.

Jong's *Sappho's Leap* takes the skeletal facts about Sappho's life, the body of Greek mythology, and what we know about the Mediterranean world to fashion a Sappho who falls in love with Alcaeus (an actual male poet from Lesbos about whom we know little except that he loved boys and, according to legend, loved Sappho). But Sappho also loves and desires women, including her slave, Praxinoa, who joins the Amazons; Isis, an Egyptian priestess; and the students she teaches the arts of song and love. Sappho bears Alcaeus's child, conceived before she is married off to an old man and separated from the love of her life. Her mother, who married the tyrant ruling Lesbos after the death of Sappho's father, snatches Sappho's daughter, Cleis, setting the bereft mother and lover off on a journey to find both Alcaeus and Cleis. Along the way, she meets Aesop, of fable fame, who falls in love with her. They encounter one mythological creature and place after another until Sappho is finally reunited with both Alcaeus and Cleis. The novel begins and ends with a reimagining of one of the stories that circulated about Sappho, clung to by those who longed to deny her love of women. In this tale, Sappho leaps to her death for love of a handsome ferryman named Phaon. In Jong's retelling, Phaon is a creation of Zeus, who bets Aphrodite that Sappho can be humbled by a mortal man. Feeling abandoned by Aphrodite, not Phaon, Sappho climbs to and then slips from the lovers' leap but is pulled out of the sea by Alcaeus, Praxinoa, and Aesop.

Jong's Sappho is not a lover of women or men but a devotee of Aphrodite and a lover of love and passion. "Did I love women or men?" Jong has Sappho ask in the prologue, knowing what history would wonder about her. "Does love even have a sex? I doubt it. If you are lucky enough to love, who cares what decorative flesh your lover sports? The divine delta, that juicy fig, the powerful phallus, that scepter of state—each is only an aspect of Aphrodite, after all. We are all hermaphrodites at heart—aren't we?"[36]

So Jong makes of Sappho a Lesbian woman in the sense of her artistry, her sexual freedom, and her birth on the island of Lesbos. And Jong's imagining that Alcaeus, a man, was the love of Sappho's life does not undermine the notion of Sappho as the voice of the lover of women. Jong represents both Sappho and her goddess and patron, Aphrodite, as feminists of a sort, championing the strength and independence of women. And she represents the changes on Lesbos as a precursor of what was to come. The cost of the long wars is that the people of Lesbos no longer want songs of love but desire patriotic tales of victory in war, and Sappho's lyrics fall out of fashion and her love of girls becomes suspicious. What Jong is suggesting fits, ironically, with the visions of Elizabeth Gould Davis and Susan Cavin: when war overtakes human society, women are devalued and love between women becomes anathema. Yet there is the fragmentary evidence about Sparta, a warlike society that valued women as the mothers of warriors.

In any case, the prophetic end of *Sappho's Leap* leads us into the Roman world, where we find further evidence of knowledge about the possibilities of love between women, but no Roman Sappho. With the development of the Roman Republic (509–27 BCE) and the rise of the Empire (from 27 BCE), Roman women had more access to public life than Athenian women had, but they remained, at least in theory, firmly under the control of men. And men found the idea of sex between women—despite their own interest in sex with other men—a frightening and monstrous thought.[37] Although Sappho's songs were much admired by ancient Roman authors, these writers increasingly seemed obsessed with—and disapproving of—her lyrics that celebrated love of women. Some insisted that there must have been two Sapphos, one the poet and the other a prostitute. A historian in the third or fourth century BCE claimed that it was the prostitute who fell in love with Phaon. Ovid (first century BCE to first century CE) embroidered the tale in his "Letter of Sappho to Phaon," which has had such a lasting effect through the centuries. Yet Jong was not the first to retell Sappho's leap into the sea, as we shall see.

The references to love between women in Latin literature consider it unnatural and represent women who have sex with women as masculine. The earliest example comes from a comedy written in the third or second century BCE in which a female slave forces sex on her mistress, a courtesan.[38] Seneca the Elder (ca. 55 BCE–40 CE) wrote of a man who killed his wife when he found her in bed with another woman making use of a dildo. Ovid told the story of a Cretan girl named Iphis who was raised as a boy and fell in love with the girl she was supposed to marry. She bemoans the fate of loving so unnaturally but is saved by Isis, who turns her into a boy. Phaedrus, a poet who lived in the first century CE, attributed the origin of tribades to a mistake of Prometheus, who, in a drunken state, slapped male genitals on women. Also writing in the first century CE, Martial described a woman as *"tribas* [the singular of *tribades*] of the very *tribades"* since she engaged in masculine pursuits and "devours girls' middles."[39] He also told the story of admiring the chastity of a woman named Bassa until he found out that she avoided men but that her "monstrous lust imitates a man."[40] Clearly the Romans knew of the possibility of sex between women.

The Roman attitude was consistent with the views of other peoples in their Mediterranean world, including the Jews. One Jewish source, written in Greek, commands women not to "imitate the sexual role of men."[41] A rabbinical commentary associated marriage between two women with Egyptian or Canaanite practices—an early example of blaming sexual deviance on foreign influence. For the rabbi, female same-sex sexuality stemmed from idolatry (harking back to associations between goddess worship and love between women). Later Jewish texts refer to women "rubbing" with one another and debate whether that constitutes harlotry. Despite disagreement about the seriousness of the matter, the evidence makes clear that female same-sex sexuality was not unknown, even if it was viewed with distaste or worse.

Why this distaste? Were Roman and Jewish and, later, Christian authors in fact responding to unsettling practices? Is there evidence that women in this world really did fall in love with other women? That is the question posed by Bernadette Brooten, who has written a groundbreaking and controversial book about female homoeroticism in the world in which Christianity was born.[42] She argues, based on a thorough analysis of a wide range of ancient sources, that disgust with women's love for other women was widespread and a reaction to knowledge, however downplayed, that such love existed. She has uncovered a wide range of ancient sources that add to what we already knew on the basis of elite literature alone.

What is controversial about Brooten's book is her perspective, for although she insists on the need to analyze ancient sources in the context of the worlds that created them, she at the same time sees the women who emerge from those sources as "ancient lesbians."[43] One of the fiercest debates in the literature on Greek and Roman same-sex sexuality centers on whether those societies had a category and concept for people who engaged in same-sex acts. The most famous proponent of the idea that they did, and that there were recognizable "gay people," was John Boswell, author of *Christianity, Social Tolerance, and Homosexuality*.[44] Brooten's argument is much more nuanced (and no less erudite) than Boswell's, but critics have nonetheless read her work as suggesting inappropriate elements of transhistorical affinity. Yet it is possible to separate the notion of "ancient lesbians" from the evidence that she contextualizes so well.

One entrancing (pun intended) source that Brooten uses is erotic spells that one woman commissioned to make another woman love her. Following the pattern of heterosexual spells, these entreaties, prepared by a professional, laid out the hopes of the client that a desired other will fall in love with her. A few surviving papyrus fragments and lead tablets from Upper Egypt, specifying the names of both parties and so identifiable as same-sex spells, call on the deities to "inflame the heart, the liver, the spirit" of another woman with love and affection, calling on the beloved to "love her with passion, longing, unceasing love."[45] Although the spells are formulaic and cannot tell us anything much about the parties involved, they do represent a rare opportunity to listen to the voices, however filtered by the professionals who prepared the spells, of women who desired women. And they indicate that such women were willing to proclaim their desire for another woman, if not in public, then at least to another person. Imagine the passion that would lead Sophia to commission this spell, with its images of violence, as a snare for Gorgonia:

> Constrain Gorgonia, whom Nilogenia bore, to cast herself into the bathhouse for the sake of Sophia, whom Isara bore, for her. Aye, lord, king of the chthonic gods, burn, set on fire, inflame the soul, the heart, the liver, the spirit of Gorgonia, whom Nilogenia bore, with love and affection for Sophia, whom Isara bore; drive Gorgonia herself, torment her body night and day; force her to rush forth from every place and every house, loving Sophia, whom Isara bore, she, Gorgonia surrendered like a slave.[46]

Astrological texts provide further evidence for the knowledge and existence of female same-sex love in the Roman world. Astrology was both a science and an aspect of religion, and it spread from Babylonia throughout the Greek and Roman world. Handbooks, treatises, and poems laying out the principles of astrology contain numerous references to female homoeroticism. The alignment of heavenly bodies at the time of birth or conception could determine a person's same-sex desire, but at the same time, such desires, especially women's love of women, could be deemed unnatural. Same-sex desire also tended to be lumped together with other kinds of sexual transgressions such as prostitution, promiscuity, and adultery. One astrologer, Dorotheos of Sidon, who lived in the first century CE, described women "who do in women the act of men," suggesting that they were masculine. Likewise Manetho, probably a contemporary, mentions "*tribades* who perform male functions."[47] In the second century CE, the famous Alexandrian Ptolemy continued the ancient Greek tradition of associating femininity with passivity and masculinity with activity. He specified degrees of the masculinization of women: some women take the active role with women in secret, but others make their desires public and even take women as their wives.

These same points reappear in other, later astrological texts, suggesting continuity across the centuries. On the one hand, we can see a notion that women who desired women were a category of person (made that way by the stars): they were tribades. Yet this was not exactly a way of dividing the world up into people who desired those of the same sex versus people who desired those of the other sex, for the crucial distinction was between people who take an active (that is, penetrating) role in sexual encounters versus those who take a passive (that is, enclosing) role, and women could fall into both categories, although that was harder for the ancients to imagine in the case of women than in the case of men. The women who fall out of the picture entirely are those who are the partners of masculine women. Unlike men who desire men but take the active role, they are not given special consideration for their gender-appropriate sexual behavior. They are not considered at all. At the end of the day, despite being made that way by the stars, women who loved other women were licentious and unnatural in the eyes of the astrologers. But they existed.

The same recognition of women who desire other women appears in Roman medical texts, which also reflect the notion that such women are masculine, in this case even physiologically, as in these writings the notion emerges that a woman with an overly large clitoris could penetrate other women. Soranos of Ephesos, a Roman physician in the second century CE, considered tribades to suffer from mental illness that caused them to "practice both kinds of love, rush to have sex with women more than with men and pursue women with an almost masculine jealousy." Soranos, in a gynecological text, recommended clitoridectomy—the removal of at least part of the clitoris—if it were "overly large" or "immoderate," indicating the concern with the possibility of a woman's penetrating another (and a persistent male lack of imagination about what two women might do to pleasure one another).[48] He provided precise directions for amputating the excess flesh of the clitoris. We have no way of knowing in what circumstances such surgeries may have taken place or what Soranos and his contemporaries thought the relationship was between the mental illness of desire for women and the physical condition of an enlarged clitoris. But in any case, his thinking, and that of his translators and successors, reinforced the idea that women's love for other women is unnatural and should be controlled.

Guides to interpreting dreams also classified female same-sex sexuality as unnatural. Artemidoros of Daldis, in the second century CE, wrote a guide to interpreting dreams.[49] Although his interest was not in sexuality per se but simply in understanding what dreaming about sex might mean, his classifications of dreams of women having sex fits with all the other ancient sources and corresponds to an Egyptian dream book that proclaimed that if a woman "dreams that a woman has intercourse with her, she will come to a bad end."[50] Dreams portended good or bad things depending on whether what was dreamed was legal, illegal, or unnatural. All sorts of sexual acts between men fell into the legal category, but all sex between women was unnatural. Dream interpretation guides, then, like the medical and astrological texts, support Brooten's argument that there was no or almost no tolerance for female same-sex sexuality in Roman times.

Brooten does suggest, at various points throughout her book, that marriage between women was a possibility in the ancient Mediterranean world, although her evidence is shaky enough that she truly suggests rather than argues the point. She cites a passage from Clement of Alexandria that refers to women "getting married and marrying women contrary to nature," Lucian's passage in Dialogues of the Courtesans in which the masculine Megilla calls another woman her wife, the astrologer Ptolemy's reference to women who have sex with other women and call them their "lawful wives," a story by a romance writer, and a funerary urn depicting two freedwomen with clasped hands, taking all these as "intriguing hints" of a real "social institution."[51] The evidence strikes me as unconvincing. Critics question the meaning of the Greek word for "marriage" and "marrying," pointing out that it is also used for the male role in sexual intercourse. They also point to the nature of ancient marriage, which had little to do with love, sexual desire, or companionship and therefore makes little sense in thinking about a relationship between two women.[52] A more nuanced position, taking off from the funerary urn (which in late antiquity

had been recut to turn one of the women into a man), points to the possibility that New Testament biblical references to pairs of women means
that two women may have formed missionary couples, comparable to
husband-wife teams, in early Christianity. In an environment of disloca-
tion from traditional family ties and sexual asceticism, the decision to live
and work with another woman would have been a social, if not sexual,
choice.[53]

This was, then, the world that launched the religion of Christianity,
which has had such a powerful impact on societal responses to love between women. Inhabitants of the ancient Mediterranean world may have
encountered references to female same-sex love in literature, through
magic and astrology, and in medical texts or guides to dream interpretation, but none of these sources accepted desire between women as natural or good. So the story of the demonization of love between women is
not, as is sometimes told, a tale of Christianity, as an antisexual religion,
overturning the culture of a sex-positive ancient world. The story is more
complicated and more controversial, as we shall see.

Ancient societies that valued rather than feared sexuality—Sparta, where
sexuality was linked to the all-important task of producing warriors; Lesbos, with its appreciation for the beauty and talents of women; the India
of the *Kamasutra*, with its multiple possibilities for pleasure—do seem to
have been more open to desire and love between women. Yet all the ancient societies, in contrast to the mythical society of the Amazons and the
imagined world of gynosociety, valued men over women. The development of stratified societies with political structures and economic dispari-
ties set the stage for increased control of sexuality. Sometimes, because
women were less important than men, what they did with one another was
of no interest or consequence; sometimes it seems to have been titillating.
But the same themes that emerged in Greek depictions of the Amazons—
masculinity and independence—could seem very threatening indeed.

What is truly striking in thinking about ancient worlds is the silence
of women. That is why Sappho continues to play such a central role in
thinking about love between women. How might our history change if the
words of other women—those who commissioned erotic spells, for example—had survived? What if we could hear women's voices? Let us end this
consideration of ancient worlds with a fragment—appropriately—from a
series of poems that Erica Jong wrote about Sappho before she began her
novel. "Sappho: a footnote" reflects on the power of words:

Sappho burned
& Christians burned
her words.
In the Egyptian desert,
bits of papyri
held notations
of her flaming heart.
Aphrodite smiles,
remembering Sappho's words:
"If death were good,
even the gods would die."

You who put your trust
in words when flesh decays,
know that even words
are swept away—
& what remains?[54]

As we move forward in time, we begin to hear a bit more from women. And we find possibilities of desire, love, and sex between women in what at first glance seem some unlikely places.

4

In Unlikely Places

(500 BCE–1600 CE)

FOR A VERY long time, from the waning of classical civilizations and
the spread of world religions to the rise of European global dominance,
the voices of women who loved women are no more than occasional
whispers. Yet if we look hard enough and listen intently, we can find places
where love between women could have flourished or—if not flourished—
at least survived. In what might seem unlikely places—in convents, harems, and polygynous households, in mystical outpourings and heretical
sects, in the practice of alternative religions—women could desire, love,
and have sex with other women. In some societies, such as those that understood that sex between co-wives might make harmonious households,
such relations were not beyond the bounds of respectability. In others,
the idea of sex between women was so horrifying that the authorities,
whether secular or religious, wavered between willfully denying that such
a thing could exist and condemning to death women who engaged in the
unspeakable. Even then, some voices break through. Listen to the love letter of one Bavarian nun to another, twelve centuries after Paul's "Letter
to the Romans" introduced into Christian doctrine the denunciation of
women's "unnatural" passion for one another:

> It is you alone I have chosen for my heart . . .
> I love you above all else,
> You alone are my love and desire . . .
> When I recall the kisses you gave me,
> And how with tender words you caressed my little breasts,
> I want to die
> Because I cannot see you.[1]

Such words of love remind us that what ought to have been was not always what was.

What's Religion Got to Do with It?

In Erica Jong's version of Sappho's life, the great singer meets and falls in love with an Egyptian priestess, Isis, who prophesies a bleak future. "In times to come, people will fear Eros and hate all pleasure. There will be a dark age in which all the sweets of life will turn bitter. It will last a very long time," she says.[2] Her words might easily evoke the rise and spread of Christianity, with its ascetic streak and renunciation of sexual pleasure. For the traditional tale of the transition from the sexual openness of the classical civilizations of Greece and Rome to a sexually repressive Christian-dominated Europe pinpoints Christian doctrine and practice as the killer of eros. But this interpretation has come under attack, especially by two scholars whom we have already briefly met, coming from diametrically opposed positions. One, Bernadette Brooten, has already provided her fascinating evidence of recognition of love between women in the Mediterranean world. But we should start with the late John Boswell, author of two controversial books on Christianity and primarily male same-sex sexuality.[3]

In *Christianity, Social Tolerance, and Homosexuality*, Boswell uses his incredible erudition and notable linguistic skills to argue that Christianity was not to blame for hostility to same-sex relations. The biblical passages that have been taken as a condemnation either meant something else or considered same-sex sexual relations a relatively trivial offence, and the Church as an institution actually fostered same-sex love. Hatred of same-sex sexuality came not from the Church fathers but only beginning in the late twelfth century from popular intolerance stirred up by the Crusades. Fear and hatred of Jews, Muslims, and heretics spread to those perceived as sexually deviant and trickled up to religious and secular elites. From a late Roman world of openness to all sorts of sexualities and a flowering of "gay culture" in the twelfth-century urban revival, late medieval Europe shut down toleration—even glorification—of same-sex love.

Boswell has been criticized from many perspectives—especially for identifying "gay people" in the past, thus suggesting an essentialist transhistorical identity—but Bernadette Brooten is notable for pointing out that his argument about the acceptability of same-sex relations in Roman times is based entirely on evidence about men.[4] She writes from a lesbian-feminist perspective that differentiates, both in the past and in the present, between the male and female forms of same-sex sexuality. As we have seen, she insists that, if we pay attention to what the sources tell us about women, the record looks entirely different. Although she provides evidence that female same-sex love existed, she is just as clear that it was viewed with disgust. So her point about the impact of Christianity is both similar to Boswell's—she does not see Christian doctrine as responsible for the condemnation of same-sex sexuality—and entirely different, since she paints a picture of persistent and continuous condemnation throughout the history of the Mediterranean world. The works of both scholars are an example of history with an agenda: absolving the Christian Church from responsibility for hatred of same-sex sexuality. Boswell, to me, sounds disingenuous about this. He says, in his preface, that it is the job of the historian "not to praise or blame but merely to record and explain." He adds, "This book is not intended as support or criticism of any particular contemporary points of view—scientific or moral—regarding homosexuality."[5] But, for me at least, it is hard to miss the passion that he puts into both defending the Church and detailing the love of men for other men. Brooten is much more forthright. The last sentence of her book reads, "By understanding our past, we may progress toward a more humane future, one in which we acknowledge the sacredness and holiness of a woman expressing her love for another woman."[6]

Perspective and agenda aside, what do these two historians tell us about the impact of Christianity on female same-sex love? In the case of Boswell, not much. He reports that Augustine told nuns that they should love one another in a spiritual rather than carnal way and that virgins and married women should not indulge in "shameless playing with each other."[7] With regard to the early medieval penitentials—lists of penalties to be doled out by confessors for all sorts of sins—that included sexual acts between women, Boswell points out that the penances were far less onerous for same-sex sexuality than for hunting by a priest. And finally there are the love letters between nuns in the monastery of Tegernsee, lines of which I quoted earlier, and a reference to "the sole extant example of medieval love poetry written in a vernacular language by one woman to another" (yet this striking example from the thirteenth century is not quoted— more on that later).[8] But most of what Boswell has to say about women concerns the passage in Romans that is the first denunciation of female same-sex sexuality and is the focus of the second half of Brooten's book.

As we have seen, Brooten pulls together a wide variety of sources from the world in which Christianity emerged to argue that Paul's denunciation of female same-sex sexuality in Romans 1:26 is consistent with Greek, Roman, and Jewish perspectives on love between women. The only real difference, she suggests, is that early Christian theology put male and female same-sex sexuality in the same conceptual category, although she also notes that condemnations targeted only those men who were "enclosers" (those who performed fellatio or received anal sex) but all women who engaged in same-sex sexuality as the violators of nature and law—leaving out men who played what the ancients thought of as the "active" or proper male role.

Paul's "Letter to the Romans," written between 54 and 58 CE, is short and to the point about female same-sex sexuality. Paul is discussing people who have turned away from God in all sorts of ways. "For this reason God gave them up to degrading passions. Their women exchanged natural intercourse for unnatural, and in the same way also the men, giving up natural intercourse with women, were consumed with passion for one another."[9] Brooten sets this passage in the widest possible context, considering the interpretations of other scholars, Paul's intentions and the context of the Roman congregation to whom he was writing, debates on natural law, Jewish law, the writings of early Church fathers, and the cultural context of the period. She rejects Boswell's argument that what Paul meant to condemn was people whose nature was heterosexual but who engaged in same-sex acts, arguing that Paul clearly saw sexual love between women as unnatural—as did the Roman world—and deserving of death.

Having described all the different contexts that the Roman congregations Paul was addressing would have brought to his words, Brooten imagines what they may have heard. A Jewish woman thinks of the denunciation of male same-sex sex in Leviticus. An old pagan man remembers discussions of natural law. His wife, who sells food at a corner stall on the street, is reminded of two young women who came to her shop with their arms wrapped around each other. A slightly drunk male customer mutters that it is not natural, that they should be married, and wonders if they strap something on. Brooten also imagines that women who loved other women may have sat in the congregation. "Did they listen silently, feeling guilty and afraid that the congregations would find out? Or did they speak up, confident in their love for one another and for Christ? We cannot know. Their voices are absent."[10] It is a lovely image, but given what Brooten has already told us, it is hard for me to imagine them confident in their love.

Critics of Brooten point out that there is one fundamental difference between Christian and earlier attitudes toward female same-sex love: it is only with the spread of Christianity that such love warrants the death penalty.[11] There is quite a difference between being the butt of a joke in a Roman comedy and suffering death and eternal torment in hell, after all. Brooten explores apocalyptic visions of those torments, ranging from having to cast oneself off a cliff over and over again to burning in a blazing pit to running in a river of fire. So despite a history of condemnation of female same-sex love, it would seem that Christianity did, in fact, have something to do with the virulence of responses to love between women.

What about other religious traditions? Was Christianity more hostile than other world religions? As we have seen, Paul's proclamations can be seen as an extension of the Hebrew Bible's call for death for a man who lies "with a male as with a woman"; Leviticus defines this as an "abomination" committed by both men but says nothing about sex between women.[12] A rabbinical commentary on Leviticus known as the Sifra prohibits for Jews marriage practices attributed to the Egyptians and Canaanites, including marriage between women, which some later commentators interpreted as referring to sexual relations. Both the Jerusalem Talmud (compiled around the fifth century CE) and the Babylonian Talmud (sixth century CE) discuss sexual practices that disqualify a woman from eating a priestly offering or marrying a priest. It is "harlotry" that is at issue, and different schools disagreed about whether two women who "'rub' with each other" are engaging in harlotry.[13] Some dismissed it simply as "obscenity." This is a pretty thin record of concern about women having sex with other women. Perhaps, as we find in so many contexts, it just was not important what women did with one another as long as they also married men and bore them children.

Islam, emerging in the seventh century CE out of Jewish and Christian traditions, also has little to say about female same-sex sexuality. The Qur'ān, like the Hebrew Bible, is silent on the subject, although it follows the Bible in mentioning five times the story of Lot in Sodom.[14] An Islamic text from the late twelfth or early thirteenth century reported that women "practiced the vice [of sodomy] for forty years among the tribe of Lot before the men took it up."[15] *Sharī'a*, traditional law based on the Qur'ān and the sayings of the Prophet Muhammad known as the *hadīth*, is considered to condemn same-sex sexuality.[16] The Prophet is reported to have included women in his pronouncements: "Doomed by God is who does what Lot's people did. . . . No man should look at the private parts of another man, and no woman should look at the private parts of another woman, and no two men sleep under one cover, and no two women sleep under one cover."[17] A decree in the *hadīth* calls for the stoning to death of both male partners, and early laws and sentences carried out this kind of harsh penalty.

Yet romantic love between men and boys flourished in early Islamic culture despite the condemnation of male same-sex sexual acts, and as Islam spread across the Mediterranean with the Arab conquest of Spain in the ninth century, depictions of male love had an impact on medieval Europe as well. Ibn Da'ud, a writer and jurist born in the late ninth century, celebrated the idea of passionate love between men in his *Book of the Flower*, dedicated to his friend Muhammad ibn Jāmī. Ibn Hazm (994–1064), who wrote a treatise on love called *The Dove's Neck-Ring, about Love and Lovers*, referred to men's love for women and for other men in the same breath. He took great pains to emphasize that, however much he may have been tempted by the beauty of men, he would not engage in any physical activity with them. Despite the existence of Arabic romances featuring female lovers, Ibn Hazm did not extend his appreciation of same-sex erotic attraction to women. He reported knowing a woman "who had bestowed her affections in ways not pleasing to Almighty God," something he called an "abomination."[18] A famous eleventh-century woman poet, Walladah bint Al-Mustakfi, daughter of the Caliph of Cordova in Spain, the "Arab Sappho," wrote poems to her female lover Muhjah, also a poet, but much of this work has been lost, presumably because of its homoerotic content.[19] Walladah, known for her sexual independence and multiple male lovers, wrote, "I give my cheek to whoever loves me / and I give my kiss to anybody who desires it."[20] Another woman poet wrote, "I drank wine for love of flirting / and I shifted towards lesbianism for fear of pregnancy" (although "lesbianism" is a translation of whatever she actually said).[21] Still, the point is that Islam, like Judaism and Christianity, paid little official attention to love between women.

The older major world religions—Hinduism and Buddhism—are less condemning of same-sex sexuality, although they also reveal contradictory attitudes. Hinduism, a diverse set of religious traditions originating earlier than any other major religion in India, has no one sacred text like the Bible or Qur'ān. A classical Hindu text from around 1000 BCE refers to "the fruitless coupling of two men or two women."[22] A text from the second century CE called the *Mānavadharmaśātra* prescribed the same penalty for upper-caste men who copulate with other men as for those who have intercourse with women in a cart drawn by oxen, in water, or during the day, and this penalty was less than the one for men who committed "an unnatural crime with a female."[23] In contrast, penalties for sex between women were more severe. A *kanya* (a young girl or virgin) who "pollutes" another girl suffered financial penalties and ten lashes with a rod. A "woman"—that is, a married woman—who polluted a girl had her head shaved or two fingers cut off or had to ride through the town on a donkey.[24] Yet the same penalty applied to a man who manually penetrated a virgin, indicating that the real crime was stealing a girl's virginity.[25] In contrast to men, higher-caste women suffered less severe punishment than lower-caste women, some authorities assigning the loss of fingers only to those from lower castes. Caste may also have played a role in deciding which *kanya* was the guilty party, since that could be difficult to determine, depending on the sexual activity involved. Some commentaries on the law refer to insertion of fingers; others suggest oral sex, since a term used to describe the activity combines the root of a word that means "enjoyment through eating and drinking" with a prefix specifying mutuality.[26]

Other Hindu texts took different and conflicting approaches. The *Arthaśāstra*, a text thought to be from the third century BCE, specified fines for different sexual offenses, with the least for intercourse with an animal, up to double for sex between women, and four to almost eight times as much for sex between men. The *Kamasutra*, as we have seen, described in a nonjudgmental way a variety of sexual activities, including oral sex, which in other texts was likened to the killing of a high-caste person. Some women, according to the *Kamasutra*, became addicted to the practice of cunnilingus and sought out women or men who would satisfy them.

Despite the contradictions, it seems fair to say that female same-sex sexuality was of relatively minor concern to classical Hinduism and was certainly not a cause for execution, as in Christianity. Later, at least in part in reaction to invasion by non-Hindus, attitudes hardened. A commentator in the late tenth to early eleventh century reported that when Kabul was conquered by the Muslims and the leader adopted Islam, he "stipulated that he should not be bound to eat cow's meat nor to commit sodomy," clearly associating such practices with Islam.[27] More blaming of foreigners . . .

Buddhism, which emerged in India from the teachings of the Buddha in the mid-sixth to early fifth century BCE, like Hinduism embraced conflicting positions on same-sex sexuality, in part, as with all religious traditions, because of variation across time and place. On the whole, however, its attitude can best be described as neutral.[28] Condemnation, when it occurred, came in the context of the renunciation of sexuality in general, since Buddhism extols the celibate life. Yet Buddhist societies did not expect everyone to give up sex, so praise for male sexual and military prowess coexisted with the monastic ideal. In texts concerning lay life, same-sex sexuality rarely appears as a transgression. There are almost no references to female same-sex sexuality except for rules against such contacts in monastic orders, about which more later.

In Indian Buddhism, condemnation of male-male sex either as a violation of a monastic vow of celibacy or in cases in which men take on the characteristics of women sit side by side with homoerotic stories from the lives of the Buddha and his companions. Neutrality mixed with ambivalence also characterizes attitudes toward same-sex sexuality in China, although we know very little about specifically Buddhist Chinese attitudes. Both Confucianism and Taoism took a neutral stance, and Chinese emperors in the Han period (206 BCE–220 CE) were known to take male lovers, so it is reasonable to assume that Buddhist monasteries may have seemed a desirable place for men with same-sex desires, whether or not they acted on those inclinations. A legend about Kūkai, the founder of the Japanese Shingon sect in the late eighth to early ninth century, credits him with bringing the practice of homosexuality from China to Japan. Unlike Hindus blaming same-sex sexuality on the Muslims, Japanese Buddhists venerated male love. So, with these differences from place to place, Buddhism can be seen as more tolerant of male same-sex sexuality than the other world religions. Even more than in other religious traditions, however, we know very little about love between women.

So what does religion have to do with it? Clearly the major world religions differ in their doctrinal positions on same-sex sexuality, Christianity seemingly the most all-encompassing and negative. But all are similar in paying less attention to sex between women—either because the male authorities did not think about it or because it did not really matter since women had little choice but to marry or to enter a religious institution or because nothing that two women could do together could really count as sexual. Yet at the same time, the sex-segregated places, both domestic and institutional, that the different religious traditions shaped created spaces in which, in fact, love and sex between women could flourish.

In Women's Spaces

What went on in women's spaces—whether monasteries or the women's quarters of private houses—has been, in the historical record, largely left to men's imaginations. Whether denied access to men or neglected by husbands busy with other women, wives in sex-segregated spaces could turn to other women, engaging in what men, when they thought of it, considered "making do." The problem is, we have almost no direct evidence of what went on away from men's eyes. So what are we to make of male fantasies?

The long stretch of time from the incursions of what the Romans thought of as "barbarians" to the discovery of the "New World" was one of increasing global integration through conquest, trade, and travel. Europe was at first a backwater; the great civilizations of the world flourished in the Middle East and Asia. As Islam, the first global civilization, spread around the Mediterranean and into central Asia from the seventh century on, the practice of secluding women in separate quarters of households (also practiced in ancient Greece) gave rise to all sorts of fervid Orientalist imaginings, especially on the part of European men who associated harem life with everything exotic and erotic in the Islamic world.

The military might of the Ottoman Empire represented a real threat to western Europe in the period when travelers began to bring home tales of life in the harem. In the mid-sixteenth century, a Venetian envoy to the Ottoman court in Constantinople described the "lustie and lascivious wenches" of the imperial harem. "It is not lawfull," he wrote, "for any one to bring ought in unto them, with which they may commit deeds of beastly uncleannesse; so that if they have a will to eate Cucumbers, they are sent in unto them sliced to deprive them of the meanes of playing the wantons."[29] Other travelers obsessed about the baths, where women "sometimes become so fervently in love the one of the other as if it were with men" that they "handle & grope them every where at their pleasures."[30] Much later, Richard Burton, the nineteenth-century British explorer and scholar who translated the *Thousand and One Nights* (which includes a story about a man seeing his beloved kissing her maid), described harems as "hot-beds of Sapphism and tribadism."[31] A British book from the mid-twentieth century reported that Iraqis believed that women in the harem kiss and make love out of sadness.[32] And in an over-the-top depiction, a 1950s account, *The Jewel in the Lotus: A Historical Survey of the Sexual Culture of the East,* ascribed wild goings-on to the harem:

> Isolated in enormous seraglios, females were generally given over to fanatic sapphism (*sehhauket*) employing the ancient substitutes for the appeasing phallus, the tongue, candle, banana, and artificial penis. . . .

In the restricted harem, *esh-sheykheh-el-bezzreh* (one who teaches the art of rubbing clitoris against clitoris) taught every girl in the sapphic sciences. To solace her in long hours of desire for the male, nearly every concubine had her own private companion whom she styled *merseeneh* or *reehauneh* (myrtle) and with whom she practices all the sapphic pleasures.[33]

The consistency of such accounts over the centuries is striking.

Despite the Orientalist fascination with the Islamic world, it was not only foreign men who imagined the goings-on in the women's quarters. Muslim historians reported that Musa al-Hadi, ruler of the Abbasid Empire in the eighth century, heard rumors that two of the women in his harem were lovers, dispatched spies who saw them embrace, and as a result had them beheaded.[34] A thirteenth-century text by a Tunisian-born jurist, Shihâb al-Dîn Ahmad al-Tîfâshî, includes a section on tribadism, including both positive and negative statements. One anecdote relates a conversation between two men. An important man says, "I want to know how women practice sex between them," and an impudent man replies, "If you would like to know that, enter your house a bit at a time."[35] In another tidbit, a man is told that his wife practices tribadism, and he responds, "Yes, I ordered her to do that," explaining, "because it is softer on her labia, purer for the opening of her vulva, and more worthy when the penis approaches her that she know its superiority."[36]

It was not only in the Middle East that women supposedly whiled away their days making love with one another. The *Kamasutra* addressed same-sex sexual activity as something that went on in women's quarters: "They dress up a foster-sister or girlfriend or servant girl like a man and relieve their desire with dildos or with bulbs, roots, or fruits that have that form." This was a practice that Vatsyayana, the compiler of the text, associated with "Oriental customs" in a colonized part of the empire.[37] A twelfth-century commentary on the erotic text connected women's domestic spaces with the households of courtesans: "Sometimes, in the secret of their inner rooms, with total trust in one another, they [women] lick each other's vulva, just like whores."[38]

Several medieval Bengali texts tell the story of how two co-wives gave birth to Bhagiratha, an important Hindu figure who brought the sacred river Ganga to Earth. In the fourteenth century, it is interesting to note, Bengal was a center of goddess worship. The stories differ in some details, but in all cases, Dilipa, the husband of the co-wives, dies without a male heir. In one version, a priest advises the wives to have sexual inter-course, with one taking on the desire of a man. In another version, the god Shiva goes to the widows of Dilipa to inform them that one will bear a son through intercourse with the other. "The two wives of Dilipa took a bath. The two young women lived together in extreme love. . . . Each of them knew the other's intentions; they enjoyed love play, and one of them conceived." In yet another version, the two women—this time with names, Chandra and Mala—are fired by Madan, the god of love, with the desire to have sex, and one of them unexpectedly conceives. "Burn-ing with desire induced by Madan, Chandra and Mala / took each other in embrace, / and each kissed the other. / Chandravati played the man and Mala the woman / The two women dallied and made love." Their son, Bhagiratha, was "born of mutual enjoyment between two vaginas."[39]

Other Indian texts also tell of love between co-wives. A Sanskrit play from the late third to early fourth century, *Swapnavasavadattam* (*Dream of Vasavadatta*), tells the story of Queen Vasavadatta, who has to fake her death and flee the county in disguise. She ends up in the care of a prin-cess, Padmavati, who is to become her own husband's new bride. The two women are attracted to each other and become very close. In a much later version of the story, the relationship is spelled out further. Padmavati sees the queen and "[falls] in love with her at first sight." She notes Vasavadatta's "shape, her delicate softness, the graceful manner in which she sat down, and ate, and also . . . the smell of her body, which was fragrant as the blue lotus." They become co-wives when Vasavadatta's identity is revealed, and they ultimately become of "one heart."[40] A slightly different version comes from a story about Brahmani, the beautiful daughter of a Brahmin, who refuses to marry because she does not want to be separated from her dear friend Ratnavati. Brahmani's mother arranges for both girls to be married into the same household. Through complicated circumstances, both end up becoming unmarriageable, so they are able to live together in "woman-to-woman bonding" for the rest of their lives.[41] All these cases from the Indian context emphasize the benefits of love between co-wives for the family and community.

Not all cultures were so welcoming. In the Siamese court during the Ayuthaya period (fourteenth to eighteenth centuries), the king forbade *len pheuan*, "playing with friends," for his concubines. "Any woman having sex with another woman like a man has sex with a woman will be punished by being whipped fifty times [and will] be tattooed on the neck and paraded around the palace."[42] Epic poems from the nineteenth century mention *len*

pheuan among concubines. In one, women expert at the practice seduce
women from another kingdom, who then delight so much in making love
to women that they refuse advances from men. A temple mural also portrays women touching each other's breasts, flirting with each other, and
being punished for sexual activity. In 1856, King Rama IV warned his
daughters not to engage in *len pheuan*, making clear that it was a known
practice.

In a variety of cultures, other kinds of sources also depicted sexual acts
between women, presumably enjoyed in the privacy of women's quarters.
An illustration from a seventeenth-century translation of a twelfth-century
Muslim Indian text shows a woman holding a bow with a dildo as the ar-
row, aiming it between the spread legs of another woman.[43] (See figure
5.) A Japanese erotic encyclopedia from the seventeenth century included
an illustration of a double-headed dildo for use by two women.[44] Chinese
sexual handbooks depicted mutual masturbation between women, and
prints and paintings featured complicated sexual acts. One handbook on
marital intercourse described two women lying

> on top of each other, their legs entwined so that their jade gates
> pressed together. They then moved in a rubbing and jerking fashion
> against each other like fishes gobbling flies or water plants from the
> surface. As they became more excited, the "mouths" widen and choos-
> ing his position carefully, Great Lord Yang thrusts between them with
> his jade root. They moved in unison until all three shared the ultimate
> simultaneously.[45]

Literary texts, too, portray women enjoying one another. A seventeenth-century Chinese short story, "The Pearl-Sewn Shirt," depicts an
older woman helping her male patron seduce a beautiful young woman by
first exciting her with "dirty and obscene" talk.[46] In another tale portraying women as likely to be aroused by other women, two sixteen-year-old
girls sharing a bed begin by touching each other "with shame," move to
kissing each other "just as a man kisses a woman with passion and without shame," and then when they observe their mothers having sex with
the same man, become so aroused that they make love with their fingers
and began regularly to engage "in sex play alternating roles as a man."[47] In
a seventeenth-century Chinese play, "Pitying the Fragrant Companion," a
young married woman falls in love with a younger unmarried woman she
met at a temple. They take vows as lovers in front of the Buddha's image,

Figure 5. Men imagine what went on in women's quarters. Image from the seventeenth-century Islamic Mughal Empire in India. Bibliothèque Nationale, Paris. From Stephen O. Murray and Will Roscoe, eds., *Islamic Homosexualities* (New York: New York University Press, 1997).

and then the married woman talks her husband into taking her lover as a second wife.[48] Late imperial Chinese literature, from the late sixteenth century to the early twentieth, abounds in tales of co-wife lovers happily married to the same man. In a comedy by Li Yu titled *Lian xiang ban* (*Women in Love*), two women who love each other work hard to persuade their fathers to allow them to marry the same man so that they can live together. It is worth noting that in some of these fictional tales, romantic love between women is primary, whereas in others, co-wives turn to each other to make their marriages work. As Li says at the beginning of *Women in Love*, "If a woman transforms the tumor of jealousy into the Embryo of passion, / It will be no ordinary infatuation."[49]

Is any of this literature a reflection of reality, or is much of it male pornographic fantasy? It is hard to know, given the available sources. Historical accounts describe slave women in the fourteenth-century harems of the *Mamluks*—slave soldiers who converted to Islam and came to rule in Egypt—riding horses, hunting (shades of the Amazons), drinking wine, indulging in debauchery with one another, and accumulating wealth, just like the *Mamluks*.[50] Another scholar reports that, in the Chinese imperial harem, "multiple concubines satisfied each other's sexual needs while on a 'waiting list' to meet with the Emperor" and that multiple wives of wealthy men also "initiated intimate alliances among themselves." Relying on erotic manuals that portray group intercourse known as "the Heavenly and Earthly Net," this scholar notes that women were likely to have had sexual contact with each other in this way, making it equally likely that they may have taken up with each other later without the presence of their common male partner. In Japan during the Tokugawa period (1600–1868), as well, the shogun's harem and a "public-access harem" of professional entertainers "were wont to engage in lesbian affairs to avoid the considerable risks of adultery." They could make use of penis substitutes, including the "dual plover" (*ryochi-dori*) that allowed two women to pleasure each other.[51]

In the Javanese court of Surakarta in the mid-nineteenth century, a scandal erupted when a woman was discovered making love to other royal women. A Dutch report on the incident explained that when the ruler discovered that "the women would be lying beside each other in various places, that among their indecencies, by way of a piece of wax which had been shaped in the form of the private parts of men they would be amidst each other," he outlawed the practice "as they might never be interested in love with men any more."[52]

In African societies, too—including among the Nyakyusa, the Mongo, the Nupe of Nigeria, the Tswana of southern Africa, and the Azande of southern Sudan—we have reports of relationships formed between the co-wives of chiefs and kings.[53] British anthropologist E. E. Evans-Pritchard, who studied the Azande in the 1930s, necessarily relied on reports from male Azande, who told him that sex-starved wives turned to one another. "Wives would cut a sweet potato or manioc root in the shape of the male organ, or use a banana for the purpose. Two of them would shut themselves in a hut and one would lie on the bed and play the female role while the other, with the artificial organ tied round her stomach, played the male role. They then reversed roles," he tells us.[54] A ruler sometimes gave his daughter a slave girl for sex. Although apparently known among Zande men, the practice was feared; in a culture in which witchcraft played a central role, sex between women could be dangerous, even fatal to a husband. Zande men reported that once a woman began to have sex with other women, she was unlikely to stop because she no longer had to wait for her husband to pleasure her. The deep connections that formed between women could be formalized through a ritual involving pledges of mutual support, and husbands, who had to give permission for their wives to take part in the ritual, found it difficult not to do so.

Still, we do not really know if such sources are accurate about what women really did. What we do know is that polygynous households provided the opportunity for desire between co-wives and that some societies considered this acceptable and others did not.

Another women's space potentially ripe for love between women was the convent or monastery. Just as religious and cultural traditions that allowed for polygyny prepared fertile ground for relationships among wives and concubines and servants, so, too, sex-segregated religious institutions facilitated same-sex relations despite vows of celibacy. The *Vinaya*, the Buddhist canon on monastic rules, referred to same-sex sexual acts between women; mutual masturbation among nuns was treated as a relatively minor offense, and not surprisingly, there were fewer references to female than to male same-sex acts in Buddhist monasteries.[55] Indian Buddhist monastic rules forbade two nuns to share the same bedcover.[56] A Japanese sexologist writing in the early twentieth century listed nuns, as well as servants in the women's quarters of feudal households, as among those who may have developed a taste for same-sex sexual acts because they could not engage in "normal sexual relations."[57] As Buddhism spread in China during the Ming dynasty (1368–1644), nuns came under increasing suspicion of having sexual connections with one another. Yet Chinese literature depicted men as accepting of or indifferent to such possibilities. A male character in one novel, *Dream of the Red Chamber* (*Hung Lo Meng*), is charmed when he comes upon a nun and another young woman in an intimate moment.[58] Disapproval stemmed mainly from Confucian rejection of Buddhist monasteries' disruption of family bonds and procreation.

As the letters between the nuns in Bavaria suggest, we know a bit more about love between women in Christian convents, if mostly from prohibitions and punishments. In Eastern Orthodox Christianity, centered originally in the Byzantine (or Eastern Roman) Empire, which survived the decline of the western part of the empire, same-sex relations were treated less harshly than in the West. Female same-sex relations merited little notice and were not punished with severity.[59] Western Christian authorities, on the other hand, took Paul's letter to the Romans to heart. Saint Ambrose, in the fourth century, explained that Paul "testifies that, God being angry with the human race because of their idolatry, it came about that a woman would desire a woman for the use of foul lust."[60] Centuries later, Peter Abelard interpreted "against nature" to mean "against the order of nature, which created women's genitals for the use of men, and conversely, and not so women could cohabit with women."[61] Most influential was Thomas Aquinas, who catalogued four categories of vice against nature under the sin of lust: masturbation, bestiality, coitus in an unnatural position, and "copulation with an undue sex, male with male and female with female."[62]

Yet early penance manuals that included sex between women as a sin did not call for severe penalties. The *Penitential of Theodore* (from England in the seventh century) specified three years' penance for an unmarried or widowed woman who "practices vice with a woman," the same amount of time as for masturbation; for married women it was a greater sin. The *Penitential of Bede*, a century later, took up the question of sexual transgressions among nuns, specifying, "If nuns with a nun, using an instrument, seven years," although whether the greater penalty was because of the religious vows or the instrument is not clear. Hincmar of Reims in the ninth century elaborated on the use of instruments, expressing the confusion that medieval authorities experienced imagining what women might do with one another: "They do not put flesh to flesh in the sense of the genital organ of one within the body of the other, since nature precludes this, but they do transform the use of the member in question into an unnatural one, in that they are reported to use certain instruments of diabolical operation to excite desire."[63] Lack of clarity about how women could have sex and what kind of sin it constituted persisted in both Church and secular law.

Monastic communities took steps to avoid nuns' falling into sin with one another. Saint Augustine, in the fifth century, instructed his sister, who was taking vows, to take care to feel spiritual, not carnal, love for her sisters. Monastic rules specified that nuns should not visit in one another's cells, should leave their doors unlocked, and should avoid ties of special friendship. In the seventh century, Donatus of Besançon warned about such friendships: "It is forbidden lest any take the hand of another for delight or stand or walk around or sit together."[64] He included the use of the endearment "little girl" and instructed that each nun should sleep in a separate bed, that lights should burn all night, and that the sisters should sleep in their clothes. Later Church councils also forbade nuns to sleep together and required a lamp to be kept lighted all night in dormitories. Such rules suggest the possibilities.

A fascinating glimpse into those possibilities can be gleaned from the letters of Shenute, the male head of the White Monastery in fifth-century

Egypt.[65] The women in the White Monastery, kept separate from the men, nevertheless lived under the same rule and the same authority. Shenute apparently relied on reports of infractions of discipline from the women in the community and meted out punishments accordingly. In one letter he listed individuals who had stolen, argued, launched physical assaults, lied, been stupid, and expressed homoerotic desire. Here is what he wrote about the latter: "Taêse, the sister of Pshai the younger. This one, concerning whom you sent to us, saying, 'She runs after Tsansnô in friendship and physical desire.' Fifteen blows of the stick." Tsansnô, too, appears in the list, guilty of even more: "This one, who says, 'It is others whom I teach.' Forty blows of the stick, because sometimes she ran after her neighbor in friendship, and sometimes she lied about empty things." The punishment consisted of blows on the bottom of the feet, a painful traditional Egyptian punishment.

The words in the original Coptic language for both "friendship" and "physical desire" refer clearly to erotic feelings. The head of a nearby monastery, a contemporary of Shenute named Horsiesios, wrote a lengthy attack on "wicked" and "evil friendship." Shenute used the term "carnal friendship" in his denunciations, stating, "And as for those among us, whether man or woman, who will be caught being friends to their neighbor in physical desire, they will be cursed in all their deeds that they do." He also warned about passion and physical contact: "Cursed is a woman among us who will run after younger women, and anoint them and is filled with a passion." And "Those, also, who will sleep, two on a mat, or those who will come too close so that they might touch or feel each other only in a passion of desire—they shall be cursed, whether man or woman."[66] The sources are silent about the actual feelings of "carnal friends."

The evidence from Egypt connects the prohibitions against "friendships" among nuns to an actual case, although we learn little about what the punished nuns, Taêse and Tsansnô, did or felt. Even more revealing, although still from the perspective of the male authorities, is the story of Benedetta Carlini, a seventeenth-century abbess of the Convent of the Mother of God in Pescia, Italy, whose mystical claims led eventually to revelations of her sexual conduct with another nun.[67] Historian Judith Brown discovered her remarkable story quite by accident, and only because Benedetta ran afoul of the Church hierarchy for an entirely different reason. Placed in a newly established convent by her parents at the age of nine, Benedetta became abbess at the young age of thirty, a result of her mystical visions and, ultimately, the appearance of the stigmata—the wounds of Christ—on her hands. Such a distinction drew attention, and favor, to the convent.

But that was not all. According to Benedetta, one night Christ came to her and removed her heart from her chest, then returned three days later and gave his own heart to her, assigning her a guardian angel named Splenditello to guard her purity. Christ returned once again to instruct her that he wanted to marry her in a public ceremony at the convent. The convent's priest and confessor, who had already permitted Benedetta in an altered state to give sermons to the nuns, agreed to the ceremony. Jesus, Mary, and a number of saints appeared to Benedetta, although not to the others, and Jesus put a ring—also not visible to anyone but Benedetta—on her finger. He spoke through Benedetta, telling of her visions in childhood and praising her virtues. After all this, Benedetta emerged from her trance and acted as if nothing special had happened. But enough was unusual—Benedetta's request for a public event, the lavish words of praise for herself that Jesus spoke through her—that the Church authorities decided to investigate. Although mystical happenings may have been rare, they were not unknown, but neither were fraudulent mystics. Because Benedetta was already attracting a following in her local community, the authorities decided it was time to confirm or disprove her claims.

It was this investigation that revealed the "immodest acts" in which Benedetta engaged with a younger nun, Bartolomea Crivelli, who had been assigned to share Benedetta's cell and watch over her during a period in which she was tormented by visions of handsome young men who beat her and tried to corrupt her soul. A first investigation, in 1619, found no cause for alarm. But in 1622 or 1623, a higher official, a papal nuncio, sent several of his men to investigate again, possibly prompted by another mystical event—Benedetta's death and return to life—or by dissatisfaction of the nuns chafing under Benedetta's firm control. The new investigation uncovered evidence of faked miracles and doubts about Benedetta's character, and this time the nuns began to talk. The real shocker came from Bartolomea, who told of the "immodest acts" Benedetta had forced on her in the guise of the guardian angel Splenditello. In handwriting presumably made shaky by the revelations, the scribe took down Bartolomea's testimony:

This Sister Benedetta, then, for two continuous years, at least three times a week, in the evening after disrobing and going to bed would wait for her companion to disrobe, and pretending to need her, would call. When Bartolomea would come over, Benedetta would grab her by the arm and throw her by force on the bed. Embracing her, she would put her under herself and kissing her as if she were a man, she would speak words of love to her. And she would stir on top of her so much that both of them corrupted themselves. And thus by force she held her sometimes one, sometimes two, and sometimes three hours.

Imagine the horror of the investigators. Sent to find out if Benedetta was a fraud, they now had to determine what else she was. They questioned Bartolomea further about the two women's relations, learning that Benedetta kissed Bartolomea's breasts and grabbed her hand "by force, and putting it under herself, she would have her put her finger into her genitals, and holding it there she stirred herself so much that she corrupted herself, . . . and also by force she would put her own hand under her companion and her finger into her genitals and corrupted her." These were immodest acts, for sure, but what kind? That was the question. Benedetta never admitted any participation in these acts, her male angel/alter-ego proving useful in this way. She did, however, in a final investigation admit that she had been tricked by the devil; she stopped having visions and took to living as an ordinary nun under the rule of a new abbess. Apparently the authorities decided that the two sisters had not committed sodomy, which would have condemned them to die at the stake. Instead, Benedetta lived out the rest of her life in prison in the convent, and Bartolomea seemingly returned to the normal life of a nun.

This case is remarkable for the description of sexual acts between women, even if that description was designed to protect the teller from the crime. We can never know what really went on, of course. Were they lovers? Benedetta, in the guise of her male angel, told Bartolomea she was "melting for love" of her and promised to "be her beloved."[68] Was she in love and expressing her love and sexual desire in the only way she knew? Was she a clever woman who found a way to get what she wanted? Or did she, too, believe in Splenditello, who in her eyes made the acts she engaged in with Bartolomea not sinful? If we cannot know what the two nuns really felt, we do at least learn something about what seventeenth-century Christian nuns may have done together.

Spanish novelist Jesús Fernández Santos, in his extraordinary dark novel *Extramuros*, imagines what went on in the story of a nearly identical case.[69] In a poor convent in Spain during a terrible drought, in the midst of the Inquisition, a nun falls ill and is attended by another sister, who narrates the novel. Death is everywhere, the convent is falling into ruin, and there seems to be no hope. The nameless sister recovers from her illness and recounts to her companion a dream, stimulated by the story of a saint that they had read together. The saint had received the stigmata, attracting attention and visitors from across the land and making her convent famous and rich. In the sister's dream, she sees their own wretched convent grow and prosper. Gradually she reveals her plan to her companion, talking her into wielding a knife to cut her palms and keeping quiet for the good of the convent. The plan works: the stigmata are accepted, townspeople flock to the convent, the nuns' patron comes to visit, and he even entrusts his daughter to the house. The "saint," as she comes to be called, is elected prioress. But jealousy and conflict within the convent erupt, and eventually the two nuns are taken away to be tried. They languish for years as the "saint" is slowly poisoned by her wounds and her lover loses her sight in the dark of the prison. But the way the story differs profoundly from that of Benedetta and Bartolomea is that the Spanish nuns are already lovers, and it is out of love that the narrator goes along with the plan. Yet their relationship never enters the investigation, despite the fact that the prioress catches them together and warns them against such a special friendship.

It is fiction, of course, but Santos provides another possible way to think of what may have happened between Benedetta and Bartolomea. He sensitively depicts the two women's relationship, how over time their "friendship ripened, bringing love in its wake shortly after." One night the "saint" arrives at her sister's cell. "When we proceeded to give each other the kiss of peace as at other times, her mouth lingered long on my cheek." The soon-to-be-saint asks if her friend loves her still. She thinks in response, "I was still flesh of her flesh, voice of her voice, breath of her breath, as I had been the very first time, back in the spring." When the narrator finally, compelled by love, tries to plunge the knife into her lover's hand, she cannot.

> Instead of wounding it I began to kiss it, beginning with her fingers, then following the path of her pale veins till both of us were lying on the bed, united and vanquished, on top of the miserable quilt. It was a dream like so many others in the past, dead now, in which love and will lost themselves till daybreak, when the two of us, locked in each other's arms, trembling, consoled, each seeking the other, the hurried pounding of our blood making us one. . . . It was like enjoying an agony eagerly desired, like wax that melts and dies in the heat of the flame,

like facing the world and sating ourselves with passion forever, a glorious madness, a splendid folly, an abundance of true carnal pleasure.[70]

It is a rapturous description of love and passion behind the convent walls,
although of course shaped by a late twentieth-century sensibility. Could
such a love have flowered between Benedetta and Bartolomea?

Less rapturous, perhaps, but historical rather than fictional are the
meager scraps of writing by nuns professing their love for a special friend.
There is the Bavarian nun who sent "all the love there is to her love":
"Why do you want your only one to die, who as you know, loves you with
soul and body, who sighs for you at every hour, at every moment, like a
hungry little bird."[71] There is a letter from Hadewijch, a thirteenth-century
Flemish beguine—a member of an uncloistered independent movement
of religious women—who wrote sensually about her love for Christ: "My
heart, soul, and senses have not a moment's rest, day or night; the flame
burns constantly in the very marrow of my soul." Yet she also expressed in
a joint letter to her sisters a special earthly love for, and disappointment
in, one of them: "Greet Sara also in my behalf, whether I am anything to
her or nothing. . . . Could I fully be all that in my love I wish to be for
her, I would gladly do so. . . . Now that she has other occupations and can
look on quietly and tolerate my heart's affliction, she lets me suffer."[72] And
there is Benedetta's reported profession of love for Bartolomea.

We know a bit more from the life of Hildegard of Bingen, an eleventh-century Benedictine abbess and visionary who formed an intensely
emotional commitment to a younger nun, Richardis, whom she "deeply
cherished" as her "dearest daughter."[73] According to the official story of
Hildegard's life, Richardis had "bound herself to [Hildegard] in loving
friendship in every way." When Richardis was elected abbess of another
monastery in 1151, Hildegard launched a letter-writing campaign to prevent her leaving. She pleaded with Richardis's mother, "[Do not] disturb
my soul and draw bitter tears from my eyes and fill my heart with bitter
wounds." When that had no effect, she wrote to the archbishop and then
the pope himself, alternately charging that Richardis's appointment represented the sale of an ecclesiastical office and insisting that it was God's will
that Richardis stay by her side. But it was to no avail—the pope threw the
matter back into the lap of the archbishop. Only one letter from Hildegard
to Richardis has survived; the younger nun died shortly after Hildegard
sent it. In it Hildegard wrote of her grief at their separation, as did the Bavarian nun to her absent friend, moving from imagery of mother–daughter

to that of widow–dead spouse. Suggesting both her conviction of the rightness of her love and her awareness of the perspective of others, she wrote, "I so loved the nobility of your character, your wisdom, your chastity, your spirit, and indeed every aspect of your life that many people have said to me: What are you doing?"[74]

So, although we may never really know what went on in women's spaces, either women's quarters or convents and monasteries, the prohibitions and the worries and imaginings of husbands and religious figures and the occasional scraps of evidence of love or sex between women are suggestive. At the very least, we might conclude, if men could imagine what two women might do left to their own devices (no pun intended), why could women not do so?

Mystics, Heretics, and Witches

In the Christian tradition, it was not only nuns who might fashion same-sex relations in the context of religious life. The line between holiness and evil—as we can see in the case of Benedetta Carlini and the "saint" of Santos's fiction—was profound but also tricky. Women mystics had the potential to challenge the gender order by behaving in unseemly ways in their altered states of consciousness—as did Benedetta in preaching to her flock. They might also express erotic desires—as did Benedetta. Were they possessed by God or the devil? That was always the question. In the case of heretics and witches, the answer was clear. Women in all these categories raise the possibility—if only that—of same-sex eroticism.

Women mystics, for example, like Benedetta, often focused on the wounds of Christ. The biographer of fourteenth-century mystic Catherine of Siena described her vision of Jesus offering the wound in his side: "'Drink, daughter, from my side,' he said, 'and by that draught your soul shall become enraptured with such delight that your very body, which for my sake you have denied, shall be inundated with its overflowing goodness.' Drawn close in this way to the outlet of the Fountain of Life, she fastened her lips upon that sacred wound, and still more eagerly the mouth of her soul, and there she slaked her thirst."[75] Scholars dispute whether this image should be understood as a metaphor for maternal nursing or cunnilingus, with the wound representing the vulva.[76] On the side of same-sex eroticism is visual evidence from a fourteenth-century close-up illustration of the wound in Christ's side, looking remarkably like a vulva.

And devotional texts designed for women encouraged them to touch, kiss, suck, and enter the wound.

Or consider the devotion to the Virgin Mary of Hildegard of Bingen, who so longed for her sister Richardis. Her musical compositions can be seen as homoerotic adoration of Mary, the counterpart to nuns' effusive love for Christ that is often described as (hetero)sexual in nature.[77] "Your innards held joy, just as grass on which dew falls when greenness floods into it; thus did it happen in you, o mother of all joy." Hildegard was also known for her knowledge of the body and herbal lore, and she wrote about female sexual pleasure: "When the breeze of pleasure proceeds from the marrow of a woman it falls into her womb, which is near the navel, and moves the woman's blood to pleasure."[78] Although Hildegard considered carnal pleasure a sign of the fall of man and explicitly denounced same-sex sexual activity—"a woman who takes up devilish ways and plays a male role in coupling with another woman is most vile in My sight"—she nevertheless connected women's spiritual devotion and sexuality in ways that can be considered homoerotic.[79]

Hadewijch, the thirteenth-century beguine we met lamenting the faithlessness of her sister Sara, wrote passionately of God as Love, using the name "Minne," also used in German and Dutch secular poetry. Like other mystics, her poetry was rapturously homoerotic:

> I greet what I love
> With my heart's blood.
> My senses wither
> In the madness of Minne.
> . . . .
> O dearly loved maiden
> That I say so many things to you
> Comes to me from fresh fidelity,
> Under the deep touch of Minne.
> . . . .
> I suffer, I strive after the height,
> I suckle with my blood
> . . . .
> I tremble, I cling, I give.
> . . . .
> Beloved, if I love a beloved,
> Be you, Minne, my Beloved.[80]

Another female mystic, Margery Kempe, a married English woman who had given birth to fourteen children, in the early fifteenth century had a vision and eventually persuaded her husband to live an ascetic life with her.[81] She began to travel around to holy sites, including to the Holy Land, and to weep and pray loudly about the passion of Christ. She was often disruptive in her shrieking and sobbing, she more than once came under investigation for heresy, and she also raised suspicions that she intended to take wives away from their husbands. In the book of her life that she dictated to a scribe, Margery told of being interrogated by the mayor of Leicester, who accused her of ill intentions: "to take our wives away from us and lead them with you." A Church official later worried that she had advised a woman "to forsake her husband."

Like Hildegard and other female mystics, Margery was devoted to the Virgin Mary, identifying with her grief at the loss of her son. She was inclined to burst out crying in the middle of sermons. During a trip to Rome, her outburst suggested passion: "she turned herself first on one side and then on the other, with great sobbing, unable to keep herself stable because of the unquenchable fire of love burning in her soul." Such drama attracted the attention of other women: "The good women, having compassion for her sorrow and greatly marveling at her weeping and crying, loved her much more." If she annoyed the men who were preaching, not so the loving women. "They, desiring to console and comfort her, . . . prayed her and in a way compelled her to come home with them, desiring that she should not go away from them." Margery's weeping and visions of Mary and the body of Christ, and the reactions of women to her, take on homoerotic overtones: "When the good women saw this creature weeping, sobbing and crying so wonderfully and mightily that she was nearly overcome by it, they prepared a good soft bed and laid her upon it and comforted her as much as they could." Christ's message to Margery in one vision suggests how important the company of women was to her: "[I will] take you by the one hand in Heaven and my mother by the other hand, and so shall you dance in Heaven with other holy maidens and virgins."[82]

Christian mystics were not the only women to express same-sex eroticism. Fourteenth-century mystical texts from India also suffuse devotion to God with homoeroticism. Janabai was a female mystic poet who depicted the deity as a woman, sometimes a devoted and intimate friend, sometimes a mother. In one verse, God washes and braids her hair, a definitely female activity. "Sitting among the basil plants, Jani undoes her hair. / God takes some butter and oils her hair, / Says 'My Jani has no one' and pours water on her. / Jani tells everyone, / My friend is bathing me.'"[83]

If appropriate spiritual devotion might be expressed erotically, in whatever religious tradition, spiritual deviance might, medieval Christian authorities believed, lead to sexual deviance. Both heretics and witches were thought to engage in lewd acts, sometimes women with women. Sexual impropriety—often heterosexual—was a charge often thrown in with accusations of inappropriate beliefs. Thirteenth-century Europe saw the rise of many heresies, a response to the intellectual and spiritual flowering of the twelfth century and reform movements within the Catholic Church. Although heretical beliefs could take a number of forms, most shared a critique of the Church hierarchy, and it is worth noting that women often played central roles in heretical sects.

One of the most important of these heresies, and the one most often connected to same-sex sexuality, was Bogomilism, which originated in Bulgaria, spread to central Europe, where followers organized the Cathar Church, and then developed a stronghold in southern France, where followers were known as Albigensians. Although heretical sects tended to emphasize asceticism, their enemies accused them of the opposite. Guibert of Nogent, a bishop in the early twelfth century, was the first to add charges of sodomy to the standard tales of orgies.[84] He described the Cathar heretics of southern France engaging in extramarital and promiscuous heterosexual relationships, adding also that "men are known to be with men and women with women."[85] Most charges focused on male same-sex sexuality, and in fact the association of heresy and sodomy can be seen in the English term *bugger*, a translation of the French *Les Bougres*, which connected the Albigensians to their origins in Bulgaria.

The Inquisition in colonial Mexico also uncovered cases in which women's intense religiosity found expression in heretical—and sexual—ways. A 1598 heresy trial of a devout Mexico City woman, Marina de San Miguel, revealed that, among other crimes, she and another woman had "kissed and hugged and [Marina] put her hands on the breast and . . . she came to pollution ten or twelve times, twice in the church."[86] In 1621, a Spanish priest reported that a young woman, Agustina Ruiz, had confessed to regular masturbation, sometimes accompanied by fantasies about the Virgin Mary in which she "came to her in her bed to hug and kiss her, they would sit with their dishonest parts rubbing against each other."[87]

The association of heresy and sexual deviation also emerges in a bizarre story about a fifteenth-century female vampire in Bohemia.[88] Barbara von

Cilli was a powerful noblewoman married to King Sigismund of Hungary and Bohemia. Toward the end of her life, in a political struggle with the powerful Habsburg family, she threw her support to the Hussites, a heretical sect similar to what later developed as Protestantism. After her death, her enemies accused her of associating with heretics, profaning Communion by drinking actual blood (thus qualifying her as a vampire), and maintaining a female harem and engaging in sex with young girls. The historical Barbara von Cilli is probably the model for a lesbian vampire tale written by a nineteenth-century Irish author, Joseph Sheridan Le Fanu—in this version there are no heretics but young girls dreaming of a lovely woman who visits them at night and kisses their throats and caresses them.[89] The fictional Count Dracula may in fact have been based on the sixteenth-century Countess Elizabeth Bathory, who wore men's clothes, spent time with an aunt known to have women as lovers, and was fond of torturing and killing female servants. Legend had it that she bathed in the blood of young girls to maintain her youthful appearance.[90]

The charges of sexual orgies, including sex with the devil, that churchmen and lay authorities leveled at heretics slide easily into the accusations of witchcraft against women in medieval and early modern Europe. In 1233, Pope Gregory IX described the orgies following initiation ceremonies of heretics and witches: "When this ceremony is over the lights are put out and those present indulge in the most loathsome sensuality, having no regard to sex. If there are more men than women, men satisfy one another's depraved appetites, women do the same for each other."[91] A tract published during the trial of witches in Arras, France, in 1460 made the same kind of connection: "Sometimes indeed indescribable outrages are perpetrated in exchanging women, by order of the presiding devil, by passing on a woman to other women and a man to other men."[92] Witches supposedly sealed their pact with the devil by having intercourse with him, and sexual deviance of all kinds was central to the supposed rituals of witches. The *Malleus Maleficarum* (*The Hammer of the Witches*), the fifteenth-century manual of witch-hunting, closely linked witchcraft to sexuality and to women's nature: "All witchcraft comes from carnal lust, which is in women insatiable."[93] A sixteenth-century tract about witches in Fez, Morocco, called them "*Sahacat*, which in Latin would be *Fricatrices*, because they have sexual relations among themselves in a damnable fashion. . . . If on occasion attractive women come to them, the witches are inflamed with love just as young men are for girls, and, in the guise of the demon, they ask that the women lie with them as payment."[94]

Witch-hunting in Europe peaked in the sixteenth and seventeenth centuries, by which time the vast majority of the accused were women. One
common accusation lodged against witches was that they caused male impotence, sometimes quite literally by separating penises from male bodies. As the *Malleus Maleficarum* put it, witches "sometimes collect male
organs in great numbers, as many as twenty or thirty members together,
and put them in a bird's nest, or shut them up in a box, where they move
themselves like living members, and eat oats and corn."[95] Representations
of witches in sixteenth-century German art portray them as independent,
meeting in groups, and often naked, calling attention to their existence
apart from men, their communal activities, and their lustful behavior.
Some scenes suggest masturbation and erotic ecstasy. Such representations seem to speak to male fear of female sexuality, especially sexuality
not controlled by men.[96] (See, for example, the homoerotic representation
in figure 6.)

Figure 6. A homoerotic
representation of witches
in early modern Europe.
Hans Baldung Grien, *Three
Witches*. Graphische Sam-
mlung Albertina, Vienna.
From Charles Zika, *Exor-
cising Our Demons* (Leiden:
Brill, 2003).

As European expansion overseas in the fifteenth and sixteenth centuries took Christianity to new lands, European conceptions of witchcraft merged with indigenous traditions. In Brazil, for example, native and African practices of magic and witchcraft confronted the importation of the Inquisition, eliciting from those accused of witchcraft confessions of sexual deviance, sometimes sex between women. In 1591, a forty-year-old woman, Paula Sequeira, confessed both to same-sex acts and to sorcery involving uttering the words of consecration used by priests during the sacrament of communion during sex with her husband. This practice, confessed by others as well, was supposedly designed to tame a man and make him "mad with love and desire."[97]

Although the witch-hunters' depictions of witchcraft are, like the reports of the activities of heretical sects, fantastic, in fact both some scholars and contemporary followers of the religious tradition known as Wicca argue that witchcraft was real, a pre-Christian pagan religion (known as the Old Religion) involving magic, healing, and worship of more than one god, including the Great Mother goddess.[98] It also involved openness to love and desire between women. In the Orthodox Church in medieval eastern Europe, female same-sex sexuality was considered a sign of paganism. Women who had sex with other women were known as "God-insulting grannies," a phrase also used for pagan women, and their sexual acts, churchmen thought, involved "praying to *vily* (female sprites)."[99] According to those who believe in the reality of the practice of paganism and witchcraft in medieval Europe, Christian and secular authorities came to view such worship, which had sexual aspects, as a pact with the devil, and through torture the authorities extorted the confessions they sought. Other scholars deny the existence of any kind of organized witch cult or pagan religious tradition, depicting those accused of witchcraft as individual women identified as deviant because they were old, eccentric, isolated, troublesome, and/or promiscuous. Or because they desired women?

Radical feminist scholars in the 1970s wrote about the witch craze as emblematic of systematic control and abuse of women. In *Woman Hating*, Andrea Dworkin connects the practice of witchcraft in early modern Europe to worship of the Old Religion, healing, and sexual independence, calling the frenzied torture and burning of witches a prime example of woman hating.[100] Self-proclaimed "Revolting Hag" Mary Daly, in *Gyn/Ecology*, counts the witch craze as one manifestation of what she calls "The Sado-Ritual Syndrome" or "The Re-enactment of Goddess Murder."[101] Both scholars see the witch hunts as a form of what Daly calls gynocide

(systematic murder of women) and the witch as an example of an independent woman in control of her body and sexuality—the exemplar of a
modern-day lesbian feminist. Contemporary practitioners of Wicca and
neopaganism, especially those who embrace feminism, make connections
to the history of goddess worship, the Amazons, and early modern witches
as healers and sexually independent women.[102]

As with mystics and heretics, most of what we know about witches as
potential lovers of women must be read between the lines. So once again
fiction comes in handy as a way to imagine the possibilities. "The Burning Times," a short story by British feminist novelist Sara Maitland, is nar-
rated by a woman who grew up in a small village alone with her mother,
a skilled lace-maker with a mass of tangled curls and a love of singing,
laughing, and storytelling. The lace-maker, who had come from another
village, was not popular, because she did not care what the other women
thought and she spurned the men who sought to kiss or marry her.

One day, as the girl was turning into a woman, a stranger named Margaret
showed up at their door. The mother shrieked and embraced her, and then
followed months during which the girl, jealous of her mother's attention to
Margaret but also enamored with Margaret, "ached and dozed and giggled
and sulked and longed with longings that [she] had no name for." She was
confused. Then one day her mother came home with the news that the Inquisitors were coming, and Margaret announced, "We can go." "Not again,"
said the girl's mother. The Inquisitors arrived, and one of them preached
a sermon about hell and witchcraft, begging the community to give up its
witches. Afterward the girl danced around a bonfire with the other young
people, but then she noticed that no one would speak to her, that people
she had grown up with were moving away from her. She ran home in fear,
and there she found Margaret and her mother, in bed and naked:

> their legs, bodies, arms, faces were entangled with each other in move-
> ment, intense and intensely beautiful. When I saw Margaret's buttocks
> in the light from the doorway, saw them lift and plunge, saw my moth-
> er's strong small butterfly hand reach across them, spread out, hold-
> ing her, then I knew what I had longed for. When I heard my mother
> moan softly I knew what I had wanted. I wanted to touch Margaret
> like that. I wanted to moan like that.

Filled with desire, and with jealousy and rage, she crept away, "and they,
wrapped in their own beauty and passion, did not even hear [her] coming

and going." She ran to the priest and denounced her mother as a witch. Margaret fled in time, but the authorities tortured and raped the mother until she confessed to all their fantasies, of flying and sex with the devil and spells to cause men's impotence. But the one thing she would not do was denounce her daughter. When they burned her at the stake, the parish priest urged the daughter to dance around the fire lest she burn too. And her mother smiled down at her as the flames consumed her.

The story begins with the agonies of the now-grown and married daughter, the mother of three sons who escapes from her house full of men to the peace of the church, where she allows herself to suffer but also remember her mother's smile and forgiveness. And it ends, playing on Paul's advice to the Corinthians that refraining from sex is best but marriage will do for those who cannot contain their lust, with "they say it is better to marry than to burn, but only just I think, only just."[103]

Whether or not witchcraft and heresy were in fact accusations flung at women who desired other women, unrestrained sexuality and independence from male control played a central role in what it was that men feared about witches and heretics.

Caught in the Act

As the historical story of Benedetta and Bartolomea and the fictional tale by Sara Maitland suggest, one of the places we can find evidence of love and desire between women is in the records of women caught in the act, few as they are. As we have already seen in the ancient Mediterranean world, exactly what women might do with one another was always a little unclear to the male authorities, thereby making female same-sex acts hard to outlaw—hence, the confusion: biblical calls for death, penances not so severe. A French compilation from 1270 stipulates punishments for women as well as men: men who commit sodomy would the first time lose their testicles, the second time lose their "member," and the third time be burned. In a puzzling parallel, "A woman who does this shall lose her member each time, and on the third must be burned."[104] What exactly a woman would lose is unclear, as is the offense for which she would be punished. In general, medieval European approaches assumed that a penis substitute was essential to anything that would count as sex, so a great deal of sexual activity between women may have gone unnoticed and, even if discovered, may have gone unpunished or may not have been punished severely.

Fourteenth-century Italian scholars, commenting on Roman law, focused on "women who exercise their lust on other women and pursue them like men" and defilement of one woman by another.[105] Throughout western Europe by the beginning of the fourteenth century, the death penalty became the norm for women convicted of what was generally considered sodomy, calling usually for burning at the stake, the same penalty as for heresy. In 1565, French jurist Jean Papon ruled that "two women corrupting one another together without a male are punishable unto death."[106] In the Orthodox Church, where sex between women was mostly considered a form of masturbation, with relatively light punishment, women who had sex with one sitting astride the other were sentenced to flogging.[107] So it is not that sex between women was unknown or ignored. Yet we have few records of women prosecuted for these crimes.

What cases there are give us some glimpses into love and desire between women. In 1405, a sixteen-year-old married woman named Laurence appealed to the king of France for a pardon for her part in sexual activities with another married woman, Jehanne. The two worked in the fields together, and one day Jehanne had said to Laurence, "if you will be my sweetheart, I will do you much good."[108] Laurence saw nothing evil in this proposition (remember, this account is her request for a pardon) but found herself surprised when Jehanne threw her onto a haystack and "climbed on her as a man does on a woman, and . . . began to move her hips and do as a man does to a woman."[109] Apparently Laurence enjoyed herself enough to have sex several more times, in her home, in the vineyards, and even by the village fountain. The case may have come to light because Laurence eventually tried to break things off, causing Jehanne to attack her with a knife. Laurence ended up in prison—we do not know what happened to Jehanne—but won release after six months, having expressed regret for her sin and depicted Jehanne as the aggressor.

In another case, in the early sixteenth century, a German domestic servant named Greta "loved young daughters, went after them, . . . and she also used all the bearings and manners, as if she had a masculine affect."[110] Greta was neither a hermaphrodite (what we would now call intersexed—the authorities checked) nor a wielder of a penis substitute, and perhaps as a result she did not arouse serious concern. The chronicler who reported on Greta noted that "among the learned and well-read one finds this thing is often encountered among the Greeks and Romans."[111]

What happened when a dildo came into the picture is clear from a number of other cases. In 1477, a woman named Katherina Hetzeldorfer was tried for a crime without a name in the German city of Speier and subsequently drowned in the Rhine. Hetzeldorfer, who had moved to the city two years before the trial with a woman she at first described as her sister, admitted in the course of the trial to having "deflowered her and . . . made love to her during two years" and also to having made sexual advances to other women in the city.[112] Witnesses, including two who confessed to having been seduced by Hetzeldorfer, described her as manlike in appearance and behavior. She gave one woman a substantial sum of money to make her submit to her "manly will."[113] Yet she had not passed as a man, despite telling at least a few people that she was a "husband" to her companion and, according to one witness, "hugging and kissing . . . exactly like a man with women."[114] Her crime was fashioning "an instrument with a red piece of leather, at the front filled with cotton, and a wooden stick stuck into it," a tool one seduced woman described as "a huge thing, as big as half an arm," with "semen . . . so much that it is beyond measure, that one could grab it with a full hand."[115] This, unlike "rubbing," was serious. Hetzeldorfer's "sister" appears nowhere in the trial transcript, so she must have gotten away. The two women who testified about having been seduced were banished from the city, a rather mild punishment. As we shall see, other women who crossed the gender lines and presented themselves as men, married women, and fashioned the tools of the trade also suffered execution in early modern Europe.

The fact that Hetzeldorfer's crime was nowhere named recalls the trial of a woman in Geneva in 1568, also sentenced to drowning for confessing to having had sex with another woman. At her execution, her crime was publicly proclaimed "a detestable and unnatural crime, which is so ugly that, from horror, it is not named here."[116] Could "female sodomy" not be named because it was so unimaginable? So threatening? Because women, so naturally lustful, might get ideas?

In other traditions as well, women who desired other women could only be conceptualized as like men. A medieval Arabic astrological treatise reported that the stars in masculine signs could make women virile, so that they would "act as if their female friends were their wives."[117] A twelfth-century text described masculine women: "They also like being the active partners. . . . When her desire is aroused, she does not shrink from seduction. When she has no desire, then she is not ready for sexual intercourse. This places her in a delicate situation with regard to the desires of men and leads her to Sapphism."[118] We have already met Shihâb al-Dîn Ahmad al-Tîfâshî, the thirteenth-century Arabic writer who addressed

ITHACA COLLEGE LIBRARY
WITHDRAWN

tribadism. He reported that tribades love one another as men do, and that they spend a great deal of money on one another, "like a man spends on his female beloved."[119] Furthermore, he envisaged the female lover on top of her beloved in their lovemaking, unless the lover was thin and the beloved heavy. An earlier Arabic text gave recipes for drugs "which make women detest lesbianism [again, surely not the exact word used] even if they madly lust for it" and others that "make lesbianism so desirable to women that they would keep busy with it and passionately lust for it forgetting all about their work."[120]

It was not only the legal authorities who had trouble conceptualizing sex between women as anything other than heterosexual in form. Andreas Capellanus, author of the twelfth-century treatise "On Love," written at the court of Marie de Champagne, herself associated with the Cathar heresy, put it this way: "The main point to be noted about love is that it can exist only between persons of different sex. Between two males or between two females it can claim no place, for two persons of the same sex are in no way fitted to reciprocate each other's love or to practise its natural acts."[121] The only known medieval text in French to depict sex between women, the twelfth-century *Livres des manières* by Etienne de Fougères, mocks and criticizes the misbehavior of different social groups, ending with elite women who sin in various ways. Sex between women, what the author calls the "vile sin," he depicts as both copying heterosexuality and failing to amount to much because of the lack of a penis: "They bang coffin against coffin, / without a poker to stir up their fire"; they "join shield to shield without a lance"; "they don't bother with a pestle in their mortar"; they play "the game of thigh-fencing." Yet "they're not all from the same mold: / one lies still and the other grinds away, / one plays the cock and the other the hen / and each one plays her role."[122]

What is striking about the stanzas on lovemaking between women in this poem is the military imagery of shields, fencing, and jousting ("In twos they do their lowlife jousting"), for these are not images that appear elsewhere in medieval French literature. They were, however, common in Arabic erotic texts, with which Etienne would probably have been familiar, given Arab rule of Spain from the eighth to the fifteenth centuries. The tenth-century *Encyclopedia of Pleasure*, by Abdul Hasan Ali Ibn Nasr Al-Katib, includes the sentence "Your vulva became like a shield." In an eleventh-century work called *The Book of Metonymic Expressions*, an Iraqi religious judge described sex between women as "a war in which there is no spear-thrusting, / But only fending off a shield with a shield." A thirteenth-century text by al-Tîfâshî, *The Delight of Hearts*, written after Etienne's poem, described "a tournament / In which there is no use of lance, / Hitting only with great noise / One shield against the other!" Al-Tîfâshî went on to provide an extraordinary detailed description of how two women might joust without a lance: "The one that must stay underneath lies on her back, stretches out one leg and bends the other while leaning slightly to the side, therefore offering her opening (vagina) wide open: meanwhile, the other lodges her bent leg in her groin, puts the lips of her vagina between the lips that are offered for her, and begins to rub the vagina of her companion in an up-and-down and down-and-up, movement that jerks the whole body."[123] The military imagery suggests not only the influence of Arabic texts on Etienne's poem but also the more open and sophisticated understanding of sex between women in the medieval Arabic tradition compared to the European tradition.

What the laws against sex between women, the trials of women caught in the act, and literary descriptions of sexual encounters tell us is how confounding sexual encounters between women could be and what a central role female masculinity played in conceptions of women's relationships.

But what of love between women? Court cases, erotic manuals, penances handed out to nuns, and the fervent imaginings of the copulation of co-wives or heretics or witches all tell us of sexual acts in such a way that love must be read between the lines, if it is visible at all. But words of love from women are rare. Women mystics poured out words of homoerotic love; the unnamed Bavarian nun expressed her love and longing for her friend; Hadewijch and Hildegard of Bingen singled out Sara and Richardis, respectively, in palpably emotional terms; and fiction tells of passion between nuns and secular women who burned for their purported crimes.

But let us return to the lone example in European medieval literature that expresses a woman's love for another woman, the one John Boswell mentioned but brushed aside. Bieiris de Romans was a woman troubadour who addressed a poem in courtly love style to a woman named Maria. Nothing is known about either woman. Not surprisingly, some scholars doubt that this is really a love poem from one woman to another—either Bieiris must really have been a man, or Maria represents the Virgin Mary.[124] Listen to the words of the first two stanzas, coming to us from the early thirteenth century:

Lady Maria, in you merit and distinction,
joy, intelligence and perfect beauty,
hospitality and honor and distinction,
your noble speech and pleasing company,
your sweet face and merry disposition,
the sweet look and the loving expression
that exist in you without pretension
cause me to turn toward you with a pure heart.

Thus I pray you, if it please you that true love
and celebration and sweet humility
should bring me such relief with you,
if it please you, lovely woman, then give me
that which most hope and joy promises
for in you lie my desire and my heart
and from you stems all my happiness,
and because of you I'm often sighing.[125]

And let us consider one more example of love, one that bridges the medieval world of the convent and the new possibilities that emerged as the world opened up. Sor Juana Inés de la Cruz, a seventeenth-century Mexican nun, was a self-taught poet, playwright, and scholar whose accomplishments shocked her (male) contemporaries. Among other things, she wrote love poems to the wife of the Viceroy and thus has come down to us as a Chicana feminist and lesbian precursor.[126] She left these lines:

Don't go, my darling, I don't want this to end yet.
This sweet fiction is all I have.
Hold me so I'll die happy,
thankful for your lies.

My breasts answer yours
magnet to magnet.
Why make love to me, then leave?
Why mock me?

Don't brag about your conquest—
I'm not your trophy.
Go ahead: reject these arms.

that wrapped you in sumptuous silk.
Try to escape my arms, my breasts—
I'll keep you prisoner in my poem.[127]

Juxtaposing words of love and evidence of women caught in the act with the contradictory religious and secular pronouncements suggests how cautiously we must evaluate the evidence. Love between women was not unknown, and in some societies it was deemed harmless or even desirable for women who lived in polygynous households. The religious institutions—especially Christian ones—that sought to proscribe love between women in fact facilitated it and provided forms of expression for passionate homoeroticism. In these different sex-segregated spaces, erotic friendships could blossom. In the eyes of the male authorities, female same-sex sexuality was at times inconsequential, at times unimaginable, at times threatening. As in ancient worlds, what separated acceptable forms of same-sex sexuality from those considered so abhorrent that the acts could not even be named was primarily masculinity—in the cases we have seen here, women who penetrated other women—and independence from male control. Women such as Katherina Hetzeldorfer, witches with insatiable lust—these were the monsters, greatly to be feared.

We turn now to consider more closely diverse manifestations of female masculinity in a wide variety of societies.

5

In Plain Sight

(1100–1900)

WHILE SOME WOMEN who loved other women kept away from pry-
ing eyes behind monastery walls or in the private quarters of their houses,
others hid in plain sight. They accomplished this feat by secretly crossing
the gender line or, where available, publicly claiming a third-gender or
"social male" role, which officially made them not-women. In either case,
they could marry and live with and, in some cases, make love to other
women. Either no one knew there were female bodies under their male
clothing, or else they knew but accepted gender crossing as appropriate. In some cases, we know about women who presented themselves as
men in societies with a rigid two-gender system because some of them
were discovered or betrayed. In other cases, we know about women in
societies with a more flexible eye for gender primarily because outsid-
ers observed and disapproved of such behavior. What we do not know is
whether women secretly became men solely for the economic and social
freedom that male dress and employment could provide, whether women
who openly crossed gender lines did so for economic or spiritual reasons,
whether sexual motivation figured into any of these decisions, or whether
some of these women conceived of themselves as something akin to transgendered, even if no such concept existed. We are particularly in the dark
about the motivations of gender-crossing women's wives. But what we
do know opens another window on women who desired and loved other
women, even if some of them may not have thought of themselves as
women at all. And of course not all women who crossed the gender lines
desired other women. It is those who did who are of interest to us here.
As we shall see, the history of gender crossing continues into the present,
when a transgender identity has increasingly become a possibility, at least
in some parts of the world.

From the very beginning, as we have seen, masculinity—sometimes
ascribed to the women in question by hostile observers, sometimes

embraced by the women themselves—played a role in the stories of women who desired women. But not until around the sixteenth century do we begin to find evidence not just of masculine women but of actual gender crossing, both secret and sanctioned. As Europeans began to encounter societies in parts of the world previously unknown to them, they were shocked to find that some allowed individuals to cross the lines of gender. They seemed not to have connected such phenomena to the kind of secret gender crossing they knew at home. The period of European expansion, beginning in earnest in the sixteenth century, witnessed not only the witch craze, with its lurid tales of sexual deviance, but also a number of cases in which women were brought to trial and sometimes executed for the crime of what one trial document called "counterfeiting the office of a husband." What third-gender or cross-gender individuals beyond the Western world made of the Europeans with their rigid notions of male and female is much harder to discern. But one thing is for certain: multiple genders and gender crossing of various kinds can be found in societies around the globe, making female masculinity a central and continuing theme in the history of sapphistries.

Beyond the Binary

The notion that there are two categories into which all people fall—women and men—and that it is always possible to place everyone in one or the other category is challenged by intersexed individuals, by those who for a variety of reasons cannot be easily categorized, and by those who object to their placement. Societies deal with such challenges in a variety of ways, including killing or "fixing" intersexed people, insisting on categorization based on genitalia, or—sometimes—recognizing the possibility of gender crossing or creating categories beyond woman and man, female and male.

A wide variety of religious traditions present deities able to transform their gender (and even turn themselves into animals), fostering rituals of worship in which their followers also invoke fluid identities. In ancient Sumer (3500–2000 BCE), for example, the goddess Inanna lived as a young man, fighting and taking multiple lovers. The Hindu god Vishnu, in his human male form of Krishna, became a beautiful woman in order to defeat a demon.[1] In the ancient Greek Dionysian rites, women dressed as men and men as women in honor of an effeminate deity. South Indian followers of the goddess Yellamma, who has the power to change people's sex, cross-dress in her honor.[2] Such divine and human gender crossings present the possibility of challenging a fixed gender binary.

In early Christianity, saintly women who dressed as men were much admired for dispensing with their inferior gender. As Saint Jerome put it in the fourth century, when a woman "wishes to serve Christ more than the world, then she will cease to be a woman and will be called man."[3] Stories about Saint Pelagia, a prostitute in Antioch who became a Christian, describe her as dressing as a man. Saint Margarita was so horrified at the prospect of marriage that she cut her hair, put on men's clothes, and became a monk. So successful was her disguise that the woman porter at the monastery accused her of fathering the child she was carrying. The same accusation confronted a woman named Marina, whose father took her with him to a monastery in the guise of a boy. In all these cases, the secret of the women's sex came to light only when they died, and what was admired about them was their virginity and their shedding of their inferior gender.

Some cultural traditions go further in recognizing not just the potential to change genders but the existence of more than two genders. In ancient Sumerian mythology, the god Ninmah created different kinds of people, one of whom "has no male organ, no female organ."[4] A Sanskrit collection of mythology and ritual from the eighth century BCE recognized male, female, and neuter genders, the latter "neither female nor male, for being a male it is not a female, and being a female it is not a male."[5] Later Indian medical texts explained such "neuter" individuals as defective, either men who were impotent or women who could not bear children, and identified the cause as flawed paternal semen or maternal blood. Such thinking underlies the category and social role in contemporary Indian society of the *hijras*, men who desire other men, are castrated, and perform femininity.[6] They present themselves as women and work as prostitutes but also take on unique social roles, including the blessing of marriages and the birth of male children.

No entirely comparable role developed in Indian society for male women, although there are traditions of women taking on male roles in a number of different contexts. A Sanskrit text from the fourth century BCE describes Amazon-like women archers who served as bodyguards for the king. Other texts refer to a *svairini* as a woman who has sex with women. A commentary on the *Kamasutra* describes the *svairini* as "a woman known for her independence, with no sexual bars," who "makes love with her own kind."[7]

A Chinese story from the early seventeenth century combines the kind of love between women in royal households we have already encountered with female masculinity. Hu Ali, one of the king's concubines, began an affair with her cross-dressed lady-in-waiting, Shenge, when the king started having sex with Hu's daughter. Shenge gave Hu a dildo, known as "Mr. Horn," which the two women used in their sexual encounters. Another lady-in-waiting saw the two together and, thinking that Shenge was really a man, told the king. Although he had had sex with Shenge himself and reportedly ordered her to wear men's clothing, he seized the opportunity to have Hu killed, after which Shenge killed herself.[8]

An example of independence, masculinity, and desire to penetrate emerges in an Arabic text from the twelfth century. Sharif al-Idrisi describes educated and intelligent women—scribes, Qur'ān readers, and scholars—who "possess many of the ways of men so that they resemble them even in their movements, the manner in which they talk, and their voice."[9] They prefer to be the active partner in sex, refuse to submit to men, and instead turn to women. But whether these different expressions of female independence, adoption of masculine roles, and desire for women constitute an institutionalized third-gender role is in question.[10]

A clearly institutionalized gender-variant role did emerge in some societies. Best known for societal acceptance of gender crossing or recognition of a third (or more) gender category are some Native American cultures, although male-to-female gender crossing was more common than female to male.[11] Manly women could be found particularly among societies in western North America, including the Kaska in the Yukon, the Klamath in southern Oregon, and the Mohave, Maricopa, and Cocopa in the Southwest.[12] These were all nonhierarchical societies with subsistence economies in which both women's and men's contributions were valued, even if differentiated. Scholars disagree about the best way to conceptualize the institutionalized role variously described as "cross-gender," "third gender," or "two-spirit." "Cross-gender" sees individuals moving entirely from one gender to the other, "third gender" describes a mixture of the masculine and feminine and a gender apart from either women or men (or, in the case of "fourth gender," manly women differentiated also from womanly men), and "two-spirit" emphasizes the spirituality connected to being a manly woman. However conceptualized, the role has to do with spirituality, occupation, personality, and gender more than sexuality, so when sex does take place between a manly woman and another woman (never another cross-gender person), it may technically be "same-sex sex" because the bodies involved are physiologically alike, but in fact the sex is more accurately conceptualized as cross-gender.[13] In some Native American societies, sex between two individuals with the same body parts was not confined to gender-crossers and their partners, making clear that recognition of gender-crossing was not just a way to conceptualize same-sex relationships.

Taking on a different gender was not something that happened suddenly or randomly. For the Cocopa *warrhameh*, the Mohave *hwame*, and the Maricopa *kwiraxame*, interest in the occupations of men in their societies began early. Girls might play with boys, hunt, and refuse to do the tasks ordinarily assigned to girls. (See figure 7 for a representation of Pine-Leaf, a Crow warrior, published in an 1856 book). Unsuited to marriage and the responsibilities of women, such individuals could be initiated into male status, allowing them to engage in men's productive tasks, fight, fulfill male ritual obligations, and marry women. Since marriages in these societies were not important for property or rank and so could be easily dissolved, manly women could acquire children from marrying a divorced woman or a pregnant woman or perhaps through extramarital sex on the part of their wives. Manly women and their female wives could engage in sexual relations, involving tribadism, the use of fingers, and a position with a special name that involved intertwined legs and vulvas rubbed together, although *hwames* did not like to have the word *vulva* applied to their genitals, since it emphasized their femaleness.[14] In every area of life, a male social role took precedence over female biology.

A few examples of manly women among Plains societies have surfaced, although earlier contact with Europeans seems to have made those societies more reluctant to discuss gender-crossing in their past or present.[15] A Crow known as Woman Chief, born in the Gros Ventre tribe and as a child captured and raised by the Crow, showed an early inclination to take on masculine habits and tasks and was encouraged to hunt and ride. She became a warrior and led successful raids against the Blackfoot, and eventually she married several wives who took care of female tasks for her. Although she was tall and strong, she did not wear men's clothing. Another woman warrior, a Piegan by the name of Yellow Weasel Woman, showed interest in masculine pursuits around the age of ten. She participated in boys' games and refused to learn women's tasks. When her father died, she became the head of the household and took in a young widow to handle domestic chores. Having shown courage and skill when caught in a raid, she became a respected warrior, earning the male name of Running Eagle. She refused

Figure 7. Pine-Leaf, a Crow warrior, 1856. From T. D. Bonner, *The Life and Adventures of James P. Beckwourth* (New York: Harper and Bros., 1856).

all suitors, declaring that the Sun had instructed her not to marry.[16] These women clearly adopted some aspects of the male role, suggesting a spectrum of gender crossing among different Native American societies.

Oral tradition among the Kutenai of British Columbia tells of a female member who married a white fur trader in the early nineteenth century but returned a year later announcing that her husband had transformed her into a man.[17] She took the name Gone-To-The-Spirits, began to wear men's shirts, leggings, and breech cloths, and armed herself with a bow and a gun. She courted women, without success, until she found one who had been abandoned by her husband and agreed to live with her. Rumor spread that she had made a phallus out of leather to pleasure her wife. When Gone-To-The-Spirits lost her bow, arrows, and canoe gambling with men, her wife left in disgust. Gone-To-The-Spirits then took up with a succession of women and also joined raiding and war parties with men. On one expedition, her brother saw her crossing a creek, having removed her clothing, and realized that she had not really been turned into a man.

With one of her wives she took up the task of delivering a letter to Fort Astoria, at the mouth of the Columbia River in present-day Oregon, where, in 1811, one of the men at the fort reported the arrival of "two strange Indians, in the character of man and wife."[18] When the fur trader who had worked with Gone-To-The-Spirits's ex-husband arrived at the fort, he recognized her and told the others that the couple "were two women, one of whom had dressed herself up as a man to travel with more security." He also reported that when he knew her in the past, "her conduct was then so loose" that he had to request her husband "to send her away to her friends."[19] Another account added, in admiring tones, "and bold adventurous amazons they were."[20]

In 1837, Gone-To-The-Spirits was mediating between the Kutenai and the Blackfoot when she was killed in a raid. According to Kutenai stories, she was shot several times with little effect, slashed with knives but miraculously healed, and died only when a warrior cut open her chest and sliced off a portion of her heart. What is clear from the accounts is that her own people came to respect her as a warrior and prophet, whereas the white traders, who called her "Manlike Woman" but also referred to her as a "lady," did not know what to make of her. Nor did the author of a 1965 article based on the oral and written sources, for he used terms such as "sexual deviation," "sexual aberrancy," "sexual inversion," and "female perversion" to describe the Kutenai "female berdache."[21]

As white encroachment on Native American lands increased, the cross- or third-gender role faded, at least from public view, and attitudes of Native American societies that had previously accepted the role hardened. Anthropologist George Devereux, who published his research on the Mohave in the 1930s, reported widespread ridicule of women who would marry a *hwame*: "No man must want her, so she went to live with a hwame," he quoted informants telling him, or "What can be the matter with that woman? She is quite terrible. What does she think she gets from that hwame husband of hers?"[22]

Devereux also recounted the story of Sahaykwisa, a Mohave *hwame* born in the mid-nineteenth century, who encountered hostility from men who tried to lure her first wife away from her. They made fun of her wife for putting up with a "husband who has no penis and pokes you with the finger."[23] At first her wife insisted that she wanted to remain with Sahaykwisa, but finally she eloped with one of the men who taunted her, although later she returned to Sahaykwisa, only to leave her once again. In the meantime people began to call Sahaykwisa "split vulvae," the term used to refer to the special sexual position between a *hwame* and her woman partner, although they did not dare say to it to her face. Sahaykwisa married another woman, who also faced ridicule from both the former wife and from men. She, too, eventually left, after which Sahaykwisa found a third wife, who abandoned her husband but then returned to him. Sahaykwisa could attract wives because she was a good provider, able to give them beads and clothes, in part through her earnings as a shaman who could cure venereal disease. But when her third wife left her and Sahaykwisa went after her, the woman's husband lay in wait for her and raped her, boasting that he would "show her what a real penis can do."[24] After that, Sahaykwisa began drinking, having sex with men, falling in love with them, and allegedly bewitching them. She was killed by two men who drowned her for her practice of witchcraft, revealing another kind of connection between magical powers and same-sex sexuality.

An intriguing story from a Saami (originally known as "Lapp") community in seventeenth-century Sweden suggests that acceptance of gender crossing may have existed in that Native culture as well. A man known as Carl Lapp died in 1694, and when the neighbors prepared him for burial, they discovered that he had a woman's body. They reported this news to the pastor, who passed it up the chain of command. A court took up the case to decide what to do with Lapp's body, and the investigation focused on his potential sexual deviance and his gender transgression. Lapp had been married twice. His second wife, who was still alive, insisted that she had never known that he was not male because they had never had sex, given that he was an old man when they married and she was barren. But his first wife had borne a son, leading the court that investigated the case after Lapp's death to conclude that he had participated "in the sin of fornication that the former wife had carried on and kept it silent and hidden it, allowed the child to be baptized and recognized it as his own."[25] Even more serious was his mutating his sex, which warranted the death penalty under Swedish law. In the end, the court ordered the executioner to bury Carl Lapp's body in the forest, rather than in a church burial ground. It was a dire punishment for a Christian, but ironically, it was a Saami practice that Swedish pastors had long opposed. Saami beliefs did not entirely separate the world of the living from the dead, and perhaps the Saami also did not draw clear lines between male and female.

Although a variety of other societies elsewhere in the world have institutionalized cross-gender or third-gender roles for men, the possibility for women to take on male ways of being seems to be much rarer. In southern Iraq, a woman could dress in men's clothing and take on some of the roles of men. Such a woman, known as a *mustergil*, would announce her decision to live life as a man shortly after she began menstruating, when ordinarily a girl would be married. She would take part in the public life of men, hunt, and be accepted in her community as a man. She would not, however, acquire the legal rights of a man under Islamic law, and she would not take a wife.[26] In fact, there is no evidence of same-sex sexual desire or behavior connected to the *mustergil*.

Another case of women taking on the social roles of men comes from the Balkans. Beginning in the nineteenth century, some Montenegrin and Albanian women from rural areas either were raised as boys because the family lacked a male heir or embraced the male role later in life. They were known as "sworn virgins" and took on the dress, occupations, and legal rights of men, although they maintained female immunity from violence despite their ability to carry arms and kill men. They were treated as social males even though their communities knew that they were biological women. Mikas Milicev Karadzic, born in the mid-nineteenth century, served as a soldier and worked as a farmer, insisting on being addressed

Figure 8. Mikas Milicev Karadzic, 1929, a "sworn virgin." From Gilbert Herdt, ed., *Third Sex, Third Gender* (New York: Zone Books, 1996).

as a man. (See his masculine appearance in figure 8). Although he never admitted to having sex with either men or women, he appreciated beautiful women and, according to one informant, was physically attracted to them.[27] Another "sworn virgin," Stana Cerovic, born into a family of all girls, also lived life as a boy from childhood and told a reporter, "I detest being a female . . . nature is mistaken."[28] At local dances, he drank with the men and remarked on the desirability of the women. Some masculine sworn virgins, however, lived with female partners in "blood sisterhood," a ritual of spiritual kinship, and some of these were at least thought to have had sexual relationships.

A somewhat similar social role for women who refused to marry emerged at about the same time in Kangra, on the edges of the Himalayas in northwest India.[29] Hinduism has a long tradition of female ascetics renouncing the world, and in a society in which women were expected to marry and bear children, the role of *sādhin* provided a small number of women the possibility of avoiding that traditional life. *Sādhini* are Hindu ascetics, but ascetic only in the sense of forgoing marriage and sexuality. They remain in their familial homes, can own property, and dress and act in some ways as men. Adopting the role is a girl's choice, supposedly made before the onset of menstruation but often in fact made close to the time when a girl would be married. Some choose the role because they do not want to marry; one father of a *sādhin* who made the choice when she was six said that when she was very young she wanted to wear boys' clothing and cut her hair short. But the *sādhin* does not become a man. She keeps her female name and continues to perform traditionally female tasks, although she may also take on the work of men. *Sādhini* are also allowed to participate in male social and ceremonial functions, although they often prefer to stay with the women. So they are like men in certain situations but are essentially women whose masculine characteristics mark them as female ascetics. Such a role shows that societies can be creative in fashioning roles for women who, for whatever reason, reject marriage to a man. In this case, unlike that of Native American gender crossers but as in the case of the Christian virgins and the *mustergil*, the price is renunciation of sexuality as well.

The question of connection between gender crossing and sexuality also arises in the case of marriages between women in some African societies. In more than thirty African groups, woman-woman marriage has been and in some cases still is a possibility. The fundamental reason for such marriages is economic and familial: if a woman cannot conceive, she can continue her family line by taking a wife who will bear children with a male consort. As among the Mohaves, a female husband could be the father of children born to her wife from a union with a biological male. In that sense, she is a "social male." In at least some cases, such a role involved, as for third-gender Native Americans, male dress and occupations. Among the Nandi of Kenya, women who have not been able to bear a son can pay bridewealth for and marry a woman to bear children for her and continue her family's line.[30] The female husband is considered a man for the important purposes of property ownership and inheritance, but she does not have to function as a man in every context. For example, it is important that she take care of her wife and children, but it is less essential that she socialize primarily with men, speak in public meetings, attend men's initiation ceremonies, and refrain from carrying things on her head, although the ideal is that a female husband will act as a social male in every way except sexually. In other words, everyone knows she is a woman, and she sometimes acts more like a woman than a man, but the fiction that she is a man and a husband must be maintained. And, like the *sādhin*, the female husband must be asexual.

Female husbands among the Nandi take this route, according to their own accounts, solely in order to gain a male heir. Elsewhere there might be additional motivations. In Nigeria in the 1990s, an elderly Ohagia Igbo *dike-nwami*, or "brave-woman," by the name of Nne Uko told an ethnographer that she "was interested in manly activities" and felt that she was "meant to be a man."[31] Although she was divorced from a husband, she farmed and hunted, joined men's societies, and married two women who gave birth to children fathered by her brother. Still, we know very little about the emotional and potentially sexual aspects of woman-woman marriages. One ethnographer who spent two years studying the Bangwa of Cameroon in the 1970s suggested an emotional component when he described his best woman informant's relationship with one of her wives, commenting on "their obvious satisfaction in each other's company."[32] Poet Audre Lorde, in asserting the importance of a history of female bonding for Black women, quoted the life history of a ninety-two-year-old married Nigerian woman; this woman spoke of her love for another woman, with whom she "acted as husband and wife," and stated outright that some woman-woman marriages among the Fon of Dahomey are lesbian relationships.[33]

Yet most scholars insist that African woman-woman marriages are never sexual.[34] In a study of gender relations in Nnobi, a town in an Igbo area of eastern Nigeria, an African scholar attacks Black U.S. lesbians, including Lorde, who interpret some African women's relationships—especially the phenomenon of female husbands—as lesbian. Such interpretations, she argues, would be "totally inapplicable, shocking and offensive to Nnobi women, since the strong bonds and support between them do not imply lesbian sexual practices."[35] She stresses the economic and cultural significance of woman-woman marriage and its erosion as a practice under colonial rule and Christianity, noting the loss of power for women that came with Western dominance. But, as the case of Native American societies suggests, there may be significant differences among various African societies, and perhaps some women found emotional and erotic satisfaction in an institution based on economic and familial needs. Lorde based her assertions on the work of an anthropologist writing in the 1930s, who admitted that "it is not to be doubted that occasionally homosexual women who have inherited wealth or have prospered economically establish compounds of their own and at the same time utilize the relationship in which they stand to the women whom they 'marry' to satisfy themselves."[36]

And what about the wives of female husbands? Nandi wives in woman-woman marriages tend to be women who cannot find a male husband, either for reasons of some perceived defect or because they are pregnant or already have a child and the father will not marry them. But wives also cite other reasons for preferring a female husband, including the possibility of greater sexual freedom, more companionship, less quarreling and physical violence, distaste for men, more input in household decisions, or more bridewealth.[37] We know little about wives in other contexts.

In all these diverse ways, some cultures have made a place for women to become men, to move into an alternative third or fourth gender, or to become social males. What ties these phenomena together is that the practices are institutionalized and accepted. In the case of Native American societies, the acceptance of gender diversity came from an appreciation for spiritual powers, a positive attitude toward sexuality in general, and, at least until the impact of European attitudes, acceptance of same-sex relations. In contrast, the examples of the *mustergil* in Iraq, the sworn virgins of the Balkans, and the *sādhin* in Kanga show that extremely patriarchal societies might allow gender crossing when it serves the interests of the preservation of a family line. Likewise, woman-woman marriages in Africa have economic and cultural importance in continuing the male line. In none of these cases was same-sex sexuality fundamental to what was at stake in a woman's taking on a male or transgender social role. Yet among manly women we can find the possibility of same-sex (if different-gender) sex, as well as histories that strike a chord among those who adopt a contemporary identity as transgendered.

Counterfeiting the Office of a Husband

In plain sight, but also hidden, were the women throughout history who adopted the dress and demeanor of men to fight, to travel, to work at occupations reserved for men, and also—perhaps as a primary goal, perhaps as necessary to their subterfuge—to marry women. Cases of this kind of gender crossing can be found especially in early modern Europe, but records from many places, continuing into the present, suggest that women who presented themselves as men and married other women were not unique to any one environment. And of course, it is only when a man was revealed to have a biologically female body that such gender crossing came to light, and if the light shone in a courtroom, self-preservation shaped the testimony in significant ways. In contrast to Native American cultures, Christian societies frowned on cross-dressing, drawing on biblical authority: "A woman shall not wear anything that pertains to a man, nor shall a man put on a woman's garment; for whoever does these things is an abomination to the Lord your God" (Deuteronomy 22:5).

At the same time, marriage records and popular accounts from England in the eighteenth century suggest that cross-dressed women did sometimes manage to marry other women without dire consequences. What were known as Fleet weddings, which until they were banned were performed by needy clergymen living in or near the Fleet prison, not only allowed men who were fortune hunters to marry with few questions asked but also opened the possibility of two women marrying. In 1737, one clergyman suspected that "John Smith," whom he married to Elizabeth Huthall, was really a woman. In the register he noted, "after matrimony my Clark judg'd they were both women, if ye person by name John Smith be a man, he's a little short fair thin man not above 5 foot."[38] But the marriage stood. In 1760, a popular newspaper reported that a woman recognized as Barbara Hill had tried to enlist in the military under the name John Brown. He had worked as an apprentice stonecutter and driver and had married a woman, "with whom she has lived very agreeably ever since. . . . On her sex being discovered after her enlisting, her supposed wife came to town in great affliction, begging that they might not be parted."[39] Such brief mentions make clear that marriages between women were not unknown and were not always severely punished.

Another intriguing legal record suggests some kind of acceptance of women marrying other women in a very different context. After the War of 1812 between the United States and England, slave owners could claim compensation for their loss of property if their slaves ran away to the British. In 1828, a witness supporting a white woman's claim described a slave woman, Minty, as having two surnames, one from her husband and another from "an intimacy with a negro woman" that she formed after she left the marriage.[40] Did slave cultures in the U.S. South recognize same-sex marriages? Was there a connection to African culture? We simply do not know.

As the case of "John Brown's" wife suggests, tales of women who passed as men were not always reported unsympathetically. An Italian professor in 1744 published the story of Catherine Vizzani, an Italian woman who took on the persona of Giovanni Bordoni and relentlessly pursued women. Although the author must have embroidered the few facts at his disposal, he tells of Catherine's surpassing "*Sappho,* or any of the *Lesbian Nymphs,* in an Attachment to those of her own Sex," connecting this story of gender transgression to the Greek past.[41] The English translator of this text found the author's admiration for his heroine too much to bear; once again linking sexual deviance to foreign others, he censored some of the sexual scenes, noting that they might be "agreeable to the *Italian Goût* [taste]" but would be offensive to English eyes.[42]

Nonetheless, the more familiar story is one of horror and repugnance when women cross-dressed and married women. One of the early modern cases that left a rather extensive paper trail is that of Catharina Margaretha Linck, beheaded for her crimes in 1721. Her story begins with echoes of the women mystics, witches, hermaphrodites, and "sworn virgins" we have already encountered. Linck, raised in an orphanage in Saxony, first put on men's clothes to protect her chastity and to "lead a holy life."[43] She was baptized by a woman prophet and joined a group, variously described as Quaker and Anabaptist, whose members fell into ecstasy, prophesied, rejected the authority of priests, and administered the sacrament of communion to one another. After she left this group, she was periodically confronted with a spirit embodied alternately as a white and a Black man, with the white man pleading with her to return to the group and remain faithful to God and the Black man tempting her with money and calling on her to unite herself with him.

Over the following years, she enlisted with various armies, fought, deserted, was captured, escaped punishment, and then returned to her hometown of Halle, where she alternated between wearing men's and women's clothes and also fluctuated between Catholicism and Lutheranism. In 1717, she went to work as a dyer and cloth maker and met her future wife, Catharina Margaretha Mühlhahn. They were married in a Lutheran church, later also in a Catholic one, and lived together as man and wife.

Listen first to Linck's testimony. According to the trial transcript, she had fashioned a penis of leather and testicles of a pig's bladder, which she tied on with a leather strap. "When she went to bed with her alleged wife she put this leather object into the other's body and in this way had actually accomplished intercourse." Attempting to downplay the relationship, Linck testified that sex "never lasted more than a quarter of an hour" because she "was unable to perform any more. At these times, she petted and fondled somewhat longer." Linck also reported—it is not clear why—that she had once put her leather penis in her wife's mouth. In a rare—perhaps unique—statement of what a gender-crossing woman felt about sex, Linck "added that during intercourse, whenever she was at the height of her passion, she felt tingling in her veins, arms, and legs." She told of having hired prostitutes while serving in the army and admitted that "often when a woman touched her, even slightly, she became so full of passion that she did not know what to do."

The trial transcript also takes up the question of Mühlhahn's role in the women's intimate relationship, reporting, from Linck's perspective and in response to her wife's testimony that the leather object had hurt her, that at first they used a thin one and only when Mühlhahn's vagina had stretched had they moved to a thicker instrument. Linck's wife "had frequently held the leather instrument in her hands and had stuck it into her vagina, which she would not have done if it had not felt pleasurable to her." Linck also asserted that the time she had put the leather object in her wife's mouth, she had been naked and Mühlhahn had caressed her breasts.

Mühlhahn's story was, not surprisingly, quite different, for if Linck did not seem intent on trying to save herself, Mühlhahn certainly did. She denied Linck's assertion that both she and her mother had known before the wedding that Linck was a woman, and her story about their first and subsequent attempts at intercourse also contradicted Linck's. She testified that "her supposed husband had been unable to insert his sexual organ into hers but had tortured and tormented her for about a week so that she endured great pains and her sexual organ had become very swollen."

Finally he got it in, but never more than the length of half a finger. He tormented her day and night, sometimes for up to an hour. "She had been a very naïve maiden," had never noticed that the organ was made of leather, and never saw her husband without his pants. She had noticed that he often urinated on his shoes and had taunted him about it. Finally one day when the "supposed husband" fell asleep without his pants on, she discovered the leather contraption, and she never allowed Linck to touch her with it again.

Linck's life as a husband came to an end when her mother-in-law accused her of being a woman. That she had had suspicions before is suggested by the fact that Mühlhahn testified that she "had followed her mother's order and after the wedding and during intercourse had tried to feel whether the defendant was a woman." After accusing Linck, Mühlhahn's mother, with help from a woman friend, cut open Linck's pants to find the leather penis and a leather horn through which she urinated. The two women "spread open her vulva and found not the slightest sign of anything masculine." They beat Linck and took the leather instruments to the authorities, who put Linck on trial for multiple crimes, including desertion, religious irregularities, and misuse of her wife's property, as well as wearing men's clothes and committing sodomy.

Linck's defense briefly raises the possibility that passing as a man required intimacy with women when she noted that, when she was a soldier, "she had to act like all the other soldiers." But, as the testimony just quoted makes clear, she also admitted to desire for women. She insisted that she had never had sex with a man nor used her penis on herself, and she ended up explaining her sodomy as a result of Satan's influence over her. In a statement that suggests some rudimentary sense of belonging to a category because of her desires, she testified that "even if she were done away with, others like her would remain."

The possibility of hermaphroditism arose in the course of the trial. Linck's mother testified that, although she had never noticed anything masculine about her daughter as a child, she "had not been perfectly female either, since in her youth the vagina had practically no opening and that because of this she might not have been capable of intercourse." The doctors who were called in to examine Linck found nothing "hermaphroditic, much less masculine," and concluded from a midwife's report on the size of her breasts, womb, and vulva that "her female member had not altogether been left alone, but that, during her extensive vagabonding, it undoubtedly had been disgracefully misused."

The judicial officials had a hard time deciding exactly what the sexual crime was and how it should be punished. Was it sodomy, given that it was not a body part that penetrated Mühlhahn and there was no semen? Did the biblical injunctions against committing abominations actually apply to women, or did they "refer mostly to Eastern women, those with a so-called flaw of nature, a very large clitoris"? Or was the act in question actually worse than that of "African women, who, after all, use members with which nature endowed them merely in a wrong and improper way"? And if capital punishment were to be applied, should it be through beheading, hanging, or burning? And if burning, should the defendant be killed first or burned alive? Such troubling questions make clear the ongoing confusion of what the Bible forbade, what sodomy entailed, and the omnipresent notion that same-sex sexuality was an invention of foreigners, often racial others.

In the end, since "the outrages perpetrated by the Linck woman were hideous and nasty," the court recommended to the Prussian king that she be condemned to death by the sword, although they left it up to him whether she should instead be flogged and sent to a prison or spinning room for life. For Mühlhahn, the court lessened the original sentence of "second-degree torture in order to arrive at the truth in her case" and sentenced "this simple-minded person who let herself be seduced into depravity" to three years in prison or the spinning room and then banishment.

The case of Catharina Linck is unusual in the details that have survived and in Linck's profession of her desire for women and assertion that "others like her would remain." But the outlines of the story are not unique, nor did her death sentence stand alone. Although executions of men were more common, women were, throughout early modern Europe, sentenced to death for having sex with women. We have already encountered the drowning of Katherina Hetzeldorfer in Speier in 1477. In sixteenth-century Spain, two nuns were burned for using "material instruments" on each other. In Bordeaux in 1533, two women were tried and tortured but released for lack of evidence. A woman from Fontaines was burned alive in 1535 after dressing as a man and marrying another woman when the "wickedness which she used to counterfeit the office of a husband" was discovered. And in 1580, in the Marne district of France, a woman was hanged when it was discovered that she had married a woman and "by illicit devices, supplied the defects of her sex."[44]

Although, as is clear from the uncertainty regarding Linck's punishment, legal codes and jurists sometimes overlooked women in defining and prosecuting sodomy, England stands out as an exception in criminalizing only male-male sex. In France, Spain, Italy, Germany, Switzerland, and Russia, death could be and was meted out to women who had sex with other women. The debate about Linck's punishment reflects the reach of the Constitution of the Holy Roman Emperor Charles V, issued in 1532, which called for death by burning for both women and men convicted of same-sex sexual acts. The uncertainty about Linck's crime echoes the work of Luigi-Maria Sinistrari d'Ameno, whose 1700 treatise argued that penetration by an object did not count as sodomy and that Paul, in denouncing women's unnatural behavior with other women, must have been thinking of the enlarged clitorises of Ethiopian and Egyptian women.[45]

A very different case of marriage between women comes from sixteenth-century Spain. Authorities in the town of Ocaña moved a prisoner, a surgeon by the name of Eleno de Céspedes, from the men's section of the prison to the women's, near but not with his wife, María del Caño, having determined that Eleno was really Elena.[46] Born into slavery of an African mother, Elena was freed at the age of twelve and given the name of her deceased mistress, but she bore brands of slavery on both cheeks. According to her own account, she was a hermaphrodite whose male member emerged as she gave birth to a son, her only child: "with the force that she applied in labor she broke the skin over the urinary canal, and a head came out [the length] of about half a big thumb, and she indicated it so; in its shape it resembled the head of a male member, which when she felt desire and natural excitement it would come out as she has said, and when she wasn't excited it contracted and receded into the place where the skin had broken."[47] This new penis did not work properly, however, because of the skin that impeded it. Undergoing surgery to remove the skin, Eleno emerged "with the aptitude to have relations with women."[48] For twenty years he worked and lived as a man, including serving in the army, and he married María with the approval of the archbishop of Toledo. But twelve days before he was arrested, his male genitals withered, he reported, after a serious accident.

The midwives who were called to examine Elena concluded from her tight vagina that she was a virgin. A midwife "stuck the candle up her female sex, and it entered a bit, with difficulty, and this witness was suspicious, so she also introduced her finger, and it entered with difficulty, and the witness, therefore, does not think that a man has ever been with her."[49] (Think how such a physical examination, like Mühlhahn's mother's exploration of Catharina Linck, must have tortured Eleno.) María, on the other hand, also examined by the midwives, "is corrupted and wide and roomy."[50] Doctors who were called to examine Eleno agreed that she was a woman, not a man or hermaphrodite: "she is not nor has she ever been a man, but a woman, which they saw and found in her natural vagina, similar to and properly that of a woman, and all the signs of woman, like breast, face, speech, and all the rest, from which it is inferred that she is female."[51] Note that her demeanor as well as her body marked her as female.

The investigation led to charges of sodomy, that "with a stiff and smooth instrument she committed the unspeakable crime of sodomy."[52] Perhaps because of Elena/Eleno's brown skin and heritage of slavery, an accusation of making a pact with the devil was added to charges of sodomy and bigamy (since Elena had been married before Eleno married María). Citing ancient sources, Elena/Eleno pleaded innocence on all charges on the grounds of hermaphroditism, since his dressing as a man, practicing as a surgeon, and marrying and having sex with María were all proper by nature. The court, however, accepted the doctors' word that Elena had always been female, but it convicted her of bigamy, not sodomy. Sentenced to two hundred lashes and ten years of confinement, Elena was sent to make use of her medical skills in a hospital in Toledo. In 1599, a physician published a translation of Pliny, one of the sources Eleno cited in his own behalf, and in his annotations described Elena as "a female slave who pretended to be a man," who "gave indications of being one, though badly sculpted, and without a beard and with some deceitful artifice."[53]

Was Eleno/Elena intersexed? Did her male member appear and disappear? How did her race and enslaved heritage, in the context of the expansion of the Spanish empire, affect the outcome of the case? We will never know, but his/her story suggests the continuing confusion over how two female-born bodies might come together and the different ways that women who married women might conceive of their desires and loves.

The military service of both Eleno and Catharina Linck was typical rather than extraordinary for women who passed as men and married women, and it reverberates with echoes of the Amazons. A seventeenth-century Dutch statesman wrote of his own experience discovering women disguised as men and fighting in uniform, asking, "are such women not also Amazons?"[54] Taking on the role of a man was an option, if an unusual one, for poor young women, especially without family, in northern Europe in the seventeenth and eighteenth centuries, and a large proportion of the cases that have come to light involve enlisting in the army or navy. Prostitution in many cases seemed to be the only other means of survival for desperately poor women.

Although the choice to fight and work as a man may have resulted most often from dire straits, even female soldiers with no erotic interest in women may have had to play the part in order to pass successfully, as Catharina Linck suggested at her trial. Marritgen Jans, a Dutch woman who enlisted as David Jans in the navy in the late seventeenth century and sailed to Africa, reported that he "sometimes visited a beautiful negress in order to remove all suspicion from her person" but nevertheless roused "wicked suspicions of doing something not befitting virtue" because he did not have sex in public.[55] Maria van Antwerpen, who was tried twice in the eighteenth century for marrying women, described in her autobiography how, as the soldier Jan van Ant, she courted servant girls and widows so as to remove any doubt about her masculinity.

A more complicated case was that of Catalina de Erauso, a Basque nun who ran away from her convent dressed in men's clothes, sailed to Peru in 1603, and spent years in the New World as a soldier of fortune. (See the representation of Erauso's masculinity in figure 9). There she used her wits to avoid marriages regularly urged on her, but she also admitted in her memoir to a taste for "pretty faces" and described lying with her head in the lap of a young woman who had taken a fancy to her: "she was combing my hair while I ran my hand up and down between her legs."[56] Her female body came to light when she was sentenced to death for murder (she committed many in the course of her career). In order to escape punishment, she revealed the fact that she was a woman and a nun, and when matrons who were called in to examine her found her to be not only a woman but a virgin, her execution was canceled.

Another woman who fled the Old World for the New was Mary Hamilton, whose story the writer Henry Fielding fictionalized in *The Female Husband* (1746). The English Hamilton had taken the name of Charles, claimed to be a physician, and married a woman named Mary Price. After two months of marriage, Price reported her husband to the authorities, claiming that Hamilton had "entered her Body several times, which made this Examinant believe, at first, that the said Hamilton was a real Man, but soon had reason to Judge that the said Hamilton was not a Man but a Woman."[57] After suffering four public floggings and six months in prison, Hamilton seems to have set sail and ended up outside Philadelphia, where in 1752, again as a doctor, she was discovered to be a woman. She was detained in case anyone came forward to accuse her of fraud, but apparently no one did. Her story makes clear that, at least in the case of Philadelphia, a woman passing as a man could be married to a woman if her wife remained happy.[58]

Figure 9. Catalina de Erauso. From Rudolf M. Dekker and Lotte C. van de Pol, *The Tradition of Female Transvestism in Early Modern Europe* (New York: St. Martin's, 1989).

As the case of Mary Hamilton suggests, some women seem to have crossed the lines of gender for more complicated reasons than the desire to work as men. Maria van Antwerpen cited nature as an explanation. Born to parents expecting a son, Maria said that "she was in appearance a woman, but in nature a man," and that she "was not like any other woman and therefore it was best to dress in men's clothing."[59] She expressed her anger, saying, "Mother Nature treated me with so little compassion against my inclinations and the passions of my heart."[60]

In cases in which women had sex with other women even before they dressed as men, the erotic motive is undeniable. Such is the case with Hendrickje Lamberts van der Schuyr, who went to trial in 1641 for having a sexual relationship with Trijntje, an older widow and mother. The affair began with Hendrickje presenting herself as a woman, but then she began to wear male dress, which improved their sex life, according to Trijntje. She testified that Hendrickje "sometimes had carnal knowledge of her two or three times a night, just as her late husband had—yes, and sometimes more arduous than he."[61] Another Dutch woman, Maeyken Joosten, was married and the mother of four children before she fell in love with a young girl, Bertelmina Wale. Maeyken wooed Bertelmina through letters signed with a male name but eventually confessed her love, convinced Bertelmina that she was really a man, and promised to marry her. She also "had sexual contact with Bertelmina in every manner as if she were a man," according to testimony at the trial.[62] Maeyken donned men's clothing and married her love at the city hall in Leiden, but—we do not know why—ended up on trial for sodomy, after which she was exiled for life. Another couple, one partner married but separated and the other unmarried, lived together for a year before one of them put on male clothing so that they could marry.

As the case of Eleno suggests, the question of hermaphroditism was never far from the surface in cases in which men married to women turned out not to be male. Cornelis Wijngraef, arrested for vagrancy in The Hague in 1732, told the court that she had been born a woman, married at fourteen, but was unable to have intercourse with her husband. Her parents committed her to an asylum, where the medical examiner pronounced her a man and released her with the instruction to wear male clothing. What she did not tell the court was that she had attacked her husband with a knife and had been sentenced to prison for her crime. There she fell in love with and began to have sex with a female prisoner, whom she told that she was really a man. When the relationship came to light, the authorities examined her and pronounced that "she was more a man than a woman," although a second investigation in a men's prison contradicted the first.[63] The widow involved with Hendrickje Lamberts testified that Hendrickje "pissed through a shaft half as long and as wide as my small finger," which disappeared when she had finished.[64] Midwives who were called in to examine Hendrickje confirmed that in her labia was something like the penis of a young boy, but thicker, which withdrew into her body when touched. Nevertheless, the court considered Hendrickje a woman and condemned her as a tribade. That the possibility of hermaphroditism may have helped women who passed as men understand themselves (as with Eleno) is suggested by Maria van Antwerpen's testimony that, when she was seventeen, "something like a shaft shot out of her body whenever nature demanded the discharge of seed."[65] Yet when medical authorities examined her at both her trials, they concluded that she had a woman's parts.

What can we make of all these women? Did passing as a man make loving and marrying a woman easier? More comprehensible even to the women themselves? Did the tradition of women who dressed as men, recounted in popular songs, suggest this possibility to women not only desperate to make a living but also desperate to express their love? Did male dress and demeanor express an inner subjectivity, and were the knowing wives attracted to female masculinity?

The Dutch historians Rudolf Dekker and Lotte van de Pol, who gleaned so many of these amazing records from the archives, report that the practice of crossing the line of gender faded away by the end of the eighteenth century, in part because the possibility of women loving and desiring one another became more comprehensible. But, as we have seen, that possibility had never been all that submerged. And cases of women changing their gender and marrying women continued.

Consider the story of Edward De Lacy Evans, born a woman, who lived as a man for twenty-three years in Victoria, Australia.[66] (See the representation of Evans in figure 10). The case came to light in 1879 when Evans was forcibly stripped for a bath, having just arrived at Kew Asylum in Melbourne. Evans had immigrated to Australia from Ireland in 1856 as Ellen Tremaye, but after working for a short time as a domestic servant, she began dressing as a man, changed her name, and married one of her shipmates. Evans went to work as a miner, and when his first wife left him for another man, explaining that Evans was actually a woman, he married a young Irishwoman. When she died, he married another young woman, who bore a child after being impregnated by her sister's husband. Although Evans claimed the child as his own, it was the birth, it seems, that sent Evans to the asylum.

What grabbed public interest was not Evans's gender crossing itself but the three marriages. Newspaper stories reported Evans's interest in women aboard ship, and one journalist concluded that "the woman must have been mad on the subject of sex from the time she left Ireland."[67] The fact that Evans had been committed may have explained his sexual deviance, but what about his wives? It was difficult to ignore the fact that his third wife had borne a child and so therefore must have engaged in sexual intercourse with a man. Although she claimed not to know either that Evans was a woman or how she became pregnant, her speculation that Evans had one night substituted a real man for himself suggests that she and Evans did indeed regularly have sex. One newspaper story reported that his wives did not expose him because they were "nymphomaniacs," a claim that reveals knowledge of the emerging medical literature that linked excessive heterosexual desire and prostitution with female same-sex sexuality. When in a bid for support Evans's wife eventually named her brother-in-law as the father of her child, Evans testified in court that he had witnessed the two in bed together but that it was so painful that he could barely speak of it. What was crucial to the public commentary was the insistence that gender transgression was a sign of mental illness, and in

Figure 10. Edward De Lacy
Evans. State Library of Victo-
ria, Melbourne. From Robert
Aldrich, *Gay Life and Culture*
(London: Thames & Hudson,
2006).

fact the doctors proclaimed Evans cured only when he submitted to wearing women's clothing. In contrast to earlier cases, in which courts meted
out punishment, sometimes harsh, the outcome in this case was decided
by the medical authorities, about whom we shall hear much more later.

The same conclusion of mental illness emerged in a twentieth-century
case from New Zealand. Amy Maud Bock, in the guise of Percy Carol
Redwood, a dapper, debonair, and well-dressed man, married a woman in
New Zealand in 1909.[68] "The Case of the Woman Bridegroom" caused a
sensation when Redwood was discovered to be a woman—and not only
a woman but one who had run afoul of the law in both New Zealand and
Australia for fraud and forgery. Despite the fact that Redwood was popular with women, more than one of whom was rumored to be eager for a
proposal, his trial and the public commentary focused on his mental state,
not sexual deviance.

The stories of Edward De Lacy Evans and Percy Redwood, as with all
the tales of women who became men and married women, leave us un-
certain what to think. Clearly, as in so many of the Dutch cases, there was

more at stake in these cases than occupational mobility. That Evans, at least, loved and desired women seems evident, but did he think of himself as male? And what about the wives? By this time, as we shall see, there were other ways for women who loved women to find one another. Are these stories more part of transgender history than of the history of love between women?

All these individuals with female bodies, in more or less plain sight, lived with and sometimes loved and made love to women. Yet the differences between Mohave *hwames* and African female husbands and "sworn virgins," on the one hand, and the exposed female-bodied men of early modern Europe and the later antipodes, on the other, are immense. We have seen that more egalitarian societies, such as those indigenous to North America, and fiercely patriarchal ones, such as the rural Balkans and southern Iraq and northwest India, both created institutionalized roles, for different reasons, that allowed women to adopt a different gender. But only in more egalitarian societies was sex between differently gendered female bodies part of the picture. Societies with a rigid notion of a gender binary—male or female, confused only by the case of the intersexed—rarely made a place for gender crossing or a third or fourth gender, forcing women who, for whatever reason, sought to leave their gender behind with no choice but to do it secretly.

It is worth noting that such gender crossing has come to light primarily in situations of increased geographical mobility. Many of the Dutch cases involved women who had been born outside the Netherlands and who moved from place to place, often, in fact, precisely to facilitate their gender change. Likewise, Catalina de Erauso, the Basque nun, sailed to Peru to live the life of a conquistador, and Mary Hamilton fled England for Philadelphia. So perhaps it is not surprising that Ellen Tremaye took advantage of her relocation to Australia to emerge as Edward De Lacy Evans. Secret gender crossing did not work well in small communities, as some of the Dutch women found out to their chagrin when neighbors and former employers recognized them. The need to travel may also explain why so many female men joined the army and navy.

Let us return again to the intriguing question of the women who married female husbands, for they certainly had other options and nothing obvious to gain if all they wanted was to marry a man. The passionate and self-incriminating words of Catharina Linck, telling a court that "when a woman touched her, even slightly, she became so full of passion that she did not know what to do," are rare, but from the wives we have only court testimony designed to project innocence of their husbands' bodies.

Taking a leap, let us consider whether contemporary fiction can help us to imagine what might have been. The novel *Trumpet*, by Scottish writer Jackie Kay, tells the story of Joss Moody, a biracial jazz trumpeter who crosses the gender line, and his white wife, Millie. Inspired by the true story of U.S. jazz musician Billy Tipton, discovered at his death to have a woman's body, *Trumpet* opens after the death of Joss Moody.[69] His adopted son, Colman, also biracial, is shocked and humiliated and enraged.

Millie is besieged by the press and drowning in her sorrow. She cannot believe that Colman is cooperating with a tabloid journalist to lay bare her life with Joss, so she escapes from London to their cottage in rural Scotland. There she remembers their life together from their first meeting in the mid-1950s. They go out, for three months they court, and at the end of the night he gives her a kiss on the cheek. She falls deeply in love, she longs for more intimacy, and one night, at a jazz club, it happens. "He grabs me up in his arms, sweeping my face towards his. He pulls me closer against him till my feet almost rise from the ground. His breathing is fast, excited. I open my eyes and stare at him whilst he is kissing me. His eyes are tight shut. He says my name as he kisses me, over and over again. I feel like I am dying."[70] But when they get to her room, everything changes; he becomes troubled and says there is something he must tell her. She imagines that he is married, has a terrible disease, has committed a crime. But she does not care; she just wants him. Finally he tells her he will show her what is wrong, and slowly he undresses, first his jacket and tie, then his shirt, next two T-shirts, then a vest, and finally bandages wrapped around his chest. Millie is relieved and feels compassion: he has been wounded, she does not care. "He keeps unwrapping endless rolls of bandage. I am still holding out my hands when the first of his breasts reveals itself to me. Small, firm."[71]

Millie is already in love, so it does not matter. "I can't remember what I thought the day he first told me. I remember feeling stupid, then angry. I remember the terrible shock of it all; how even after he told me I still couldn't quite believe it. I remember the expression on his face; the fear, that I would suddenly stop loving him. I remember covering his mouth with my hand and then kissing it. But I don't think I ever thought he was wrong. I don't think so."[72] She imagines explaining it to Colman: "that his father and I were in love, that it didn't matter to us, that we didn't even think about it after awhile? I didn't think about it so how could I have kept it from him if it wasn't in my mind to keep?"[73]

Fiction allows us to hear the imagined voice of a woman in love with a man with a woman's body, in a way that history does not. We hear also the familiar explanations in the press: "Millie Moody must have felt lonely and frightened."[74] One article is titled "Living a lie."[75] Millie worries that they will call her a lesbian. How wrong the stories that have come down to us may be is suggested when the journalist working with Colman interviews an old school friend of Josephine Moore, who became Joss Moody. May Hart suddenly remembers the crush she had on Josephine, although she does not tell the journalist about it. When she learns that Josephine became a man and looks at a picture of Joss with his trumpet, "all the old love came spilling back. . . . As a girl, May Hart would have died for Josie. She loved everything about her. . . . Looking at Josie all dressed up as a man, May realized that she'd missed her all her life. . . . She was moved to tears." Later, the journalist writes in her notebook, "May Hart was so upset at the deception of her old schoolfriend that she burst into tears."[76]

But what lingers is the image of two people in love, without concepts or identities and without the need for them: two people who desire each other. Millie remembers their Sunday-morning lovemaking, how Joss's breathing excites her, how she shakes with desire, how he holds her and tells her he loves her again and again, how he takes her to their "other world": "Our secret world that is just his and mine. Nobody else's, just his and mine."[77] Does this novel help us to understand the possibilities?

As the early modern world grew more connected—with European voyages of exploration and an increase in global trade, including the trade in human beings—the possibilities for women who desired women changed. Beyond polygynous households and convents and marriages to women, we begin to find the origins of communities of women able to find one another, and not just one by one—although some of those earlier forms of relationship remained as well, as the story of Percy Carol Redwood reminds us. For female masculinity remains a salient theme, not just in the ways that different societies conceptualized women who desired women but also in the ways that some women fashioned themselves.

6

Finding Each Other

(1600–1900)

WHETHER HIDDEN OR in plain sight, some women who loved or desired other women found ways, since the earliest recorded history, to be together. But the woman who made love with a co-wife, the nun who fell in love with another nun, or the woman who married a soldier with a female body could not be said to be part of any kind of community, despite Catharine Margaretha Linck's assertion to the authorities that "even if she were done away with, others like her would remain." She may have known that other such women existed, but she would have had no way to find them, much less to find a group of women willing to marry female-bodied men.

But that began to change with the growth and increasing complexity of cities such as Paris, London, and Amsterdam, along with economic developments that brought groups of women together in public places. We have already seen that geographical mobility made possible gender changes in Europe and European settler colonies, and the continuing growth of cultural contact—beginning in the fifteenth century between the so-called Old and New Worlds—spread knowledge of different kinds of thinking about gender, sexuality, and intimate relationships. Same-sex sexuality already had a long history of attribution to a foreign other, so it is no coincidence that early modern European authorities associated women's ability to penetrate other women without the help of fingers or artificial aids with Africa or the Middle East, or that European men continued to fantasize about lurid sexual scenes in all the places they visited or invaded.

So beginning around the seventeenth century, we start to find evidence of the first nascent communities of women with same-sex desires. In European cities, respectable women had little access to public space, but in the emerging sexual underworlds thieves, pickpockets, and prostitutes made a living in the streets. At the other end of the class spectrum, royal and aristocratic women became the target of attack for their lascivious natures. A couple centuries later, groups of Chinese women who worked in the silk factories organized as marriage resisters, opening up space for intimate female contacts. Around the same time, a form of poetry in India celebrated love between women and their precious friends, suggesting at least the knowledge of such possibilities. And, throughout the Euroamerican world, the phenomenon of romantic friendship emerged, eventually creating a context in which women with the option to forgo marriage found a way to make a life with one another. Through tales of "roaring girls" in London or Urdu poetry or literary odes to romantic friends, women began to find a way to find each other.

Roaring Girls and Randy Women

Let us begin with a "delightful lesbian romp," published in 1985 and based on the stories about a late-sixteenth-century Londoner by the name of Mary Frith, a.k.a. Moll Cutpurse.[1] Frith was a notorious denizen of the London underworld, known as a pickpocket and teacher of her trade, and she reportedly wore a strange mixture of male and female clothing, as perhaps befitted a woman who took to the streets but not as a prostitute. Her fame was such that she served as the model for the heroine of the comedy *The Roaring Girl*. (See figure 11 for the representation of Frith from the cover of the published play.) Ellen Galford, author of the lesbian romp, cited the existing (limited) historical sources about Frith but added, "Some of the episodes in this story are derived from these sources; the others may be as close—or closer—to the truth."[2]

What Galford, I surmise, thinks is closer to the truth is Moll's lust for women. From her gender-transgressive appearance—"halfway between man and woman"—Galford spins out a tale of Moll's same-sex desire, and in the process she touches on stories of Amazons and witches, recalling earlier tales of woman-loving women. The novel is told from the perspective of Moll's lover, Bridget, who says at the outset that Moll, who was not one for keeping secrets and relished the rumors and lies that flew around about her, kept this secret out of love for her. Bridget, whose father is an herbalist with an interest in spells and potions, meets Moll when she shows up one day pleading for a potion that will turn her into a man. She looks like a man and thinks she was not meant to be a woman, having hated women's work and passed as a boy for a time with a traveling troupe of players. Her parents sent her off to work as a servant, and there she fell

Figure 11. Mary Frith, a.k.a. Moll Cutpurse. From Alan Haynes, *Sex in Elizabethan England* (London: Wrens Park, 1997).

in love with the kitchen maid, only to find herself scorned and vilified for her desire. Bridget's father decides to take advantage of Moll, promising that his elixir might do the trick if she keeps coming back each week.

Bridget finds herself eagerly awaiting Moll's return, her interest having "passed beyond the purely professional." For Bridget too has a transgressive history, having fallen in love with a neighbor girl who died: "And it was good to feel the old stirrings in my belly once again."[3] When Moll escapes from being shanghaied by a sea captain and arrives wet and shivering at Bridget's door, Bridget makes her move. She gives Moll something to help her sleep, tucks her in her bed, and then joins her. She begins to caress Moll's breast, wondering why she would ever prefer the chest of a man, undresses her and licks "the dark tips" of her breasts, then snuggles up to her and falls asleep.[4] When Moll awakens, she accuses Bridget and her father of cheating her with their elixir, which has yet to turn her into a man. Moll confesses that her desire to become a man has much to do with the fact that she lusts after women and her belief that women do not want her without a man's equipment. Bridget retorts, "if you looked farther than the end of your nose, you'd find a lot of us about. . . . For there are those of us who know that such machinery but gets in the way of a woman's true pleasure."[5] Subsequently Bridget shows Moll exactly what she means.

The love and desire between Moll and Bridget is lesbian feminist fiction, shaped by the late-twentieth-century world that put it in print, but Galford may be on to something. Women in the kind of underworld through which Moll moved with such style may have met others with the same desires. Although it is difficult to know what Mary Frith was really like, the 1611 play based on her life hinted that her gender transgression may have gone along with sexual interest in women. A biography published three years after her death portrayed her as someone who "delighted and sported only in Boys play and pastime" and who refused to marry because "above all she had a natural abhorrence to the tending of children."[6] One character in the play notes that the lack of clarity about Moll's gender (or her possible hermaphroditism) would allow her to "first cuckold the husband and then make him so as much for the wife."[7] Records of the arrest of the real Moll make clear that her combination of men's and women's attire led the authorities to suspect her of lewdness and to question whether "she had not byn dishonest of her body & hath not also drawne other women to lewdness by her p[er]swasion," although they meant prostitution.[8] And if the playwrights of *The Roaring Girl* downplayed Moll's sexuality, portraying her as scorning the men who found her in-betweenness enticing, she appeared herself onstage at the end of a performance, sang a song, made "imodest & lascivious speaches," and promised to expose her femaleness to the curious if they showed up at her lodgings.[9] Here the real Moll—not a male actor portraying her, as was required on the Elizabethan stage—insisted on her right to define herself.

What is even harder to know is whether, indeed, the fictional Bridget was right when she told Moll, "you'd find a lot of us about." The prologue to the play places Moll above other roaring girls: "None of these Roaring Girles is ours; shee flies / with wings more lofty."[10] Especially compared to the emerging subcultures of men who desired other men, we have little evidence of female same-sex subcultures as European cities grew in the seventeenth and eighteenth centuries. The emergence of terms such as *tommy* and *sapphist* in England to describe women with same-sex desires suggests the identification of a kind of woman who desired other women, but the historical record is quite silent on the "roaring girls" who in literature modeled themselves after Moll.[11]

In eighteenth-century Amsterdam, court records of women charged with indecency provide some evidence of an emerging subculture of women who desired other women. The documents use the term *lollepotten*, a word meaning "randy women" in the sense of sexually loose women.[12] Most of these women were poor women living in the Jordaan neighborhood of Amsterdam, and they lived by begging or prostituting themselves—in that sense, like members of the underworld in which Moll Cutpurse flourished. Four women arrested in 1796 lived together in a house reputed to be a place where disreputable people came together, apparently a reference to a brothel, since the owner was tried as a madam rather than a tribade. Gesina Dekker admitted to the authorities that she had been lying on the floor with Engeltje Blauwpaard, "and when they were caressing one another, Blauwpaard had put her finger in her womanliness, moved that finger up and down, which lasted about a quarter of an hour."[13] The owner of the house, Willemijntje van der Steen, was present during this activity, and the fourth woman, Pietertje Groenhof, testified that she had been seduced with coffee and alcohol and succumbed to caressing as well.

In 1798, five other Amsterdam women who shared an apartment were arrested after neighbors heard a noise in the attic, went to investigate, peeked through a hole in the wall, and saw two of the women making love—an activity that went on for two hours (they said), long enough for other neighbors to come and see for themselves. The neighbors testified that the women had "lain with their lower bodies nude and had kissed and caressed one another, like a man is used to do to a woman," that they had lain on top of each other and one of them "had lifted her leg across the shoulders of the other" and "had licked the womanliness of the other with her tongue." One of the women, Anna Schreuder, reported that her mother had initiated her into prostitution when she was fourteen, and the cause of her arrest was "street-whoring."[14] Although these two group arrests do not necessarily provide evidence of a full-fledged tribade subculture, they do suggest that women could meet others with similar desires in urban underworlds.

Some of the Amsterdam women who dressed as men and sought relationships with women also seem to have been part of this kind of underworld. Trijn Jurriaens, a woman born in Hamburg whose story ended up in popular songs, was a forger and swindler who, in the guise of Hendrik Brughman, slept in a bed with another woman and promised to marry her. She was arrested when she impersonated a recently deceased woman in order to will all the old woman's wealth to herself and an accomplice.[15]

And then there are the tales about women pirates. Anne Bonny and Mary Read, the two whose stories have come down to us, seem very like the roaring girls and randy women in the historical sources. Anne Bonny, born in Charleston, South Carolina, in 1710, was reputed to be a rowdy tomboy with an uncontrollable temper who hung out with buccaneers at taverns in the port.[16] When her wealthy father disinherited her for marrying, she tried to kill him by burning down his plantation. Mary Read, born in England, passed as a boy in order to inherit from her grandmother, a plot designed by her mother, although Mary's continuing penchant for masculine attire subsequently caused her mother to disinherit her. She joined the army, married a soldier, and opened a tavern with him. When he died, she went to sea, where her ship was captured by pirates, whom she promptly joined. Anne was already well launched on a career of piracy in the Caribbean, and it was there that the two met.

According to a 1724 text, *A General History of the Pyrates*, attributed to Daniel Defoe, Mary was successfully passing as Mark Read: "Her sex was not so much as suspected by any Person on board till *Anne Bonny*, who was not altogether so reserved in Point of Chastity, took a particularly Liking to her; in short, *Anne Bonny* took her for a handsome young Fellow, and for some Reasons best known to herself, first discovered her Sex to *Mary Read*."[17] Although Defoe did not suggest that the two women were lovers, he did note that their "Intimacy so disturb'd Captain *Rackam*," Bonny's lover, "that he grew furiously jealous, so that he told *Anne Bonny*, he would cut her new Lover's Throat."[18] One version of the story has Rackham bursting into Read's cabin to do away with her, only to find her lying on her bed in front of Anne, partially clothed.[19] Whatever the truth of their relationship, it seems clear that the two were so close that a jealous lover assumed they were having a (heterosexual) affair. In any case, their story continues the thread of women on the wrong side of the law as sexual outlaws, of one kind or another.

Two institutions connected to sexual and criminal underworlds—the brothel and the prison—had the potential to bring together women with same-sex desires or to facilitate the realization of those desires. Note the connection to prostitution in both of the Amsterdam group arrests. (And Moll Cutpurse, in Galford's fictional tale, takes a turn serving as a bodyguard for a traveling group of prostitutes.) The association between prostitution and sexual acts between women goes way back, as we have seen, to Lucian of Samosata's *Dialogues of Courtesans*, with its tales of Leaena and Megilla, and to the term *hetairistria*, meaning women who have sex with women and derived from the word for "courtesan." (See figure 12 for an eighteenth-century pornographic representation of a young woman being initiated into a brothel.) The connection between commercial sex and same-sex sex crosses cultural boundaries as well: as we have also already seen, a twelfth-century commentator on the *Kamasutra* compared erotic activity in women's quarters to what went on among prostitutes. In Japan, a group of young girls in the seventeenth century were trained as dancer-prostitutes to take on the male role; before they began to service men, they worked as drinking companions for women, in this way originating the contemporary *onabe* role for female-bodied, male-identified hosts in special women's bars.[20] (See figure 13, a Japanese erotic woodcut, possibly a brothel scene.)

It is not surprising, then, that pioneering sexologist Alexandre-Jean-Baptiste Parent-Duchâlet, in his 1836 study of prostitution in Paris, concluded that a high proportion of prostitutes engaged in sex with other women. He thought it was "repugnance for the most disgusting and perverse acts . . . which men perform on prostitutes" that drove "these unfortunate creatures" into each other's arms.[21] A study of prostitution commissioned by the city council of Amsterdam in the 1890s found that half the

Figure 12. An eighteenth-century representation of a young woman being initiated into a brothel. John Cleland, *Memoirs of a Woman of Pleasure*. From Robert Aldrich, *Gay Life and Culture* (London: Thames & Hudson, 2006).

Figure 13. Japanese erotic woodcut, possibly a brothel scene. Hokusai, 1821. From Robert Aldrich, *Gay Life and Culture* (London: Thames & Hudson, 2006).

prostitutes questioned had sex with women, sometimes for money.[22] In the eyes of investigators, what women who had sex with men for money seemed to share with women who avoided sex with men was hypersexuality. Parisian street songs from the late nineteenth century connected a famous brothel to same-sex sexuality:

> The girls from la Farsy's place
> Are lezzies (*gougnottes*), my girlfriends.
> Happy the girl to whom God gives
> A real tough dyke (*gousse*) from la Farsy's place.[23]

Stories in the popular press in France around the same time told lurid tales of woman-loving prostitutes. Mélie Hélie, who gained fame when two men fought over her and ended up in court, had been taken under the wing of a streetwalker by the name of Hélène de la Courtille, known for her same-sex desires. Another Parisian, Thérèse V, served time in a penal colony before working in a brothel and taking up with a woman named

Berthe. A "passion against nature soon welded these two women together," as the tabloid press put it.[24]

A case from San Francisco in the 1870s connected prostitutes to a masculine woman. Jeanne Bonnet, born in Paris, had from the time she was fifteen "cursed the day she was born a female instead of a male," according to a story in the local paper. Described as a "man-hater" with "short cropped hair, an unwomanly voice, and a masculine face which harmonized excellently with her customary suit of boys' clothes," she visited brothels to lure women away from their pimps.[25] Arrested often for wearing male attire, she was killed by an angry man who shot her through a window as she prepared to climb into bed with her lover, Blanche Buneau.

So the connection between prostitution and same-sex sexuality persists throughout history and across cultures. A San Francisco madam in the 1940s insisted that "just about all prostitutes are lesbians and tribades," and courtesans in Lucknow, India, in the 1970s reported that their closest emotional connections were to other courtesans, and some even admitted that their most satisfying physical relationships were also with other women.[26]

Another institution connected to criminal and sexual underworlds, the prison, also came to be associated with female same-sex sexuality. In sixteenth-century Seville, the Royal Prison housed women who reportedly fashioned dildos and strutted around crowing "like roosters."[27] In 1750, an embroideress in Paris, Geneviève Pommier, was sent to prison, where another woman proclaimed her love for her and expressed surprise that Geneviève did not yet know what a "good friend" was or about "the friendly favours they gave each other," meaning kisses, caresses, and "brisk and violent movements."[28] Another Parisian street song from the next century painted a vivid portrait of a jail:

> You've got to see this at night in the holding cell,
> The little women kissing like mad
> On the straw.
> And when the sun goes down,
> They go down too,
> Without a fuss.
> It's a helluvah lot more fun.[29]

The reputation of same-sex sexual deviance continued to cling to prisons as well as brothels. In nineteenth-century Japan, a radical political activist, Fukuda Hideko, formed a close relationship with a beautiful cell-mate, a tie she described as like parent and child. The authorities, however, saw the intimacy differently and separated Fukada from the woman, whom a guard contemptuously called her "wife." Fukada vehemently denied that hers was an "indecent and immoral" relationship but admitted that many of the prisoners formed such attachments.[30] Reports from southern Africa also mention sexual relationships between institutionalized women. In the 1930s, a psychologist reported that women in the Queenstown Mental Hospital engaged in mutual masturbation and other "perverse homosexual activities," linking these acts to witchcraft, although the women may simply have been engaging in traditional adolescent labia stretching.[31]

In the United States, too, prisons from the early twentieth century on attracted attention for the sexual relationships women formed with one another.[32] What is particularly striking in this context is the pattern of interracial relationships between Black and white women, for prison was one place where segregation did not reign. Investigators in the 1950s reported that imprisoned Black women in relationships with white women took on a masculine role, but despite the tendency in mainstream U.S. culture to perceive Black women and other women of color as hypersexual, observers also noted that feminine white women actively pursued their Black prison mates. Love notes between women in prison make clear how passionate such relationships could be, despite the attempts of the authorities to classify the women as "making do" without men. Both brothels and prisons, despite vastly different conditions across time and space, were places where women could develop same-sex desires or find others with similar erotic interests.

Another space in which women could find others interested in same-sex sexuality was in servants' quarters, if not exactly a public underworld, at least a working-class world largely hidden from the eyes of the better-off. The fictional Moll Cutpurse so desired one of the kitchen maids during her brief stint as a servant that she made the mistake of kissing her on the lips one night as they shared a bed together, only to be greeted with a blow that knocked her across the room. A court in the Massachusetts Bay Colony in 1642 found Elizabeth Johnson, a servant, guilty of "unseemly practices betwixt her and another maid" and sentenced her to a whipping and a fine.[33] At the end of the nineteenth century, French writer André Gide remembered as a ten-year-old child being awakened by two women servants making noises that seemed to him "like nothing on earth; a pathetic chant, spasmodically interrupted by sobs, clucking sounds and cries."[34]

Servants could also be involved, willingly or unwillingly, in sexual relationships with their mistresses. A woman by the name of Anna Grabou, arrested in Amsterdam in 1797, bragged about the beauty of her maid, whom she claimed she woke up every morning "to scratch her poverty" and who, she also claimed, preferred Grabou to a man.[35] The following year in the same city, Susanna Marrevelt and her maid stood accused of embracing, making "unnatural movements," and baring their bodies below the waist and touching each other's "shameful place."[36] A seventeenth-century Japanese story, "Life of an Amorous Woman," tells of a young woman who works as both a servant and courtesan and finds herself employed by a seventy-year-old widow who orders her into bed: "I expected that she would tell me to scratch her hip, or something of the sort. But that wasn't the case. I performed the woman's [part], and my mistress assumed the male [role], and we played around all night."[37] In 1845 in Norway, a sixty-eight-year-old woman, Simonette Vold, went on trial for having sex with her two young servants, something that had been going on for years, according to the testimony. Vold admitted to "slapping flat-cheek," a reference to tribadism, but her servants reported that she had made a dildo of velvet, called a "loose fellow," that she used on them, and a witness testified that one of the servants had yelled at Vold, "You are never more satisfied than when you can ride on the girls with both the loose one and the fastened." Vold, according to both the servants and a physician, did not have an enlarged clitoris, so the reports of the dildos seemed likely to the court. Vold was sentenced to one year's hard labor and her servants to fifteen days' seclusion with nothing but bread and water.[38]

Women in urban underworlds, in brothels, and in prison came mostly from the bottom of the class structure, and most of what we know about them comes from court documents or the pens of men. One place where women did leave their words was in notes written to lovers in prison. From a French jail in the early twentieth century comes the following smuggled letter from La Pincette to her "darling Cloclo": "Oh, if only you knew how much I suffer when I think of you, my sweet girl! If I could go and console you, I would do so most gladly, but we are separated by walls, and the doors are double locked. . . . I end this letter by rolling a thousand and one kisses in your little mouth, on your little tongue. Your woman [wife] for life."[39] U.S. prisoners also had a penchant for secret love notes. "Mild and wild passion surges through my body aching for your touch. Never before has every nerve tissue in my entire being been ever so on fire with desire," wrote a California fem to her butch lover. "Chiquita Diablo" in

West Virginia told "Mi amor," "I want you to hold me and run your fingers through my hair and kiss me sweet and tenderly."[40]

The voices of poor and working-class women who moved through sexual and criminal underworlds cannot be much heard in the historical sources, but the evidence that has come down to us suggests that women who had access to the streets, as cross-dressers, prostitutes, criminals, or workers, could find, if they so desired, others who shared their sexual interests.

Aristocratic Depravity

At the same time that tales of roaring girls and randy women—on the streets of European cities, in brothels, and in prisons—began to reveal a sexual underworld in which women who desired other women could find one another, tales of depraved desire also began to circulate at the other end of the social scale. Sexual license had long been associated with the ruling classes in Europe. Pierre de Bourdeille, Seigneur de Brantôme, who chronicled the French court in the sixteenth century, reported that women could often be seen "sleeping together, in the fashion called in imitation of the learned Lesbian Sappho, *donna con donna* [woman with woman—he had to put it in Italian]"; he thought that women were especially likely to engage in such practices in France, Italy, Spain, Turkey, and Greece.[41] Queen Anne of England in the early eighteenth century became the target of attack by an aristocratic former favorite replaced in Anne's affections by a poor relation. According to one popular ballad about the new favorite, "Her Secretary she was not, / Because she could not write; / But had the Conduct and the Care / Of some dark Deeds at Night."[42] Seventeenth- and eighteenth-century pornography merged with political propaganda to use stories of sex between women to attack the aristocracy or an opposing political party. Pamphlets and popular tracts spread lurid tales of women with insatiable desires for other women, culminating in the portrayal of Marie-Antoinette, the French queen guillotined in the course of the French Revolution, as a tribade. (See figure 14 for a pornographic portrayal of Marie Antoinette having sex with the duchess of Pequigny.)

Consider two popular pornographic novels, *L'Academie des dames* (1680) and *Secret Memoirs and Manners of Several Persons of Quality of Both Sexes from the New Atalantis, an Island in the Mediteranean* [sic]

par les baisers excite mes defirs,
je luis, ma bonne, au comble des plaisirs.

Figure 14. "With your kisses, excite my desires, I am, my darling, at the height of pleasure." Eighteenth-century pornographic portrayal of Marie Antoinette and the Duchess of Pequigny. Louis Binet. From Marie-Jo Bonnet, *Les Deux Amies* (Paris: Éditions Blanche, 2000).

(1709). *L'Academie des dames* is made up of dialogues in which a married nineteen-year-old girl instructs her fifteen-year-old cousin about sex. The instruction is not only verbal, as is clear from this description: "Ah god! What game do you want to play, in stretching yourself out on me in this way? What, mouth against mouth, breast to breast, stomach to stomach . . . Ah! Ah! Tullie how you press on me, ah Gods! Such thrusts? You set me all afire, you are killing me with these agitations."[43]

Such scenes of sex between women, sometimes set in convents, became a staple of libertine literature. *The New Atalantis*, as the 1709 novel is known, told the story of a "new Cabal" of women lovers. Delarivier Manley, the Anglo-Dutch woman author, in satirizing the politics and sexuality of prominent members of the Whig Party in England describes a secret society committed to homoerotic passion. Although some of the members had to accept marriages of convenience, such relations with men were unimportant. With satirical disbelief in the sexual connection that permeates the novel, an observer describes one pair in the cabal: "Two beautiful Ladies join'd in an Excess of *Amity* (no word is tender enough to express their new Delight) innocently embrace!"[44] The initials and pseudonyms used referred to members of the aristocracy, making the connection between libertine sexuality and the depraved ruling class. Although lurid tales of sex between women were not new, the collectivity of the "Cabal" suggests the possibility of the formation of communities.

In England, rumors about sexual deviance seeped out about Anne Conway Damer, an aristocratic sculptor whose husband's suicide left her independent and relatively wealthy. Scandalous tales about Damer emerged immediately after her husband's suicide, at first because she seemed not sufficiently grief stricken and eventually because she remained unmarried and chose women for her closest friends. *A Sapphick Epistle, from Jack Cavendish to the Honourable and Most Beautiful Mrs. D*****, published around 1778, included the lines, "For if report is right, / The maids of warm Italia's Land, / Have felt the pressure of your hand, / The pressure of delight," with their innuendo of the touching of genitals, once again in a foreign land.[45] The rumors reemerged in the 1790s when Damer formed an intimate friendship with Elizabeth Farren, a leading comic actress. The writer and gossip Hester Thrale linked the two, writing in her diary that "Mrs. *Damer* a Lady much suspected for liking her own Sex in a criminal Way, had Miss Farren the fine comic Actress often about her last Year" and recording verses written about the two women by another: "Her little Stock of private Fame / Will fall a Wreck to public Clamour, / If Farren leagues with one whose Name / Comes near—Aye very dear—to *Damn her*." A later political pamphlet attacking the Whig Party, which Damer supported, repeated the charges and named others in aristocratic circles involved in "amorous passions" with other women.[46] Thrale commented that "'tis now grown common to suspect Impossibilities—(such I think 'em)—whenever two Ladies live too much together" and added that in London one expressed suspicions about "Sapphism" by saying "such a one visits *Mrs Damer*."[47] What is important about these attacks, in both private writings and the popular press, is that love between women came to be painted as a vice infecting aristocratic circles.

On the other side of the English Channel at about the same time, much the same process was at work. The lieutenant general of police in Paris reported that Madame de Murat, a noblewoman, among other scandalous and shameful behavior had "a monstrous attachment to persons of her sex" and that "the horrors and abominations" of her "reciprocal friendship" with a Madame de Nantiat "justly horrify all their neighbors."[48] The Duchess de Villeroy reportedly surrendered herself "to strange whims that exclude all male creatures," engaging in what the French called the "Italian taste."[49] One figure much written about in the French context was Mademoiselle de Raucourt, an actress at the Comédie Française. Appearing on the stage for the first time in 1772 and praised for her beauty and intellect, although also described as somewhat masculine, she reportedly refused to follow the common practice of other actresses of selling herself to male admirers. Instead, she gained the reputation of a taste for tribades and earned the title of a "young priestess of Lesbos."[50] An illustrious opera singer, Sophie Arnould, who reportedly staged orgies with groups of women, applauded Raucourt as an "illustrious sister," and the two were linked sexually.[51] In fictional guise in a pornographic text called "Confession of a Young Girl," Raucourt asserted that tribades had existed throughout time and that Turks, Chinese, and Jews (once again, the "Others") had allowed sex between women in the interests of male sexual arousal. Raucourt makes an address to "the Anandryne Sect" in another pamphlet, in which she tells her "Cunt-Sisters" about a plot hatched by prostitutes to reduce tribades to their rank.[52] The fictional Raucourt states, "We, actresses, dancers, figurants, galley-rowers of the Opera, the Comédie-Française, the Italians, etc., having renounced fucking in the usual forms to take refuge from the consequences that result from them, and having taken an oath to make use of pricks and balls no longer, . . . agreed to fuck and tongue each other so as to pick the roses of pleasure without being exposed to the prick of the thorns."[53]

Mademoiselle de Raucourt, like other actresses, including Elizabeth Farren, moved between the disreputable world of the stage and the world of the court. Titled ladies reportedly offered to buy her favors, and Marie-Antoinette herself took an interest in her, leading to Raucourt's inclusion in a list of the queen's woman lovers, along with the Comtesse de Polignac and the Princesse de Lamballe.[54] It was the Austrian-born queen, symbol of the frivolity and heartlessness of the French monarchy, who came to represent depraved female lust in popular and pornographic texts. "The court lost no time going à la mode; / Every woman turned both tribade and slut; / No children were born; it was easier that way: / A libertine finger took the place of the prick."[55]

What is noteworthy in the political pornography featuring Marie-Antoinette, which intended both to undermine the monarchy and to police sexual boundaries, is that it pictured the queen moving in a crowd of tribades. The Comtesse de Polignac, for example, offered her supposed confession in a pamphlet titled "The Grievances of the Fucking Bitch de

Polignac, or Regrets on the Loss of the Cocks of France": "More than one pretty virgin / Lying on my bed, / Gave up pricks altogether, / Chose my lovely hand instead."[56] The tribades in revolutionary pornography appeared feminine but took male sexual roles; sometimes they had enlarged clitorises, sometimes they used fingers and dildos. And the pamphleteers made them into "public women," in the sense of prostitutes or actresses or roaring girls, by exposing their reputed sexual misdeeds to an increasingly wide reading public. No longer portrayed as women who took their pleasure together two by two, tribades, in the revolutionary imagination, cropped up everywhere in aristocratic households and the court.

The sources about aristocratic women making love to one another and to actresses were, of course, based on little beyond rumor and political propaganda. We know relatively little about what the women charged with lewd behavior did or felt. Marie-Antoinette wrote loving letters to Madame de Polignac when the revolutionary turmoil separated them. In 1789, she wrote, "I console myself by embracing my children and thinking of you, my dear heart."[57] We do know that Raucourt survived the revolution and lived out her years with another woman, Marie-Henriette Simonnot-Ponty, whom she met in prison. Raucourt wrote to her, "you are so necessary to my existence that far from you I am nothing but a shadow" and "I will love you until my last day."[58]

Lesbian scholar and novelist Emma Donoghue took the historical information about Anne Damer, Elizabeth Farren, and the woman to whom Damer ultimately devoted her life, the writer Mary Berry, and crafted a novel, *Life Mask*, which imagines Damer and Mary Berry discovering the joys of sex together. The fictional actress pulls away from her friendship with Anne Damer (as had the historical one) because of the talk, fueled by the rumors about Marie-Antoinette across the channel. Anne is already forming an equally intimate friendship with Mary, whose late-in-life offer of marriage throws Anne into despair. When the marriage is called off, Anne and Mary go away to the seaside for Mary to recover, and one night in bed together they kiss, and things go on from there. Night after night, they make love; in the daytime, they avoid talking about what they are doing. Anne

> looked back over the years and saw that she'd always wanted this but hadn't seen it for what it was. She'd been confused, terrorized by the grotesqueries of the pamphleteers, the obscene silhouettes on black sofas. . . . *I am this way,* she thought, *as simply as a stream flows down*

a hill. It has always been women. How many years of my life have I spent chiseling their beautiful cheeks? This wasn't evil, this wasn't debauchery. It was love made flesh.[59]

Perhaps women were confused and terrorized by the pamphlets, or perhaps the political attacks and pornography of eighteenth-century Europe called their attention to the possibility of loving another woman. In any case, such publicity made known the existence of women at both ends of the social scale who came together in groups of tribades, making it clear that "Sapphism" was not a rare or isolated phenomenon.[60]

Sworn Sisters and Sweet Doganas

Beyond the streets and courts of European cities, women came together in altogether different ways. Access to public worlds made contact possible for the poor and transgressive women of London, Paris, and Amsterdam, as well as the aristocratic women of London and Paris, but the domestic worlds within which most women everywhere lived also held possibilities, as we already know from the love between co-wives and female monastics.

In the Guangdong province of China, from the early nineteenth century to the early twentieth century, an unusual pattern of marriage resistance developed. This took two forms: women either married but delayed or refused going to live with their husbands, or they took vows never to marry. Explanations for marriage resistance focus on the importance of unmarried women's employment in the silk industry in that region, which gave them the possibility of supporting themselves, the emergence in villages of "girls' houses" where young women lived until they married or took vows of spinsterhood, and the influence of a religious sect with a mother goddess and a commitment to sexual equality.[61]

Commentators at the time and contemporary scholars as well have associated both forms of marriage resistance with same-sex practices. During the May Fourth era, a period of nationalist and cultural ferment following on the heels of the First World War, a debate between male intellectuals in a Shanghai feminist magazine connected delayed transfer marriage, in which a woman remained with her family of origin for several years after marriage, to same-sex desire. According to one writer, women put off moving in with their husbands because they "acquired intimate friends with whom they practiced homosexual love."[62] Another author disputed the origins of the unusual marriage pattern but also connected it to same-sex sexuality.

Another, more permanent kind of marriage resistance was *zishu*, "sworn spinsterhood" or "sworn sisterhood." Women performed ceremonies known as "the union of sisters" or "bonding with an understanding friend" and refused to marry at all.[63] A novel described a group of Shanghai prostitutes taking the name "Mirror-polishing Gang"—referring to the Chinese term for tribadism—and loving and having sex with one another. Members took vows not to marry except within the group and to kill themselves or their husbands if forced into marriage with a man.[64] Other sources refer to the Golden Orchid Association, a semisecret group of sworn friends modeled after a Buddhist nuns' community who took vows not to marry after performing a traditional premarital hairdressing ritual that marked a woman as mature.[65] They would go through a marriage-like ceremony during which they would be given money by relatives, "sisters," and friends, and a banquet would follow. Sworn spinsters would then move in with their "sisters," and together they would save money to pay for celebrations, emergencies, eventual retirement in a spinsters home, or funeral expenses. Some women reportedly took this step to avoid the economic and social consequences of marriage, out of dislike for heterosexual relations, or because they feared childbirth.

According to some sources, sworn sisters not only vowed not to marry men, but they also married one another, one taking on the role of husband and the other serving as wife. A book on Chinese customs published in 1935 reported such a practice: "Whenever two members of the association develop deep attachments for each other, certain rites of 'marriage' were performed. For such a 'marriage' to be permitted, one partner has to be designated as 'husband.'" Once an offering of food was accepted by a woman, "a night long celebration which is attended by mutual female friends follows. From then on the couple will live as 'man and wife.' Sexual practices including genital contact called 'grinding bean curd' or the use of dildoes are practiced." As with some Native American and African female husbands, children could be adopted and could inherit property from their parents.[66] A disapproving male commentator described the marriages this way: "Two women dwell together, always existing as if they were one woman. They are as close as a stalk of grain coming through a stone. . . . All women who take this oath get to know one another, arranging eventually to unite."[67]

Even sources that do not portray women marrying one another in their sworn sisterhoods admit that women might have sex with one another. One informant explained that a woman is predestined to marry the same person repeatedly in different incarnations, and if one of those happens to be as a female, she will want to marry him in that guise. Others agreed that women might engage in "grinding bean curd" or use a silk dildo filled with bean curd.[68] A tale of a virgin who gave birth to a baby-shaped sack with nothing inside because she had imitated intercourse with her sworn sister suggests that the possibility of sex between marriage-resisting women was in people's minds.[69] Stories of women who committed suicide when they could not stay with their beloved friends reveal another kind of marriage resistance. In the story "The Affinity between Five Young Women," five teenagers drown themselves to avoid having to marry and separate from one another.[70] The extremity of the solution reveals the strength of the connection among women.

From the pens of elite Chinese women in the late imperial period come expressions of love for and attraction to other women. Wu Zao, born in the late eighteenth century, wrote a sensual ode "To the Courtesan Qinglin of Suzhou":

On your slender body
Your jade and coral girdle ornaments chime
Like those of a celestial companion
Come from the Green Jade city of Heaven.
One smile from you when we meet,
And I become speechless and forget every word. . . .
You glow like a perfumed lamp
In the gathering shadows.
We play wine games
And recite each other poems.
Then you sing "Remembering South of the River"
With its heart-breaking verses.
We both are talents who paint our eyebrows.
Unconventional as I am,
I want to possess the promised heart of a beautiful woman like you.
It is spring.
Vast mists cover the Five lakes.
My dear, let me buy a red painted boat
And carry you away.[71]

Such lyrics express appreciation for another woman's body, dress, and talents, as well as Wu Zao's longing, as an "unconventional" woman, for the love of a beautiful woman. In a play by the same author, the protagonist imagines life as a male scholar with a lovely woman by her side, suggesting yet again a connection between masculinity or masculine privilege and desire for women.[72] What might such poems mean about the possibility of love between a woman writer and a courtesan? That is harder to tell.

Equally difficult to interpret is a genre of late-eighteenth- and early-nineteenth-century Urdu poetry from northern India known as *Rekhti*. Urdu is a language that has become increasingly associated with South Asian Muslim culture, and *Rekhti* is a genre of poetry written and performed by men (sometimes dressed as women) but in the voice and guise of elite secluded women. Highly popular as well as respected in the nineteenth century, more recent collections of Urdu poetry have excluded *Rekhti* because of its female voice, eroticism, and mixed Muslim and non-Islamic conventions.[73] Literary scholar Ruth Vanita argues persuasively that *Rekhti* has something important to tell us about love between women.

Rekhti spoke of love and desire between a woman and her *dogana*, a term referring to an intimate companion, with connotations of sexual intimacy between the two. (See figure 15 for a representation of female intimacy from the eighteenth-century Islamic Mughal Empire in India.) As explained by Sa'adat Yar Khan "Rangin," the Urdu poet reputed to have invented the form, "these relationships usually exist mutually among those women who engage in Chapti," a term for female same-sex sexual activity.[74] He went on to describe rituals that determined who "considers herself the man" and who is "compelled to become the woman," both known as *dogana*.[75] "Then they get married among their [female] companions," signifying a special tie between the two, although they may also have been married to men.[76] Havelock Ellis, the British sexologist who, as we shall see, had so much to do with defining female homosexuality in the early twentieth century, told of an Indian Medical Service officer who connected *Rekhti* to same-sex sexuality: "The act itself is called *chapat* or *chapti*, and the Hindustani poets, Nazir, Rangin, Jan Saheb, treat of Lesbian love very extensively and sometimes very crudely."[77]

Relationships between women needed to be kept secret in order not to damage a woman's honor. "People will say / That you and I are having an affair, *Dogana*, this is awkward." So poems refer to lovers sneaking into each other's rooms: "At night I scaled your rooftop with a ladder / And hid behind the parapet. / I wish your hinge would break, / You wretched,

Figure 15. A scene of intimate friendship between women in the Mughal Empire, eighteenth century. From Robert Aldrich, *Gay Life and Culture* (London: Thames & Hudson, 2006).

unmelodious door."[78] The ambiguity of terms could also mask love as friendship. But the secrecy would enhance the delights of a relationship: "How to describe the taste of sweets eaten in secret?"[79]

But the poems make clear—as does the vocabulary used to describe love and sex between women—that such relationships were not unknown. Verses describe sexual acts, including tribadism, stroking with fingers, the use of dildos: "When I take your tongue in my mouth and suck on it / with what tongue shall I describe the state I am in?" And "The way you rub me, ah! It drives my heart wild / Stroke me a little more, my sweet *Dogana.*"[80] In a poem about two women, Sukkho and Mukkho, a servant tells their husbands about their relationship. "When their husbands forbade them to do what they were doing / They said, We are now famous everywhere as *chapatbaz* / Why not act upon it then—when going out to dance, why wear a veil?"[81] Poems even compare female same-sex lovemaking favorably to heterosexual intercourse: "Let her go to men who wants stakes hammered into her / Can she ever get these hours and hours of pleasure?" Says another, "There's no pleasure in the world like clinging to a woman. . . . However much 'daring' a man may have / However much energy and lustful desire / I'd rather see a face that gives me pleasure— / I'd give anything for this intimacy, which I much prefer."[82]

Although, as Vanita argues, scholars have tended either to ignore *Rekhti* altogether or to dismiss it as pornographic, we should not assume so easily that representations of love and sexual activity between women, even if intended in whole or in part to titillate men, bear no relationship to behavior. A poem by Rangin, describing a woman telling another of watching two prostitutes making love under a tree, certainly seems designed to arouse:

> One would tease and excite the other.
> When she got hot and began to writhe
> The other would slow down her movements . . .
> "Do rub your breasts against mine
> So that your nipples are not seen. . . ."
> When they both came together
> They began to say to one another,
> "One who has a dildo
> Only such a one has the whole game."
> The one below said, "O *Dogana*, my life,
> I would sacrifice myself for this rubbing of yours.
> Go below me and rub my body now
> Water the garden of my vulva.
> Press hard and squeeze into me."[83]

Rangin says in the introduction to his collection of *Rekhti* that he learned female language from married women who also worked as prostitutes in Lucknow. That, along with the fact that courtesans and other women in Lucknow in the early nineteenth century were not entirely secluded, suggests that *Rekhti* was not meant just for male audiences. One poet recounted a conversation between another poet and a Lucknow courtesan about Rangin, saying that he "used the language of whores" and that "all the people of Delhi and Lucknow, whether women or men," were reciting his verses. "So good men's daughters and daughters-in-law would read it and grow impassioned."[84] One explicit poem even depicts a kind of community of *Dogana*. "Chaptinamas," or "Tribad Testimonials," by Shaikh Qalandar Baksch, who wrote under the name Jur'at, portrays two women complaining about their "wretched husbands" while they "play at doubled clinging," a pleasure beyond compare: "This rubbing above,

below, is intercourse wondrously rare, / Making love with one's own like-
ness is a strange, delightful thing":

> Let's invite all the women in town who are given to clinging,
>   Welcome them to our house with flowers and betel, embracing,
> Performing each other; when of their husbands they start to
>   complain,
>   That's when you and I begin our chant; teach them our refrain:
> Come, let's play at doubled clinging, why sit around, better labor
>   free.[85]

So whatever the relationship between *Rekhti* and the lives of women,
the poetry reveals a conception of love and desire between women that
transcended individual households and suggests the possibility of a nascent community. Rather than swearing off marriage as did the women
of Guangdong, the women of *Rekhti* combined marriage with the love of
a sweet *Dogana*. That was a model that also flourished elsewhere in the
world at the same point of time.

Romantic Friends

In the Euroamerican world in the late eighteenth and early nineteenth centuries, a phenomenon known as "romantic friendship" began to flourish.
Ironically, the attacks on aristocratic women's sexual license that emerged
around the French Revolution played a role in creating the possibility for
women to love one another in a changed social context. An ideology of
sexual difference between women and men that took hold among the urban middle classes turned upside down the traditional Western notions
of women's sexual nature as potentially excessive and dangerous. As economic development and the emergence of democratic political institutions transformed the landscape of western Europe and the newly independent United States, a new Ideal (read "white, middle-class") Woman
emerged. Assigned the domestic sphere of the home and assumed to be
emotional and essentially asexual, she was defined as the polar opposite
of the Ideal Man. He was, depending on his class and race or ethnicity,
characterized by the head or the hand, she by the heart. Because women
were perceived as fundamentally different from men and because middle-
class society tended to separate female and male social worlds, it seemed

natural that women would find their soul mates among other women. At the same time, marriage was what made a complete whole out of complementary female and male parts. Romantic friendship, in theory, could coexist with marriage. So it is not surprising that society condoned, even celebrated, relationships among women, although scholars disagree about the acceptability of romantic friendship and the sexual nature of such relationships.[86] The ideology of profound sexual difference, in conjunction with economic and social sex segregation, very much like the physical sex segregation in other societies, opened up spaces for passionate, intense, loving, physically affectionate relationships between women. (See figure 16 for a typical representation of romantic friends.)

One of the sex-segregated places that fostered romantic friendships was the girls' school, an institution that emerged as education for women became more acceptable. Often residential, such schools facilitated intense relationships among students. Crushes between schoolgirls were so common that they acquired a multitude of names, including *rave, spoon, pash, smash, gonage,* and *flame.*[87] Not only did many of the students form

Figure 16. Romantic friends. Danske Kvinders Fotoarkiv. From Karin Lützen, *Was das Herz Begehrt* (Hamburg: Kabel, 1990).

passionate attachments with one another, but they also fell in love with their teachers, often single women themselves in relationships with other women. Danish school pioneer Natalie Zahle, for example, who sought to make the role of teacher an acceptable alternative to marriage, in the 1850s formed a relationship with one of her students, Henriette Skram, who declared, "we belonged together," and devoted the rest of her life to "serving" Zahle.[88] Constance Maynard, an English teacher and school founder, in the 1870s fell in love with a series of admiring students. When one spoiled girl revolted against the pressure to do well, Maynard wrote in her diary, "Oh, Mary, Mary, I loved you, *loved*—do you know what that means? . . . Oh my child my child, are you lost to me indeed?"[89] As the case of student-teacher relationships suggests, intense attachments between women were not always between peers.

According to the ideal, female romantic friendship existed alongside and enriched marriage. Consider the famous friendship of Frenchwomen Anne-Louise-Germaine Necker, better known as Madame de Staël, and Juliette Récamier. Both married and also pursued affairs with other men, but they nevertheless loved each other and expressed that love. "I love you with a love surpassing that of friendship. I go down on my knees to embrace you with all my heart," Madame de Staël wrote. Or in another letter, "My angel, at the end of your letter say to me *I love you*."[90] Such expressions of love, longing, and commitment were central to romantic friendship.

Across the Atlantic, fourteen-year-old Sarah Butler Wister met sixteen-year-old Jeannie Field Musgrove in Massachusetts in 1849. Sarah, who took on a male pen name, kept flowers in front of Jeannie's portrait when they were in school together. The intensity of their friendship continued uninterrupted by Sarah's marriage. At the age of twenty-nine, Sarah wrote to Jeannie, "I can give you no idea how desperately I shall want you," and after one precious visit, Jeannie poured out her love: "Dear darling Sarah! How I love you & how happy I have been! You are the joy of my life." She urged Sarah to "just fill a quarter page with caresses & expressions of endearment" and ended her letters with such expressions as "Goodbye my dearest, dearest lover" or "A thousand kisses—I love you with my whole soul."[91] Jeannie finally married when she was thirty-seven, provoking anxiety on Sarah's part about the impact on their relationship. But their love lived on.

If in theory and sometimes in practice romantic friendship coexisted successfully with heterosexual marriage, that was not always the case. The Dutch female writer Aagje Deken, who lived with author Betje Wolff for twenty-seven years and in death was buried with her, lost her third *ziels-vriendin* ("soul friend") to a man.[92] When Molly Hallock Foote met her romantic friend Helena in New York in 1868, she expressed her hope: "for a time, at least—I fancy for quite a long time—we might be sufficient for each other. . . . Imagine yourself kissed many times by one who loved you so dearly." They planned to live together, and Molly wrote of what she longed for: "to put my arms round my girl of all the girls in the world and tell her . . . I love her as wives do love their husbands, as friends who have taken each other for life." That plan fell apart when Helena married. Before Molly herself followed suit, she wrote, "You know dear Helena, I really was in love with you. It was a passion such as I had never known until I saw you." And, suggesting the incompatibility of her love with marriage but at the same time making clear the lack of stigma attached to expressing that love, she wrote to Helena's fiancé, "Do you know sir, that until you came along I believe that she loved me almost as girls love their lovers. *I know I loved her so.* Don't you wonder that I can stand the sight of you."[93]

And perhaps many romantic friends, especially if they remained single, truly could not stand the sight of their friends' husbands. Geraldine Jewsbury, an English writer, formed an obsessive romantic attachment to Jane Carlyle, who was married to the famous historian Thomas Carlyle. Jewsbury valued her independence and disapproved of Thomas Carlyle's belittling of his wife's intellect. She wrote to Jane, "I love you my darling, more than I can express, more than I am conscious of myself, and yet I can do nothing for you." She longed to live with Jane and hoped that someday that would be possible: "I believe we are touching on better days, when women will have a genuine, normal life of their own to lead. There, perhaps, will not be so many marriages, and women . . . will be able to be friends and companions in a way they cannot be now."[94]

Or what about the poet Emily Dickinson, who fell in love with her friend Sue Gilbert, who later married Dickinson's brother? What must it have been like to have her beloved become her sister-in-law? In 1852, Dickinson wrote to Gilbert, "Susie, will you indeed come home next Saturday, and be my own again, and kiss me as you used to? . . . I hope for you so much, and feel so eager for you, feel that I *cannot* wait, feel that now I must have you—that the expectation once more to see your face again, makes me feel hot and feverish, and my heart beats so fast."[95] Such expressions of desire were also an accepted facet of romantic friendship.

When, in certain privileged circumstances, both parties to a romantic friendship could choose not to marry as expected, they sometimes formed

Figure 17. The Ladies of Llangollen. Lady Leighton, ca. 1813, National Library of Wales. From Martha Vicinus, *Intimate Friends* (Chicago: University of Chicago Press, 2004).

marriage-like relationships that became known in the United States, because of their prevalence in the Northeast, as "Boston marriages." One such marriage joined French artist Rosa Bonheur to Nathalie Micas, the daughter of Bonheur's patron. Micas's father proposed and blessed the union days before he died.[96] But the most famous marriage between romantic friends, and one that became a model for others, was that of Eleanor Butler and Sarah Ponsonby, who ran away together from their aristocratic Irish homes in 1778, when they were thirty-nine and twenty-three. When they were at first caught and brought home, a family member reassured a correspondent that the elopement did not appear "to be anything more than a scheme of Romantic Friendship."[97] Although they dressed oddly, sometimes in matching riding habits, they lived together respectably, if eccentrically and not without occasional criticism, in a rural retreat in Wales for fifty-one years. (See figure 17 for a famous representation of the ladies.)

As the "Ladies of Llangollen," Butler and Ponsonby came to embody romantic friendship and the possibility of marriage, in practice if not in name, between two women. They called each other "my Better Half," "My Sweet Love," and "my Beloved."[98] Visitors flocked to their home, newspaper accounts described their house and garden, and other women who loved women viewed them as icons of female love. Sophia Jex-Blake, an early woman doctor, invited the object of her passion, philanthropist Octavia Hill, to visit Llangollen with her. The very idea made her heart "beat like a hammer," and she recorded Hill's response: "She sunk her head on my lap silently, raised it in tears, then such a kiss!"[99]

But the social acceptance of loving and intimate friendship between middle- and upper-class women did not erase knowledge of the history and possibility of female gender and sexual transgression. As we have seen, Hester Thrale, the English writer and diarist who noted her suspicions of Anne Damer's friendships, knew the term *Sapphism* and applied it to Damer. She first mentioned sexual deviance in connection with Marie-Antoinette, who she had heard was "the Head of a Set of Monsters call'd by each other *Sapphists*."[100] She alternated between praising romantic friendship and condemning "Sapphism," suggesting the complexity of societal views in distinguishing between what was admirable and what was abhorrent. Thrale was a close friend of the Ladies of Llangollen and visited them often in their home, yet in her diary she described them as "damned Sapphists" and reported that women would not stay the night with them unless they had a man to accompany them.[101] She seemed to suspect her own "first of friends in every sense of the word," Sophia Weston, of illicit tendencies when Weston expressed reluctance to marry, and Thrale urged her to give up her "romantic Friendship" for "romantic Love" of a man.[102]

Anne Lister, an English gentrywoman who kept a diary in code that recorded her loves and lusts for women, visited the Ladies of Llangollen in 1822 and felt a connection. In response to her own lover's question, Lister mused about the Ladies' relationship: "I cannot help thinking that surely it was not platonic. Heaven forgive me, but I look within myself & doubt. I feel the infirmity of our nature & hesitate to pronounce such attachments uncemented by something more tender still than friendship."[103] Because of her own passion for women, Lister had a nose for the slightest whiff of similar desires among other women. She thought Ponsonby at first "altogether a very odd figure" but concluded that she was "mild & gentle, certainly not masculine, & yet there was a *je-ne-sais-quoi* striking."[104]

The Ladies of Llangollen, and other female couples who admired and sought to imitate them, had one strike against them in forgoing marriage to men. As Thrale's encouragement of Sophia Weston's marriage suggests, refusal to accept a proposal, if one were proffered, might raise suspicions. So too might a too-masculine demeanor or any hints of sexual desire. It is striking that Butler, who was short and round, at fifty-one was described in a local paper as "tall and masculine . . . and appears in all respects as a young man, if we except the petticoats which she still retains."[105] Presumably the petticoats saved her from condemnation as a cross-dresser.

The question of sexual desire is a tricky one. Lillian Faderman, as we have seen, in her pioneering book *Surpassing the Love of Men*, suggested that romantic friendships probably did not involve genital sex, and in *Scotch Verdict* she presented arguments both for and against a sexual component.[106] What did it mean that romantic friends regularly expressed longing to be with, to touch, and to kiss a romantic friend? Certainly some of what romantic friends wrote to one another sounds like declarations of desire. There is Alice Baldy, a white woman from the U.S. South, in 1870 writing to her beloved Josie Varner, "Do you know that if you only touch me, or speak to me there is not a nerve or fibre in my body that does not respond with a thrill of delight?"[107] Or there is nineteenth-century Czech writer Božena Němcová writing to Sofie Rottová, another author and Czech patriot, "Believe me, sometimes I dream that your eyes are right in front of me, I am drowning in them, and they have the same sweet expression as they did when they used to ask: 'Božena, what's wrong? Božena, I love you.'"[108] Or there is African American poet Angelina Weld Grimké writing in 1896 to her school friend Mamie Burrell, "Oh Mamie if you only knew how my heart beats when I think of you and it yearns and pants to gaze, if only for one second upon your lovely face."[109] Are these expressions of physical desire? Formulaic expressions of friendship? Or sometimes one, sometimes the other, sometimes both? What might it mean that a woman would imagine traces of another's kisses on her face when the two had never met?[110] And what, after all, counts as "sex"?

As more evidence emerged about different women's relationships, it became increasingly clear that sexual desire and acts were part of romantic friendships. Consider the story of two African American women, free-born domestic servant Addie Brown and schoolteacher Rebecca Primus, who formed a passionate friendship across the chasm of class in Hartford, Connecticut, in the 1860s. Some of their correspondence echoes the expressions of love and longing of other romantic friends: "Rebecca, when I bid you good by it's seem to me that my very heart broke. . . . My Darling Friend I shall never be happy again unless I am near you."[111] Addie associated their relationship with romantic friendship, commenting on Grace Aguilar's 1850 book *Women's Friendships*, which told the story of an aristocratic and a middle-class British woman. But there was more. Addie reported, from her post at a girls' school, to Rebecca, who had gone south to teach freed slaves after the Civil War, the "girls are very friendly towards me. . . . One of them wants to sleep with me. Perhaps I will give my consent some of these nights." How Rebecca responded we do not know, but in her next letter, Addie explained, "If you think that is my bosom that captivated the girl that made her want to sleep with me, she got sadly disappointed injoying it, for I had my back towards all night and my night dress was butten up so she could not get to my bosom. I shall try to keep your f[avored] one always for you. Should in my excitement forget, you will partdon me *I know*."[112]

Addie was no stranger to heterosexual desire, for she compared Rebecca's kisses to those of her male employer, concluding, "No *kisses* is like youres." She refused to kiss her employer one morning, reporting to Rebecca that because of her, "I don't want anyone to kiss me now." And Addie clearly thought of their relationship in terms of heterosexual marriage: "You are the first girl that I ever *love* so and you are the last one. . . . If you was a man, what would things come to? They would come to something very quick. . . . What a pleasure it would be to me to address you *My Husband*." That Rebecca's family recognized the depth of their feelings comes through when Addie wrote Rebecca about what her mother had said: "I thought as much of you if you was a gentleman. She also said if either one of us was a gent we would marry."[113] African American communities, both slave and free, regularly extended kin ties to non-family-members, so Addie's welcome in Rebecca's family is not surprising. Rebecca's aunt, however, warned Addie not to tell her suitor that she loved Rebecca more than him. In the end, Addie's dream of living with Rebecca was not to be. Addie married her suitor, stopped writing to Rebecca, and died of tuberculosis at age twenty-nine. Rebecca also married but lived into old age, saving Addie's letters. It would seem that this romantic friendship was neither compatible with heterosexual marriage nor innocent of sexual pleasure—at least the caressing of breasts.

In the case of Anne Lister, who suspected that the Ladies of Llangollen shared more than simple companionship, romantic friendship served as a convenient disguise for her fierce sexual desires. Lister was especially interested in the relationship of the Ladies because she longed to marry her own lover, Mariana Belcombe, who for economic reasons ended up married to a man. While the two women waited for Mariana's husband to die, they carried on an active sexual relationship when they could be together. But Lister—a "female rake" if ever there was one—was unwilling to put aside pleasure as she waited.[114] In 1824, despite her continued love for

Belcombe, Lister visited Paris and began to court a widow, Maria Barlow, who wanted to be Lister's wife but had to settle for the status of "mistress." Barlow thought that Lister, with her masculine appearance, could pass as a man and marry her publicly and openly. "It would have been better had you been brought up as your father's son," Barlow told Lister, but Lister was not keen on the idea of having no access to women's company, since she found so many lovers that way.[115] Instead, Lister recommitted herself to Belcombe, exchanging pubic hair to wear in lockets, and Barlow sadly accepted her "divorce."[116]

Lister, at the end of her life, got her wish to marry a woman when she courted Ann Walker, an heiress whose property adjoined hers, although she was never really in love with Walker.[117] At first Walker described their relationship as "as good as a marriage," and later they exchanged rings, moved in together, rewrote their wills, and in every other way acted as husband and wife.[118] Although Lister was considered odd in her community, she also held economic and social power. Despite gossip and even incidents in which neighbors witnessed Lister and Walker kissing, the two women lived as if married without censure.

Lister was explicit in her diary about her sexual exploits. Using "kiss" to mean orgasm, she wrote of her lovemaking with Belcombe: "From the kiss she gave me it seemed as if she loved me as fondly as ever. By & by, we seemed to drop asleep but, by & by, I perceived she would like another kiss & she whispered, 'Come again a bit, Freddy.' . . . But soon, I got up a second time, again took off, went to her a second time &, in spite of all, she really gave me pleasure, & I told her no one had ever given me kisses like hers."[119]

Belcombe was not the only lover to enjoy kisses with Lister. In 1820, while Lister was taking up once again her sexual relationship with the lover who had introduced her to Belcombe, she also flirted with two of Belcombe's sisters. Of one, she wrote, "Kissed her [in this case, meaning what she says], told her I had a pain in my knees—my expression to her for desire—& saw plainly she likes me & would yield again, without much difficulty, to opportunity & importun[ity]."[120] In Paris, Maria Barlow, the widow whom Lister courted, came to her room one night and climbed into bed with her. "I was contented that my naked left thigh should rest upon her naked left thigh and thus she let me grubble her over her petticoats. All the while I was pressing her between my thighs. . . . Now and then I held my hand still and felt her pulsation, let her rise towards my hand two or three times and gradually open her thighs, and felt . . . that she was excited."[121] After a night of lovemaking, Lister described getting out of bed and Barlow's "touching my queer" and promising to "do to you as you do to me." Lister was astonished and tried to explain that she did not want to be touched in that way.[122]

Anne Lister's frank reports of her conquests leave no doubt about the possibilities of sexual activity in the guise of romantic friendship. Her exploits seem to have been a kind of open secret in her social world, where she was considered eccentric but tolerated. Her masculine appearance and demeanor sometimes earned her taunts. Her aunt called her "a queer one," and in one diary entry Lister reported, "people generally remark, as I pass along, how much I am like a man. . . . Three men said, as usual, 'That's a man' & one axed 'Does your cock stand?'"[123]

But Lister had no doubt about her sexual and emotional nature, writing in her diary in 1821, "I love and only love the fairer sex and thus, beloved by them in turn, my heart revolts from any other love than theirs."[124] She considered this her nature, reassuring Belcombe, who had a horror of the unnatural, that her "conduct & feelings" were "natural to [her] inasmuch as they were not taught, not fictitious, but instinctive."[125] In a conversation with Maria Barlow, she contrasted her own nature to "Saffic regard," which for Lister had "artifice in it." Barlow claimed not to understand, but Lister claimed, "[I] told her I knew by her eyes she did & she did not deny it, therefore I know she understands all about the use of a ——."[126] Elsewhere Lister thinks of another woman "using a phallus to her friend," so presumably that is the word she omitted in this entry.[127] I understand Lister as contrasting her own natural sexual nature and her practice of tribadism and the use of fingers with the "Sapphism" of French and English pornography.[128]

Another woman whose sexual desire for women seemed to be an open secret was Charlotte Cushman, a famous and much admired nineteenth-century American Shakespearean actress who arrived in Rome in 1852, forming a community of expatriate artistic and intellectual women with similar erotic desires. Members of her circle included boyish sculptor Harriet Hosmer, who flirted with both women and men before forming an erotic relationship with Louisa, Lady Ashburton, a Scottish aristocrat; Cushman's first partner, writer, translator, and feminist Matilda Hays; her second partner, sculptor Emma Stebbins; Emily Faithfull, a masculine woman involved with a woman whose marriage ended in a scandalous divorce case; and African American and Native American sculptor Edmonia Lewis, who left Oberlin College under a cloud of suspicion that she had drugged a female classmate in her room.[129] Elizabeth Barrett Browning wrote to her sister about Cushman's circle: "there's a house of what I call emancipated women—a young sculptress—American, Miss Hosmer, . . . very clever and very strange—and Miss Hayes [*sic*] the translator of George Sand who 'dresses like a man down to the waist' (so the accusation runs)."[130] Despite such gossip, the members of Cushman's circle were notable and admired for their achievements and independence.

Known for playing Romeo onstage, Cushman romanced women off-stage as well. Not only did she form two long-term and public relationships with women, but she also carried on more secret affairs with younger female fans. Not long after Cushman exchanged rings with Stebbins, while touring in the United States she met Emma Crow, the young daughter of Harriet Hosmer's patron, and fell madly in love. She told Crow from the outset that she was "already married" and that she wore "the badge upon the third finger of [her] left hand," but she also expressed her passion: "I love you dearly, my own darling. . . . *I love you! I love you!* Goodbye, I kiss your pretty soft loving eyes and hands."[131] Harriet Hosmer wrote to Crow's father to say about Cushman, "I perceive that she and Emma are what we this side of the ocean call 'lovers'—but I am not jealous and only admire Emma for her taste."[132] Crow came to Rome and stayed with Cushman and Stebbins for three months, and then Cushman came upon the perfect solution to her love triangle: Crow would marry her nephew and adopted son, making her part of the family. Before the marriage, Cushman and Crow met in Paris, where they could be alone, a rendezvous Cushman remembered later: "ah what delirium is in the memory. Every nerve in me thrills as I look back & feel you in my arms, held to my breast so closely, so entirely mine in every sense as I was yours."[133]

Cushman's secrecy about her relationship with Crow, in contrast to her publicly accepted marriage to Stebbins, makes clear that it was the adultery rather than the same-sex relationship that was to be hidden. In an 1860 letter, Cushman warned Crow, "there are people in this world who could not understand our love for each other, therefore it is necessary that we should keep our expression of it to ourselves."[134] Crow's marriage made real Cushman's practice of naming lovers as family members, and Emma Crow became "Dearest and Sweetest daughter, niece, friend and love."[135] But the arrangement was not easy for anyone. Although one friend called Cushman and Stebbins "as firm in their friendship as the ladies of Llangollen," Stebbins fell apart emotionally and Crow never had enough of Cushman.[136]

In light of Anne Lister's and Charlotte Cushman's stories, the case of Scottish schoolteachers Jane Pirie and Marianne Woods is puzzling, for it suggests a societal ignorance of—or willful disbelief in—the possibilities of sex between romantic friends. Of course, neither Lister's nor Cushman's sexual exploits were made public. In the early nineteenth century, Pirie and Woods fulfilled a dream by establishing a school together in Edinburgh. Then it all came crashing down one day when one of their students, Jane Cumming, born of a liaison between an Indian woman and an aristocratic Scottish man who died in the service of the empire, reported shocking behavior to her grandmother, Lady Cumming Gordon. According to Jane Cumming—once the case came to court—the teachers visited each other in bed, lay one on top of the other, kissed, and shook the bed. Further, Cumming reported that Jane Pirie said one night, "You are in the wrong place," and Marianne Woods replied, "I know," and asserted that she was doing it "for fun." Another night, she said, Pirie whispered, "Oh, do it, darling." And she described a noise she heard as similar to "putting one's finger into the neck of a wet bottle."[137]

Pirie and Woods, their school ruined when Jane Cumming's grandmother withdrew Jane and recommended that all the other students leave as well, took the unimaginable step of suing the powerful Lady Cumming Gordon for libel. The judges then found themselves forced to make what they seemed to have found an impossible choice between believing that respectable Scottish schoolteachers might engage in sexual behavior or that decent schoolgirls could make up such tales. As one judge put it, making clear the acceptability of normal romantic friendship, "Are we to say that every woman who has formed an intimate friendship and has slept in the same bed with another is guilty? Where is the innocent woman in Scotland?"[138]

Yet despite the insistence of the same judge that "the crime here alleged has no existence," various parties in the trial referred, directly or indirectly, to the history we have already encountered.[139] The nursery maid of one of the students reportedly remarked that the schoolteachers should be burned as punishment for their crimes, invoking early modern legal punishments as well as witchcraft, and Lady Cumming Gordon's counsel referred to the medieval regulations prohibiting nuns from sleeping together. Other testimony referred to cross-dressing, "digitation," "Tribades," and classical literature, suggesting that however much the judges protested that they knew nothing about same-sex sexuality among females, they did.[140] One of the judges, who had spent time in Paris and India, admitted that "women of a peculiar conformation, from an elongation of the *clitoris*, are capable both of giving and receiving venereal pleasure, in intercourse with women, by imitating the functions of a male in copulation. . . . Nor is it to be disputed that by means of tools, women may artificially accomplish the venereal gratification." But he nevertheless thought the teachers innocent because "the imputed vice has been hitherto unknown in Britain."[141]

Ultimately, the judges had to decide if Pirie and Woods kissed, caressed, and fondled "more than could have resulted from ordinary female friendship," suggesting a line between affectionate behavior and sexuality that could be crossed.[142] The only way out of the dilemma was provided by Jane Cumming's heritage and childhood in India, where surely, many of the judges decided, she must have learned not only about sex but also about sexual relations between women, something no respectable Scottish schoolgirl would be able to imagine. As one judge put it, "The language of the Hindoo female domestics turns chiefly on the commerce of the sexes. . . . It is impossible to live in Indostan without learning through observation and instruction, by the age of eight or nine, something about venereal intercourse."[143] As usual, the national/racial Other provided a convenient explanation for deviance. The outcome of the case is not particularly instructive: Lady Cumming Gordon won the first round, the schoolteachers won on appeal and in review by the House of Lords, but it really did not matter. Pirie and Woods's school and lives were ruined. What is important for us is that this case suggests the complexity that romantic friendship cast on relationships between women.

The stories of Addie Brown and Rebecca Primus, Anne Lister and Mariana Belcombe and Maria Barlow, Charlotte Cushman and Emma Stebbins and Emma Crow, Marianne Woods and Jane Pirie complicate the notion that intense and passionate relationships between women found acceptance in the Western world in the long nineteenth century because no one could imagine that women might be sexual together. These stories represent what historian Anna Clark calls "twilight moments," half-understood expressions of sexual desires or acts that are prohibited by society but at the same time are an open secret.[144] This does not mean that all romantic friendships involved the caressing of breasts or the exchange of "kisses." But they do open up the possibility that more romantic friends than we know acted on their erotic desires, however they may have thought of such activities.

What remains to be said, then, is that romantic friendship was a socially approved form that allowed women who sought an intimate friend or life partner or lover to find one another. Anne Lister, in her diary, recorded meeting a woman a little too masculine for her taste who, through hints about a woman friend and a discussion of classical literature, admitted to knowledge that neither of them named. As Lister recorded in her diary, "Asked Miss Pickford if she now understood me thoroughly. She said yes. I said many would censure unqualifiedly but I did not. . . . If it had been done from books & not from nature, the thing would have been different. . . . There was no parallel between a case like this & the Sixth Satire of Juvenal," the latter being Lister's favored reference for classical knowledge about same-sex sexuality. Yet Lister (for Belcombe's sake) deceived Pickford about her own nature, insisting that she did not "go beyond the utmost verge of friendship." With what sounds like some regret, Lister wrote, "I am now let into her secret & she forever barred from mine." And significantly, Lister ended her diary entry wondering, "Are there more Miss Pickfords in the world than I have ever before thought of?"[145] Certainly she knew that there were many romantic friends and many women who might succumb to the seductions of a female rake. What she wondered was whether there were many who had what she saw as "natural" masculine sexual passion for other women.

So, in an entirely different context and for different reasons, romantic friendships bring to mind the sweet lovers depicted in *Rekhti* and the marriage-like bonds of sworn sisters in Guangdong. Roaring girls and randy women, aristocratic tribades, Chinese marriage resisters, lovers in Urdu poetry, and romantic friends had little in common except that they lived in environments where they could find other women with similar erotic tastes. It was not the first time, of course, that women found one another, as we know from the tales of women lovers in polygynous households and monasteries. What was different was that at least some of these women found one another in nascent communities of women. Women of lower social classes—women in the underworlds of European cities and, later, Chinese factory workers—had access to spaces beyond the domestic realm. Women in brothels and prisons continued the tradition of forming relationships in sex-segregated spaces. As middle-class women gained access to education and employment, they could meet at school and even choose, like the women of Charlotte Cushman's circle, not to marry. But private spaces remained important as well, as we can see in the case of the women in *Rekhti* as well as the U.S., British, and European women who met in elite social circles, private homes, collective houses, or *pensions*.

What was new was the beginning of a sense of a community of women with common interests, as well as public awareness of more than lone women engaging in sexual activity. From the fictional Moll Cutpurse insisting that "you'd find a lot of us about" to the oaths sworn in English pornography to "make use of pricks and balls no longer" to Charlotte Cushman's Rome community to Anne Lister's wondering if there were more Miss Pickfords about in the world, some women, however they conceptualized their own natures and desires, began to think that there might be ways to find others like themselves. What that meant was wildly different in different contexts, as Lister's dismissal of those with "Sapphic regard" makes clear. Soon enough some women would have to contend with definitions imposed on them whether they embraced them or not— and the increasing integration of far-flung parts of the globe would make a difference.

7

What's in a Name?

(1890–1930)

IN DEEPA MEHTA'S controversial 1996 film *Fire*, Radha and Sita, sisters-in-law living in loveless marriages in a joint-family household, fall in love with each other. (See figure 18 for a still from the film showing Radha and Sita.) After a first surprising kiss, they discover passion in each other's arms. When they make love for the first time, Sita, who is younger and the instigator, asks Radha, "Did we do anything wrong?" to which Radha replies, after a moment, "No." One day Ashok, Radha's celibate husband, discovers them in bed together. Sita is not sorry, but Radha wishes she had told him first. "What would you have said?" Sita asks. "'I love her, but not as a sister-in-law?' . . . Now listen, Radha, there's no word in our language that can describe what we are, what we feel for each other." Radha responds, "Perhaps you're right, seeing is less complicated."[1] Neither in this context nor in thinking about the naming of desire between women cross-culturally and historically is the statement that "there's no word in our language that can describe what we are, what we feel for each other" a simple one. It is important to remember this as we turn to a consideration of the naming of lesbianism by Western sexologists and the impact, and lack of impact, of that naming on various other parts of the world. For there have been many names for love, desire, and sex between women, and there has also been a great deal of unnamed love, desire, and sex between women. Both naming and leaving unnamed have their histories.

A once-familiar tale had it that until around the late nineteenth century, when sexologists categorized and named "the lesbian," there was no notion of a kind of woman who sought out sex with other women—in some times and places, any woman might fall prey to such a sin or crime; in other times and places, sex between women just did not happen. This idea was largely an echo of one about men's sexuality, since in the Western world (and elsewhere) there was a long tradition of elite men taking the right to penetrate anyone lower in the social scale, including not only

Figure 18. Radha and Sita in *Fire*. From Gayatri Gopinath, *Impossible Desires* (Durham, NC: Duke University Press, 2005).

women but boys, slaves, servants, and members of lower classes. Only an adult elite man enclosing another man, or desiring to do so, had consequences. This conception of male sexuality is what, according to the standard story, changed so dramatically in modern Western history, when as a result of the spread of new ideas, any man having sex with another man, no matter the part he played in the encounter, became a "homosexual."

Our understanding of this trajectory for men has become increasingly more complex, but what is most important here is that no similar change in the idea of sexuality applied to women. That is demonstrated by the fact that the crucial question about the wives of women living as men was whether they knew about the actual physical equipment of their husbands. If they did know, their willingness to enclose male women as well as men did not make them blameless.

Nor was the notion that some women desired and had sex with other women a novel idea in the nineteenth century. Consider what we have encountered already: in ancient Greece, tales of what Aeschylus described as "the warring Amazons, men-haters," who according to Diodorus of Sicily, were "greatly admired for their manly vigor"; Plato's fable of half-females searching desperately for their lost female half; the Aztec *patlācheh,* who "has sexual relations with women"; in ancient China, women engaged in *tui-shih* ("eating each other") and *mojingzi* ("rubbing mirrors"); "tribades" in ancient Greece and Rome, in medieval Arabic texts, and in medieval, early modern, and modern Europe; *hetairistria* in ancient Greece, women who had sex with women; Sappho, to whom the association of same-sex desire has clung for centuries; *sahacat,* witches in sixteenth-century Fez, who "have sexual relations among themselves in a damnable fashion"; "God-insulting grannies," as the Orthodox Church in medieval eastern Europe called women who had sex with women; Indian *svairini,* Cocopa *warrhameh,* Mohave *hwame,* Maricopa *kwiraxame,* Montenegrin and Albanian sworn virgins, all of whom became social males and sometimes pursued sex with women; roaring girls and randy women; the "new Cabal" and "Anandryne Sect" in eighteenth-century England and France; Chinese sworn sisters and Urdu *Doganas* and *chapatbaz.* Sapphists.

Lots of names. Lots of conceptions, not only that women might make love to other women when no men were in sight but that some women might desire and seek out other women. And yet some important new developments were in the works as the world became increasingly interconnected. It is to those we turn next.

Before the Sexologists

Where there seems to have been little idea of a person with same-sex desires as a "kind of person" was outside Europe. In China, the Taoist tradition envisioned two forces, *yin* (associated with femininity and passivity) and *yang* (a masculine and active force), which need to exist in harmony. What mattered was not the biological sex of sexual partners but the preservation of *ch'i,* the life energy found in semen or vaginal secretions. Since women's *yin* is limitless, no sexual activities between women could sap *ch'i.*[2] Taoist ideas about sexuality had an impact on Japan, as well, where male-male love flourished alongside heterosexuality. In all these contexts, sexual relations between women as well as between men did not meet with condemnation, nor did they mark a woman engaged in sex with other women as a particular kind of being.

Some scholars have argued that what is essential for the emergence of the notion that people with same-sex desires are a kind of person is the concept of women and men as fundamentally different. In both the

Chinese and European traditions, according to recent scholarship, the idea of women's and men's bodies as polar opposites is of relatively modern origin. Chinese physicians from the Song to the Ming dynasties (960–1644) conceptualized the body as androgynous, viewing male bodies with too much *yang* and female bodies with too much *yin* as out of balance.[3] In a similar way, ancient Greek texts presented male and female bodies as quite similar, and that model had staying power in European history, although how dominant it was and how long it lasted is disputed. According to ancient Greek thinkers, bodily fluids were the same and reproductive organs comparable, with women's inside instead of out, making woman a lesser but not diametrically opposed man.[4] Anne Lister, the turn-of-the-eighteenth-century female rake, read about Aristotle's concept of the female body as inside-out male and took from it confirmation that her sexual desire for women was natural.[5]

In addition to changing ideas about gender difference, another scientific development that played a role in European conceptions of women's desire for women was the "rediscovery" of the clitoris in the sixteenth century.[6] With the practice of dissection, European anatomists began to notice this mighty organ, which the doctors, if not women themselves, had forgotten since ancient times. Now recognized as the source of women's sexual pleasure, the clitoris became the counterpart of the penis, a role formerly reserved for the uterus.[7] The doctors even agreed that the clitoris was essential to reproduction, for if women did not emit their seed during orgasm, they could not conceive. Knowledge of the clitoris gave rise to fears, as we have already seen, of what women with enlarged organs might do. Jane Sharp, a seventeenth-century midwife in England, described the possibilities: "sometimes it grows so long that it hangs forth at the slit like a Yard [the term for the penis], and will swell and stand stiff if it be provoked, and some lewd women have endeavoured to use it as men do theirs."[8] Sharp, like others before her, thought this mostly happened in Asia and Africa, but by the seventeenth century, as the cases of hermaphrodites and women passing as men make clear, the image of the tribade and her active clitoris was firmly entrenched in the Western world.

The question for us here is, was the tribade "a kind of person"? A seventeenth-century English medical text would suggest so, going on from a description of an enlarged clitoris to add, "And this part it is which those wicked women doe abuse called *Tribades*."[9] A travel text from the sixteenth century connects "feminine wantonness" in Turkish baths to the activities in "times past" of "the Tribades, of the number whereof was Sapho the

Lesbian."[10] And we have already encountered the denunciations of English and French aristocratic women as tribades and sapphists. But what caused tribadism was unclear: perhaps women with unnaturally large clitorises pursued sex with other women, but perhaps it was use of the clitoris that made it grow. And, in any case, what were the limits of a normal clitoris?

There is no agreement, then, about when in the Western world we can begin to talk about women who desired other women as belonging in a discrete category.[11] But, whether or not the sixteenth-century tribade or the eighteenth-century sapphist represented a new conceptualization, what is clear is that these categories did not have the same global reach as the naming of the lesbian by the nineteenth-century sexologists.

A Name That Stuck

By the late nineteenth century, European and U.S. doctors interested in what they defined as deviant sexuality began to talk across national borders about the problem of individuals who desired and had sex with others with biologically alike bodies. Medical and scientific attention to same-sex sexuality was part of the process of growing state involvement in civil society as a result of economic transformation across the industrialized world. The sexologists did not, of course, make up their ideas out of thin air. The emerging visible subcultures and communities of women and especially men with same-sex desires both piqued the doctors' interest and provided material for their theories. The doctors differed on the question of whether people were born with same-sex desires or acquired them for a variety of reasons, but all contributed to the notion that having such desires and engaging in same-sex sexual acts defined one as a particular kind of person.

Richard von Krafft-Ebing, the Viennese psychiatrist whose monumental and influential work *Psychopathia Sexualis* appeared in German in 1886, defined same-sex desire as a symptom, rather than the defining characteristic, of what he termed "inversion." What was inverted, or reversed, was gender: a woman would think, act, and feel as a man, and vice versa. Krafft-Ebing distinguished four kinds of female inverts with increasing degrees of deviance. One category consisted of women who "did not betray their anomaly by external appearance or by mental (masculine) sexual characteristics" but who were responsive to masculine women.[12] Here we finally meet the wives of female husbands. The second category was made up of women "with a strong preference for male garments." Next came women who assumed "a definitely masculine role." And finally, the "extreme grade of degenerative homosexuality" encompassed women who possess "of the feminine qualities only the genital organs; thought, sentiment, action, even external appearance are those of a man." Note that female masculinity, either as a characteristic of a woman or as her object of attraction, defined the female invert. Krafft-Ebing described one woman as "quite conscious of her pathological condition. . . . Masculine features, deep voice, manly gait, without beard, small breasts; cropped her hair short and gave the impression of a man in women's clothes."[13]

If Krafft-Ebing paid more attention to dress and manner than to sexual desire, sex came clearly into the picture with Havelock Ellis, a British sexologist whose early-twentieth-century writings both opposed sexual repression and labeled women's desire for women perverted. Ellis, married to a lesbian woman, differentiated between the congenital invert, who could not help her condition and should therefore be tolerated, and women in Krafft-Ebing's first category, who possessed a genetic predisposition for responsiveness to the advances of other women. These women, in an atmosphere such as a boarding school or women's club, had the potential to become homosexual, and Ellis feared that the advances in women's education and legal rights, along with the work of the women's movement, were creating a hotbed of potential homosexualization. The crushes so prevalent in girls' schools no longer seemed so innocent. As Ellis explained, "While there is an unquestionable sexual element in the 'flame' relationship, this cannot be regarded as an absolute expression of real congenital perversion of the sex-instinct."[14] But if crushes between schoolgirls did not point to a congenital condition, the atmosphere of the school or the women's movement might put women in danger of being seduced. Here is how Ellis, with no evidence whatsoever, described the women who would attract and be attracted to true inverts: "Their faces may be plain or ill-made but not seldom they possess good figures, a point which is apt to carry more weight with the inverted woman than beauty of face. . . . They are always womanly. One may perhaps say that they are the pick of the women whom the average man would pass by."[15]

Swiss neurologist August Forel, like Ellis and Krafft-Ebing, differentiated between women with a "hereditary disposition to inversion" and "sapphism acquired by seduction or habit."[16] The "pure female invert," he wrote, "feels like a man." He cited a case in which such an invert, "dressed as a young man, succeeded in winning the love of a normal girl." Even after the invert was discovered and sent to an asylum, the "normal girl" "continued to be amorous" when she visited her lover. Forel "took the young girl aside" to express astonishment at her feelings for the one who had deceived her. "Her reply," he wrote, "was characteristic of a woman: 'Ah! You see, doctor, I love him, and I cannot help it!'"

Forel's and Ellis's attention to sexual desire moved closer to the notion of homosexuality as defined by the sex of one's chosen sexual partner, although they still placed great emphasis on gender inversion in the case of those born "that way." In 1913, Ellis described inversion as referring to sexual impulses "turned toward individuals of the same sex, while all the other impulses and tastes may remain those of the sex to which the person by anatomical configuration belongs."[17] When Sigmund Freud introduced the distinction between sexual aim and sexual object—"aim" referring to a preference for genital, oral, or anal sex or for an enclosing or penetrating role, and "object" to the desired sexual partner—it marked a shift away from a focus on gender inversion. But this was truer in the case of men than women, for the sexologists continued the long tradition of associating female same-sex sexual desire with masculinity.

It is not surprising, given the history we have already encountered, that the sexologists at the end of the nineteenth century returned to a consideration of hermaphroditism, either physical or psychological. Perhaps, they thought, those masculine women were partly men; perhaps they had enlarged clitorises. Or perhaps they had a mind of one sex in a body of the other—making them a "third" or "intermediate" sex. Such was the concept embraced by a number of male sexologists who themselves desired other men, including Karl Ulrichs and Magnus Hirschfeld in Germany and Edward Carpenter in England. In the Netherlands, the director of the Dutch Institute for Research into Human Heredity and Race Biology in the 1930s sought to prove through analysis of identical twins that homosexuality was genetically determined. The female twins he found through the Dutch Scientific Humanitarian Committee, a spinoff of Hirschfeld's pioneering German organization, fit the traditional description of masculine women who preferred male activities, had deep voices, and felt no sexual attraction to men.[18] The biological argument of a "third sex" was an appealing concept for people with same-sex desires, for punishment made no sense if they could not help being who they were.

At the other end of the explanatory continuum, Sigmund Freud and his followers gave an enormous boost to the idea that social factors produced same-sex desire. Freud's attention to dynamics within families to explain homosexuality took same-sex desire out of the realm of the biological. Yet both kinds of explanations—the biological and the social—lived on (and continue to linger). One sexologist in 1919 claimed that people who had homosexual sex but in an appropriate sexual role—that is, "passive" lesbians and "aggressive" homosexual men—did so as a result of social factors, whereas "aggressive" lesbians and "passive" homosexual men could only be explained by "biological anomalies of development which are often coupled with unmistakable physical signs."[19] But whatever the cause of same-sex sexual desire, those who had it increasingly came to make up a category of person labeled "homosexual" or "lesbian."

The thinking of European scientists of sex reached beyond the United States to Japan and China, becoming a transnational conversation about sexuality. In Japan, the importation of Western science followed the end of Japanese resistance to contact with Western "barbarians" and the development of a more centralized state.[20] The Japanese Forensic Medicine Association sponsored a Japanese translation of Krafft-Ebing's *Psychopathia Sexualis* that appeared in 1894, and ideas about legal rights for individuals becoming known as "homosexuals" also filtered into Japan. At the same time, German sexologists made use of knowledge about Japanese male same-sex sexual practices gleaned from Western travelers to Japan or Japanese visitors to Europe to describe a culture, like that of ancient Greece, accepting of male same-sex sexual acts.

Japanese thinking about same-sex sexuality focused almost entirely on male-male love: the concept of *homosexuality* as referring to both male-male and female-female interactions was, literally, quite foreign. When Japanese forensic pathologists first encountered Western texts, they coined a term in Japanese meaning "same-sex intercourse" to translate *homosexuality*, giving precedence to sexual acts, particularly anal intercourse. By 1887, Japanese texts mentioned "obscene acts" between women, using the German term *"Tribadie."*[21] Yet Japanese authorities merged the concepts from the European sexologists with Japanese tradition, asserting that "intercourse between females" was most likely to occur when young women lived closely together without access to men, as in prison or wealthy households. Eventually the sexologists did place male and female same-sex sexuality in the same conceptual category, by the 1920s adopting as the standard term *dōseiai*, "same-sex love." As a result, Japanese experts began to pay more attention than they had previously to female same-sex love. Loanwords such as *lesbian* (*rezubian*) and *garcon* (*garuson*, from the French word for "boy"), meaning a masculine woman, became household words.[22] By the 1920s and 1930s, same-sex love had come to seem a peculiarly female phenomenon, as "modern institutions of entertainment" distracted schoolboys from homoeroticism.[23] This was one of the major ways that Western sexology affected Japanese thinking in this realm.

Japanese sexologists, like their European colleagues, disagreed about whether same-sex love was a biological or sociological phenomenon. Habuto Eiji, a well-known early-twentieth-century expert, distinguished between common feelings of love among preadolescent girls or directed at a teacher and a "hereditary element of mental disease" if such love lasted beyond puberty.[24] The concept of sexual inversion emerged in the assumption of gender difference between partners, that one would be masculine and the other feminine. Some Japanese sexologists rejected such a notion and emphasized that it was sex segregation in schools, textile mills, prisons, convents, nurses' quarters, and hospitals that treated prostitutes for venereal disease that caused girls and women to turn to one another. Whatever the cause, same-sex love might cause physical problems, including vaginal cramps and sterility, or insanity or lead to suicide or murder.[25] One sexologist even blamed same-sex love in girls' schools for "declining birth rates in civilized nations."[26]

In China, as in Japan, the introduction of European sexologists' concepts accompanied other forms of Western importation and fostered the new notion that male and female forms of same-sex love formed a conceptual unity, embodied in the term *tongxing ai* (same-sex love). As we have seen, female same-sex bonds had a place in Chinese culture, but "sisterhood" and "friendship" characterized such relationships, and sex acts between women did not signify a personal taste or an independent eroticism.[27] That changed in the course of the political, cultural, and intellectual flowering of the post–First World War May Fourth era. Western-oriented intellectuals embraced European sexology, sometimes imported through Japan, and spread a new term, *female same-sex love,* which encompassed older concepts of relationships between women such as those between co-wives. Terms such as *nüzi tongxing lian'ai* (female homosexuality), *qingyu zhi diandao* (sexual inversion), and *biantai* (perversion) came into the Chinese language.[28]

Havelock Ellis's influence can be seen in the emerging distinction between sexually inverted women, who displayed masculinity, and the pseudo-homosexuality of feminine schoolgirls who grew up to marry. Shan Zai (a pseudonym) published an article in a Shanghai women's journal in 1911 that quoted German and British sexologists and used German sexological terminology. He both asserted the similarity of male and female same-sex love—"when a woman falls in same-sex love with another woman, it is in fact the same as a man's being fond of having sex with beautiful boys"—and differentiated between inverts and women who "want to satisfy their erotic desire but have no opportunity to associate with men."[29] He also mentioned Sappho, tribades, and nuns.

Ellis was not the only sexologist translated into Chinese. Magnus Hirschfeld visited China in 1931 and lectured, in German with Chinese translation, to thirty-five audiences. In addition, the texts of Krafft-Ebing, Freud, and Edward Carpenter were translated and published in China. As in Japan, traditions of sex segregation came together with economic and social changes that were transforming gender and sexuality in a way that made distinctions between heterosexuality and homosexuality and ideas of sexual inversion make sense. As in the case of Japan, intellectuals took what was useful from Western thinking and translated it, in both a literal and figurative sense, into Chinese culture.

The writings of the sexologists, then, did three transformative things. They presented homosexuality, whether the result of biology or social context, as a condition that defined certain individuals. They combined what had often been viewed as quite disparate phenomena—male and female same-sex love—into the concept of homosexuality. And their ideas had resonance in diverse cultures where other Western influences and processes of economic development created receptive audiences. It is ironic that European thought about same-sex sexuality, which had long associated it with foreign cultures, beginning in the late nineteenth century created the conditions that underlie the contemporary notion in much of the world that homosexuality is a Western import.

New Ways of Seeing

It is easy to exaggerate the impact of the writings of a handful of elite European men, and it is important to remember that they developed their ideas of sexual inversion and homosexuality from observations of and contact with individuals and groups of people who experienced same-sex desire. Despite the reach of Krafft-Ebing, Ellis, Hirschfeld, and others across national and linguistic boundaries, there was no immediate earth-shaking transformation in the ways that people thought about same-sex sexuality. Sometimes the new ideas came into play, sometimes they did not. In the mass-circulation British press, for example, stories of women who dressed as men and married women took a tone of admiration for the boldness of such masquerades and did not refer to sexual deviance well into the twentieth century.[30] A look at some famous cases allows us to see the complex mixture of old and new ideas in different societies.

Consider the story of Alice Mitchell and Freda Ward in late-nineteenth-century Memphis, Tennessee.[31] Mitchell, a middle-class white nineteen-year-old, fell in love with her seventeen-year-old friend Freda (known as "Fred") Ward. At first their attachment seemed, to their families, to fall into the familiar pattern of romantic friendship. Then Ward's family intercepted and read some of their letters and discovered Mitchell's plot to dress as a man, run away, and marry her beloved. Alarmed, they sent back the engagement ring and other tokens of love, forbidding them to see each other. Even worse from Mitchell's perspective, Ward began to be courted by a man. Early on in their plans to run away, Mitchell had said she would kill Ward if she backed out of her promise to marry her, and in 1892 she acted on this threat by slashing Ward's throat on the streets of Memphis. Found insane, largely because her family's social prominence made a conviction of murder unpalatable, Mitchell died in an asylum, either of tuberculosis or suicide.

The case attracted attention from doctors and the popular press not only because of its drama but also because it seemed to fit so perfectly the newly emerging paradigm of gender inversion and sexual deviance as inextricably linked. That is, Alice Mitchell became the embodiment of the "invert" or "lesbian" in American medical and popular discourse. Her family's strategy for the defense was to have her declared insane, and so her attorneys constructed a case that portrayed Alice's mother as having had "mental trouble" while pregnant and Alice as a tomboy with no interest in the expected activities of girls and with an "extraordinary fondness" for Freda. "They were very different in disposition. Fred was girl-like and took no pleasure in the boyish sports that Alice delighted in. . . . Time strengthened the intimacy between them. They became lovers in the sense of that relation between persons of different sexes."[32] But by this description, the defense meant that the relationship was neither one of "sexual love" nor of the kind of romantic friendship that might lead to a Ladies of Llangollen–like marriage. Rather, Alice's feelings represented "perverted affection," "insane love," or "morbid perverted attachment."[33] Press coverage of the case raised the issue of hermaphroditism, avoided in the trial itself, suggesting the confusing mixture of old and new ideas that swirled through public opinion. One report noted that the insanity defense rested on the idea that Alice's insistence that she could be Freda's husband was delusional: "The only apparent defect in this reasoning is the fact that it has not been proved that Alice could not perform the duties of a husband. None of the experts who have testified before the court have made an examination for the purpose of ascertaining that point."[34] So even in the midst of language about perversion and morbidity stemming from the discourse of the sexologists, older images of hermaphroditic bodies and enlarged clitorises remained.

In a case from Tokyo in 1888, many of the same developments can be observed. The daughter of an elite family named Fukuda had been romantically involved with her former maid, Maeda Otoki, for thirteen years when Maeda tried to kill Fukuda, thinking that she had lost interest in her.[35] She planned then to kill herself as well. The prosecutors tried to determine which of the women was the "husband," whether either of them had an unusual anatomy, or whether they had used some kind of "instrument."[36] The two women were guilty of the "obscene act" of mutual masturbation, but that was not in itself a crime. A forensic pathologist concluded that Maeda suffered from "sexual inversion," indicating the impact of the new diagnosis.

In between Memphis and Tokyo, at about the same time, the Hungarian count Sandor Vay was accused by his father-in-law of forgery and fraud, since he "was only a woman, walking around in masculine clothes."[37] Unlike Mitchell, Vay was a "passing woman" who was raised as a boy, had affairs with women, and worked as a journalist and writer. In Budapest, where Sarolta Vay grew up, people knew that she was a girl passing as a boy. As the family solicitor testified at the trial in 1889, "In Budapest nobody was bothered by that, because everybody knew her."[38] Vay met his wife elsewhere, and both she and her family claimed to have had no idea that he was not what he seemed. His father-in-law testified that one could see the shape of (rather large) male equipment between Vay's legs, and Vay's wife reported that she had given herself to him and had no idea prior to his arrest that he was not biologically a man. Yet other witnesses, including servants, testified that they knew that the count was a woman. Other testimony alluded to the opinion that Vay was a hermaphrodite. The midwife who was called in to examine Vay's body reported on "the female sex of the Countess and her small sexual parts."[39]

In the past, such a finding would have been the end of it: Vay's deceit would have been revealed, and he would have been either executed or

restored to his proper sex. But here we see the emerging ideas of the sexologists beginning to change the story. The doctor who reported on the case
to the court was himself confused, finding it difficult to deal with the masculine countess as a lady and much "easier, natural, and more correct" to
think of Sandor as "a jovial, somewhat boyish student."[40] He and another
forensic doctor asked all kinds of questions about Vay's sex life, wanting to
know what kinds of women attracted him, whether he had read anything
about sexual inversion, whether he allowed his sex to be touched, whether
he used his fingers or tongue in making love to women. Vay was no longer
a passing woman; he was becoming an invert. The examining doctor concluded that he suffered from "a congenital, hereditarily determined disorder of the whole nervous system" and a "congenital pathological disorder
of the mental capacity," meaning "sexual inversion."[41] As in the case of Alice Mitchell, the doctors worked to uncover a family history of mental illness that would support the idea of hereditary disease, and they made use
of the new concept of sexual inversion.

Both the Mitchell and Vay trials stimulated extensive discussion in the
mass-circulation press and among experts—Krafft-Ebing and Ellis added
discussion of the cases to their work—illustrating the way that actual cases,
sensational stories, and scientific analyses interacted in a complicated way
to create different versions of the modern "lesbian." In both of these cases,
as well as in that of Maeda in Tokyo, we see medical and legal authorities
shifting from earlier frames of romantic friendship or gender crossing to
a diagnosis of inversion and mental illness. Yet the process is complex, as
the loves and desires of women such as Mitchell and Maeda and Vay drive
the narrative as much as the abstract theories of the doctors.

What Women Thought

We still need to ask, once the sexologists undertook the process of naming
and defining the kind of people who loved others of the same sex, what
did such definitions mean to women who loved other women? There is no
simple answer to this question. Whereas language of perversion and morbidity offered little for them to embrace, the concept of a third sex could
have its appeal. At the same time, even the positive pronouncements of
the homosexual sexologists carried the potential to expose women living
respectably in Boston marriages. For example, Magnus Hirschfeld's *The
Homosexuality of Men and Women*, published in 1914, noted the frequency

of same-sex couples creating "marriage-like associations characterized by the exclusivity and long duration of the relationships, the living together and the common household, the sharing of every interest, and often the existence of legitimate community property."[42] So for some women, the medicalization of same-sex love brought unwanted attention and shame. Some fell into the clutches of those who hoped to cure them of their desires. Others differentiated their romantic friendships from deviant lesbian love or ignored the new concepts altogether. Still others embraced the new definitions as providing an identity—even if a disparaged one—that made sense of their lives.

Ethel Smyth, a British composer, feminist, and masculine woman who formed passionate relationships with women and with one man, seemed to be referring to the medicalization and deviance of same-sex love when she wrote to her male lover in 1892, "I wonder why it is so much easier for me, and I believe for a great many English women, to love my own sex passionately rather than yours? . . . How do you account for it? I can't make it out for I think I am a very healthy-minded person and it is an everlasting puzzle."[43] Clearly reflecting the concepts of the doctors, in her memoirs she characterized her eroticized mother-daughter relationship with the wife of her music teacher as a "blend of fun and tenderness that saved it from anything approaching morbidity."[44] And late in life she considered whether an incestuous love for her mother was behind her passion for women.[45]

Jeannette Marks, a professor of English at Mount Holyoke College in Massachusetts, who lived in an intimate relationship for fifty-five years with Mary Woolley, the college's president, was one who worried that others might see her as a lesbian. In an essay she wrote in 1908, she denounced as "abnormal" "unwise college friendships" such as the one she had shared with Woolley and insisted that the only relationship that could "fulfill itself and be complete is that between a man and a woman."[46] British writers Eliza Lynn Linton and Vernon Lee reacted in different ways to medical theories of gender inversion. Linton was masculine and erotically attracted to women but considered gender inversion a sign of degeneracy and could only resolve her feelings by portraying herself as a man in her writing. Lee embraced the notion of a divided self, a masculine intellect with feminine feelings.[47]

Lu Yin, a May Fourth writer in Republican China, wrote about same-sex love and expressed unease about her desires. "Lishi's Diary," written in 1923, tells the story of a woman who does not wish to marry and whose feelings for her school friend Yuanqing change from "ordinary friendship" to "same-sex romantic love." They make plans to live together, and Lishi that night dreams that they are rowing a boat in the moonlight. Then Yuanqing's mother forces her to move away and plans to marry her off to her cousin. Yuanqing writes to Lishi, "Ah, Lishi! Why didn't you plan ahead! Why didn't you dress up in men's clothes, put on a man's hat, act like a man, and visit my parents to ask for my hand?"[48] In the end, Yuanqing repudiates their plan and Lishi dies of melancholia. Lu Yin herself married twice, but her writings suggest that she struggled with desire for women and worried that others might have "dreadful suspicions" about her.[49]

Others were less tortured but worked to distinguish themselves from the pathologized subjects described by the sexologists. In a 1930 autobiography, the pseudonymous American "Mary Casal" described her sexual relationship with another woman as "the very highest type of love" and "on a much higher plane than those of *the real inverts.*"[50] In the same vein, U.S. prison reformer Miriam Van Waters, in an intimate relationship with her benefactor Geraldine Thompson from the 1920s to Thompson's death in 1967, struggled to differentiate her own "normality" from the gender inversion and pathology of lesbianism that she denounced in the women's reformatory that she supervised.[51] And yet other women forged ahead with their relationships, despite their familiarity with the writings of the sexologists. M. Carey Thomas, president of Bryn Mawr College in Pennsylvania, kept lists of books labeled "Lesbianism" and "Books on Sapphism" and admired and followed the trial of Oscar Wilde, yet she never expressed any unease over her overlapping relationships with the two loves of her life.[52] German feminists Anita Augspurg and Lida Gustava Heymann, who lived together as a couple for forty years and moved in transnational women's-movement circles familiar with the language of the sexologists, reported unselfconsciously in their memoirs about marriage proposals they were offered by their farmer neighbor: "It took all of our effort to remain serious and make clear to the man the hopelessness of his desire. As he left, we shook with laughter."[53]

On the other hand, the concept of lesbianism as a defining characteristic allowed some women to embrace their own sexuality more fully. One of the women whose case histories appear in Havelock Ellis's *Sexual Inversion* credited sexology with being "a complete revelation" of her nature, and another credited Krafft-Ebing with cluing her into the fact that her "feelings" were "under the ban of society," although she rejected his notion that she was "unnatural and depraved."[54] British feminist Frances Wilder

Figure 19. Radclyffe Hall and Una Troubridge, 1927. Hulton Archive by Getty Images, New York. From Martha Vicinus, *Intimate Friends* (Chicago: University of Chicago Press, 2004).

expressed her gratitude to homosexual sexologist Edward Carpenter, since his work made her realize, "I was more closely related to the intermediate sex than I had hitherto imagined."[55] Radclyffe Hall, who was "overjoyed and proud" that Havelock Ellis put his stamp of approval on *The Well of Loneliness,* had her famous character Stephen discover her true nature when she finds a copy of Krafft-Ebing's *Psychopathia Sexualis* with her father's notes in the margins.[56] Hall, a masculine woman herself, hoped that her novel would help young women come to terms with their desires as well as elicit sympathy from heterosexual readers.[57] (See figure 19, the masculine Radclyffe Hall and her feminine lover, Una Troubridge, 1927). When the book went on trial for obscenity and Hall's lawyer sought to convince the court that "the relationship between women described in the book represented a normal friendship," Hall was furious.[58]

A particularly fascinating source on lesbian reaction to sexology can be found in the research of the Committee for the Study of Sex Variants, a group of experts who undertook a large-scale study of homosexuality in the 1930s in New York.[59] Women (and men), who were recruited largely from an urban bohemian context, provided family histories and underwent psychiatric and physical examinations. Following in a tradition we have encountered before, the gynecologist Robert Latou Dickinson set out to confirm his hypothesis that a woman's genitals would reveal innate sexual deviance as well as deviant sexual experience. In incredibly intrusive examinations, which involved measuring the clitoris with a ruler and the vagina with fingers, as well as tracing the vulva on a glass plate, the researchers sought to detect such signs as a large vulva, erectile clitoris, insensitive hymen, and small uterus. Not surprisingly, they found just what they were seeking, along with the expected signs of "inversion."

What they did not expect, however, was what they heard from some of the subjects, who insisted on the pleasures of their sex lives and bragged about their ability to satisfy their lovers. Ursula, described appreciatively by her lover, Frieda, as "a big, bold, mannish, fat woman who heaves into a room like a locomotive under full steam," confuses the doctor, telling him that she finds Frieda "tiny and very feminine, . . . very virile and aggressive." Refusing to confine sex to the genitals, she insists that "every part of the body becomes beautiful—caressing and kissing all parts of the body. . . . My sex life has never caused me any regrets."[60]

Perhaps playing with both traditional notions about lesbians and the experts' belief in the hypersexuality of Black women, a number of African American subjects boasted of their sexual technique: "I insert my clitoris in the vagina just like the penis of a man. . . . Women enjoy it so much they leave their husbands."[61] Or as another put it, "I think they are fond of me because of my large clitoris. I think that's the chief reason. They comment upon it. They whisper among themselves. They say, 'She has the largest clitoris.'"[62] And Marian J. insisted, "I became so expert in lingual caresses that I was noted in theatrical circles and in the fringe of polite society for my excellence. . . . Sometimes I put my tongue in the vagina to increase the sexual excitement." Although the subjects of this study sometimes adopted the negative spin of the sexologists, we can see that at least some of them played with those ideas and proudly asserted the superiority of their abilities and the rightness of their desires.

So, across the globe, in different locations, women who loved women ignored, rejected, feared, or welcomed the idea that they were a kind of person who could be named. But it is important to remember that not everyone, even in societies where the ideas of the sexologists circulated relatively freely, knew the names. One young British woman in the 1950s who was involved with another woman in college remembered telling a mutual friend about the relationship: "She said in surprise, 'But you're clearly the most obvious lesbian I've ever seen.' And my response was, 'The most obvious what?' I'd never heard the word; I didn't know what she was talking about. She said, 'Well, women who fall in love with other women.' And for the first time in my life I had to sort of sit back and think, 'Oh, there's a word for something that I must be.'"[63]

The name *lesbian* was not the first to be applied to women with same-sex desires, but it was a powerful one. The women who formed romantic friendships or lived in marriages with other women or showed their masculinity or expressed desire for other women represented the source of the ideas of Krafft-Ebing and the others, and the stories of women such as Alice Mitchell and Maeda Otoki and Sandor Vay circled back from the courts and the doctors' offices to the newspapers, in the process fashioning the concept of the "female homosexual" or "lesbian."

It is hard to resist ending this chapter with Radclyffe Hall's *The Well of Loneliness*, which is all about the power of naming: Stephen Gordon's loving and sympathetic father finds Karl Heinrich Ulrichs's work and takes "to reading half the night, which had not hitherto been his custom."[64] He is coming to understand that his daughter Stephen is what Ulrichs called an *Urning*, or member of the third sex. He means to explain to his wife, Anna, who is cold toward Stephen, but he never can bring himself to utter the words. When a male suitor tells Stephen that he loves her and wants to marry her, and she reacts with terror and repulsion and outrage, she goes to her father to ask him if there is anything strange about her. He thinks, "Merciful God! How could a man answer? What could he say, and that man a father?"[65] So he lies, and then he dies before he can tell Anna or Stephen what she is. Stephen's teacher, Puddle, also finds herself unable to utter the truth. And then Stephen "fell quite simply and naturally in love, in accordance with the dictates of her nature," with a married woman neighbor.[66] Puddle sees, and she longs to help. She imagines going to Stephen and saying, "I *know*. I know all about it. . . . You're neither unnatural, nor abominable, nor mad; you're as much a part of what people call nature as anyone else; only you're unexplained as yet—you've not got your niche in creation. But some day that will come."[67] But she does not.

And then Stephen's married lover betrays her, and her mother turns against her. That is when she discovers the books locked away in her father's study. "For a long time she read; then went back to the book-case and got out another of those volumes, and another . . . Then suddenly she had got to her feet and was talking aloud—she was talking to her father: 'You knew! All the time you knew this thing, but because of your pity you wouldn't tell me. Oh, Father—and there are so many of us."[68] Stephen recognizes herself as an invert and goes on her self-sacrificing way, ultimately giving up the love of her life, one of Ellis's "pick of the women whom the average man would pass by," forcing her into the arms of a male suitor.

A Chinese literary scholar, Zhao Jingshen, in 1929 wrote about the banning of *The Well of Loneliness*, finding humorous the fact that an ordinary love affair between two women so upset the authorities.[69] Yet he was perfectly aware of the language of abnormal sexual psychology and thought "same-sex love" "perverse." Such distinctions, like Hall's naming and Radha and Sita's inability to name their love, remind us of the complexities.

So the naming of the "lesbian" was both momentous and not. It was not momentous because, in some ways, the term simply replaced older names for women who made love to one another, combining masculinity (or attraction to masculinity) with the propensity to engage in same-sex sexual acts. It was not momentous because the new ways of viewing women who loved women did not reach everywhere, and not all women exposed to the work of the sexologists claimed or even reacted to the concepts.

On the other hand, it *was* momentous because the "lesbian," in all her cultural and linguistic variations, had a wider global reach as the ideas of the European sexologists spread to other parts of the world and merged with different cultural traditions. It was momentous because not only did it create a new conceptual unity between male and female same-sex sexuality in places such as Japan and China where they had previously been distinct, but it also gave the concept of lesbianism a Western origin. As we shall see, this change had its own momentous consequences, as the European notion of sex between women as a non-Western perversion gave way to the idea of lesbianism as a Western import. And it was also momentous because the concept of the lesbian underlay the development of different kinds of communities of women who desired women, beginning in the early twentieth century.

8

In Public

(1920–1980)

IMAGINE, FOR A moment, that you are in Berlin in the 1920s. After a devastating loss in the first near-global war, followed by hyperinflation that had workers paid daily or even twice a day in wheelbarrows full of soon-to-be-worthless currency, in the midst of political violence between right and left—in the face of all this defeat and humiliation and turbulence, the culture of the new Weimar Republic has burst into bloom, perhaps only so vibrant because of the economic, political, and social turmoil. So you are in Berlin, it is nighttime, and you are out on the town. You wander into one of the many clubs catering to gender ambiguity and sexual freedom. There are masculine women with feminine women, feminine men with masculine men. The entertainment is risqué, the atmosphere a little seedy (think *Cabaret*). Numbers include "O Just Suppose" (*"Gesetz den Fall"*) and "When the Special Girlfriend" (*"Wenn die beste Freundin"*), the latter a number performed by Marlene Dietrich in 1928. Both of these hint that presumably straight women might at any moment fall into each other's arms.

At some point in the evening, a woman comes onstage (here definitely think Marlene Dietrich), and the song she sings stirs a response in the world-weary crowd. It is "The Lavender Song" (*"Das lila Lied"*), a rousing anthem of queer pride flaunted in the face of the rising Nazi threat. This is what sets your heart pounding:

> We're not afraid to be queer and diff'rent
> if that means hell—well hell we'll take the chance
> they march in lockstep, we prefer to dance
> We see a world of romance and of pleasure
> all they can see is sheer banality
> Lavender nights are our greatest treasure
> where we can be just who we want to be

Round us all up, send us away
that's what you'd really like to do
But we're too strong proud unafraid
in fact we almost pity you
You act from fear, why should that be
what is it that you are frightened of

the way that we dress
the way that we meet
the fact that you cannot destroy our love
We're going to win our rights
to lavender days and nights.[1]

The scene is a far cry from the mostly private interactions between women that we have encountered so far. As we have seen, the conceptions of the sexologists, as they spread from Germany around much of the globe, made elements of an already existing world of same-sex desire more public. Schoolgirl crushes, traditionally either ignored or validated as innocent, came under new scrutiny. Explosions of creative energy in cultural movements—from the May Fourth movement in China to the salon of Natalie Barney in Paris to the Harlem Renaissance in New York—publicized in the written word, in the visual arts, and in song the existence of women who loved women. And the flourishing of commercial entertainment in urban areas created spaces where women as well as men with same-sex desires could meet.

But this is not simply a triumphal story of secret lives coming out into the light of day, for private connections remained important in the history of women who loved women. Lack of access to public space in many cultures meant that the new vibrant public worlds that flourished in some cities were only part of the global story.

Schoolgirls in the News

In the early twentieth century, the intimate friendships between girls in school, which had blossomed and seemed so admirable in many societies, suddenly found themselves in the harsh glare of sexological theory. Havelock Ellis, in his "The School-Friendships of Girls," an appendix to the third edition of *Studies in the Psychology of Sex*, published in 1920, warned about the dangers of the passionate relationships between girls in schools in Italy, England, the United States, and Latin America. Known as a *flamma* (flame) in Italy, such a relationship was, according to Ellis, "non-sexual," yet at the same time it had "all the gradations of sexual sentiment." He quoted an informant for Italian researchers who described a flame relationship developing "exactly like a love relationship; it often happens that one of the girls shows man-like characteristics, . . . the other lets herself be loved" as would "a girl with her lover."[2] Although such relationships involved passion and kissing and caresses, Ellis and his Italian source did not see them as homosexual but, rather, as "love-fiction, a play of sexual love."[3]

In England, such relationships were known as *raves* or *spoons,* and Ellis quoted an Englishwoman who insisted that such passionate ties were "far commoner than is generally supposed." "From what I have been told by those who have experienced these 'raves' and have since been in love with men," she told Ellis, "the emotions called forth in both cases were similar."[4] Students might have raves on teachers or on one another. In the case of two schoolgirls, "there is more likely to be a sexual element, great pleasure being taken in close contact with one another and frequent kissing and hugging."[5] But girls were so ignorant of sexuality that they did not recognize this activity as sexual. Ellis leaves judgment in the English case to his informant, who thought that if there was no actual sexual activity, then such relationships did more good than harm.

For the United States, Ellis relied on answers to a questionnaire sent out by a professor at Clark University. He reports much the same thing: that girls in school and young women in college are likely to fall in love with one another. One woman wrote about falling for another girl at fourteen that "it was insane, intense love," just like her first love for a man; in both cases, her "whole being was lost, immersed in their existence."[6] And from Buenos Aires, Ellis cites a researcher who found that as soon as schoolgirls left their classrooms, "they were found in pairs or small groups, in corners, on benches, beside the pillars, arm in arm or holding hands. . . . They were sweethearts talking about their affairs." One was active, the other passive, expressing "her affection with sweet words and promises of love and submission."[7]

Because such relationships were so common in so many places—60 percent of students according to the Italian researchers—Ellis seemingly could not wrap his head around the notion that they represented "an absolute expression of real congenital perversion of the sex-instinct," even though he admitted that "there is an unquestionable sexual element."[8] Yet it is clear from his descriptions that gender difference (masculinity/ femininity, or in his terms "active"/"passive") sometimes entered into the picture and that, however much he and his sources tried to deny it, sexual feelings, if not actual genital activity, played a part in schoolgirl friendships.

If Ellis agonized over what to make of passionate attachments among girls, over time such relationships did come to seem a sign of "congenital perversion." A 1928 novel about Vassar College, We Sing Diana, described a veritable sea change from the days in which the women's college was a breeding ground for acceptable "smashing." By 1920, a character in the novel noted, "intimacy between two girls was watched with keen distrustful eyes. Among one's classmates, one looked for the bisexual type, the masculine girl searching for a feminine counterpart, and one ridiculed their devotions."[9] As the novel suggests, the language of sexology had in some places infiltrated the world in which young women fell head over heels in love with no self-consciousness.

Attention to schoolgirl intimacy brought love between women into the public eye, not only in the United States, England, western Europe, and Latin America but especially in Japan and China, where girls' schools represented a relatively new development. In Japan, intimacy between women had never been roundly denounced by religious, medical, or legal authorities, but the spread of sexology changed all that.[10] A 1911 newspaper article listed a whole slew of words referring to "passionate love" between classmates or to the young women themselves: goshin'yū (intimate friends), ohaikara (stylish, from the English term "high collar"), onetsu (fever or passion), ome (possibly a combination of the words for "male" and "female"), and odeya (an honorific attached to the Japanese version of the English word "dear"). In the 1920s and 1930s, the term S, from the English word sister, had become publicly associated with both schoolgirls attached to their friends and the friendships themselves. Girls' schools were elite institutions in Japanese society, which the references to English words confirmed. Connections to the "raves" and "smashes" and "flames" of young women's friendships in the Western world suggest a nascent cross-cultural schoolgirl culture.

Some Japanese sexologists emphasized the romance rather than the sexuality of schoolgirl friendships, considering them a "normal" phase, harmless "love play," a "preliminary step" or "practice run" for heterosexuality.[11] Freud's theories of same-sex attraction as a part of normal sexual development influenced Japanese sexologists' thinking on this question. Such attachments might involve no more than kisses or caresses. In contrast to schoolboys, who were assumed to have a stronger sexual drive that would result in anal intercourse, schoolgirls' same-sex love was more "mysterious" and "platonic."[12] Sex researcher Yamamoto Senji criticized male teachers who saw in "platonic love" among girl students who "simply hugged each other without any carnal trick" the same kind of deviance as in boys' mutual masturbation and sodomy.[13] Habuto Eiji, in 1921, described relationships in this way:

> As love between the female couple begins to heat up, their letters start to read like love notes, which they send under pseudonyms for no reason. They have their photographs taken often. . . . They leave the house early, visit each other inordinately, and stroll hand in hand in parks and at shrine and temple affairs. They exchange meaningful smiles on almost any occasion. Their conversations are invariably long, and they scribble their partner's name in their books and notebooks.[14]

Some feminists took up the defense of schoolgirl relationships by arguing that they were positive and spiritual, rather than carnal, although other feminists denounced them as unwholesome. Furuya Toyoko, a founder of a girls' school, published an article in a women's journal in 1923 titled "The New Meaning of Same-Sex Love in Female Education."[15] She differentiated same-sex love of a student for a teacher, which encouraged a girl to work hard and model herself on her beloved, or between students, which facilitated emotional development, from "sordid" love between women in the past, referring to Buddhist nuns or ladies-in-waiting in women's quarters. In making that contrast, she denied any physical involvement through "base passion" on the part of schoolgirls.[16]

But some sexologists linked "S" ties directly to sexual perversion. At the outset of the twentieth century the Japanese sexologist Ishikawa Kiyotada thought that prostitutes were the main practitioners of female same-sex love, but by 1920 Sawada Junjirō gave the honor to students in girls' schools (although in addition he suspected it among factory workers, nurses, aristocratic ladies, unmarried daughters, married women, concubines, widows, prisoners, maids, sales girls, clerical workers, teachers, actresses, geishas, prostitutes, and nuns—hardly a select list). Sexologists noted signs that ordinary school friendships might be developing into sexual perversion, following the example of an Italian psychologist and psychiatrist. But what were parents to make of the fact that friends' choosing to wear their hair in the same style meant excessive affection, and if one bobbed her hair, they might be having sex? Or that sexologist Sawada Junjirō assured them that "these things are immediately visible to the eyes of those with experience, but to those with none, they cannot easily be apprehended"?[17]

Sawada, along with other sexologists, claimed to know something about the sexual practices of schoolgirls, including genital activity. He thought girls became increasingly sexual beginning at around age fifteen. Another sexologist reported a past incident in which graduates of a girls' school had drowned and their genitals were found to resemble those of prostitutes. And yet another sexologist announced that the renovation of a dormitory revealed a secret supply of dildos hidden away, presumably for the enjoyment of the girls together. Ironically, as schoolgirls replaced schoolboys as the main practitioners of "same-sex love," they came to resemble them more in their presumed sexual practices.

As with the case of Alice Mitchell's murder of her lover Freda Ward in Memphis, scandal resulting from schoolgirl relationships alerted the public to what was going on and also served as "evidence" for the sexologists. We can see this dynamic in the case of the 1911 double suicide that gave rise to the sexologist's report on the state of the drowned girls' genitals. Sone Sadako and Ikamura Tamae, both twenty years old and graduates of a Tokyo girls' school, left their homes, tied themselves together with a pink sash, weighed themselves down with stones, and threw themselves into the Sea of Japan. While at school, their classmates reported, they were a clear case of *ome*, and since graduating they had seen each other daily. Perhaps unhappy that one of their fathers had tried to curtail their meetings and that Sone was to be married, they planned what was a traditional performance in Japan known as *shinjū*, "what is in the heart." On their last voyage, they used the same family name, Tanaka, and signed a note they left "Two Pine Needles."[18]

Although female double suicides were not entirely novel in Japan, most were among factory workers, prostitutes, and maids, not well-educated elite young women. The press, including a women's magazine and widely read newspapers, reported avidly on the incident, bringing to public attention the phenomenon and vocabulary of schoolgirl friendships, sexological concepts of perversion, and the notion of "same-sex love." A masculine woman, Sakuma Hideka, who was thwarted in a suicide attempt with her feminine partner in 1924, told the press, "I don't hate men, I've just felt closer to women since graduating from girl's high school."[19]

At the height of the Great Depression in the early 1930s, female double suicides became a "phenomenon of the age," according to sexologist Yasuda Tokutarō.[20] One well-publicized case, although not involving schoolgirls, nevertheless called attention to what one account called the "recent, disturbing increase . . . in lesbian affairs between upper class girls and women."[21] The star-crossed lovers, both in their twenties, were Saijō Eriko—who played a woman's part in the all-female Shōchiku Revue, where both masculine and feminine performers inspired crushes in their fans, many of them girls in school—and Masuda Yasumare, an upper-class masculine fan who had taken a male name.[22] Because Masuda had short hair, wore mannish dress, and sported round glasses, she bore the brunt of the negative publicity about their double suicide attempt. A national daily newspaper treated the incident in its humor column, and a ballad appeared with the title "Suicide Journey of a Flapper and a Mannish Woman." The hostile publicity contrasted with the reverent treatment of heterosexual lovers who killed themselves rather than submit to arranged marriages to others.

Saijō and Masuda met backstage in 1934, and Saijō admitted in her account of the affair that she found the fan handsome and that the two began to see each other every day. Masuda wrote letters expressing her longing to spend every minute with Saijō, which the actress (no doubt disingenuously) reported that she wrote off as fan mail. The two took off on an extended trip together, during which Masuda refused to return home and Saijō, according to her account, began to tire of Masuda's intensity. After Masuda's mother tracked her down and took her home, she escaped the family home, "re-entering the fickle world of sexual desire," according to a press account.[23] She went to Tokyo and called Saijō, who came to her hotel room accompanied by her father. He felt sorry for the distraught young woman and—making clear how differently their relationship could be viewed—urged Saijō to spend the night with her. Saijō's account makes no mention of the suicide pact and tranquilizers they took, as reported in the press, admitting only that she was surprised to wake up in the morning. Masuda recovered, and her family allowed her to live independently, a privilege reserved for sons; Saijō left the revue to pursue a career in film. In conjunction with the stories of schoolgirl romances, the attention accorded this case because of Masuda's class standing and Saijō's celebrity introduced the Japanese reading public to a world of same-sex love and sexual desire.

In Japan, as elsewhere, publicity about schoolgirl lovers resulted from anxieties about social and economic change. In contrast to the idealized traditional Japanese wife and mother, the schoolgirl, and especially the masculine young woman, represented the deleterious effects of Westernization. Saitô Shigeyoshi, a physician, insisted that mannish women were "more prevalent in the West," and other sexologists associated "permanent" female homosexuality with the West and the "transient" variety with Japan.[24] In fact, it would seem that fear about what was going on in the dormitories and halls of girls' schools was a transnational phenomenon, as suggested by the popularity in Japan of *Mädchen in Uniform*, a 1931 German film about sexual desire in a girls' school.[25] As we have seen in so many other times and places, love between women carried all sorts of implications for the health and authenticity of a culture or nation.

The debate about girls' schools in Japan, as well as the writings of German and British sexologists, including Krafft-Ebing and Ellis, had an impact in China as well. A 1911 article in a women's journal, *Funü shibao* (*Women's Times*), titled "Same-Sex Erotic Love between Women," described attempts to eliminate "same-sex mutual love" in Japan. "To prevent this fashion by abolishing the dorms in women's schools or forbidding close female friends to sleep in the same room is easy to say but difficult to carry out."[26] As in Japan, experts disagreed about the nature of girls' friendships, some emphasizing the emotional qualities and others worrying about perversion. In 1927, a Chinese translation of Ellis's "The School-Friendships of Girls" appeared under the significantly altered title "Same-Sex Love among Female Students."[27] Pan Guangdan, who translated Ellis's *The Psychology of Sex* into Chinese in 1946, thought that the rise in coeducational schools had greatly limited same-sex love between male students but that "we can find many instances of same-sex love between female schoolmates. Some women even make a mutual agreement not to get married or to marry the same person in the future."[28] (See the representation of Chinese women's friendships in figure 20).

One of the ways that romance between girls at school came to public attention in China was through literature. As in Japan and elsewhere, education for girls beyond elementary school was a privilege of the Chinese elite in the early twentieth century. Educated women struggled to free themselves from traditional roles as wives and mothers if they sought to pursue a career as a teacher, doctor, reformer, or writer. We have already encountered Lu Yin, whose story "Lishi's Diary" depicted classmates in love. Another of her works, *Old Acquaintances by the Seaside*, imagines a community of women at college who long for a house by the sea where they can live and work together. But as they graduate, they marry and give

Figure 20. Chinese
friends, early twentieth
century. From Tze-lan
Sang, *The Emerging Les-
bian* (Chicago: Univer-
sity of Chicago Press,
2003).

up their dreams, and the protagonist, Lusha, is left depressed by the loss
of a loving women's world.[29] An alternative scenario to life after school appears in "Summer Break," by another May Fourth writer, Ding Ling. In
that story, two women teachers who had spent their days in school seeking girlfriends, sending love letters, kissing, and embracing find themselves
uninterested in their chosen careers. Although they regret not marrying,
they continue their same-sex romance, doing "with each other whatever
newlyweds do."[30]

In yet another example of May Fourth fiction, Ling Shuhua recast
a story published by a male member of her circle. Both tales, written in
1926, tell of a relationship between two girls who play Romeo and Juliet
in their school production. The original story, "Why Did She Suddenly Go
Crazy" explains their "same-sex love" as a result of "Romeo's" masculinity
and the lack of heterosexual opportunities. In Ling's version, with the intriguing title "Rumor Has It That Something like This Happened," the two
girls fall in love, embrace and kiss, and even share a bed in the dorm. Gu

Yingman, who plays Romeo, argues for the superiority of female same-sex love, pointing to the example of two of their teachers, who live together. "Why can't we follow their example?" she asks Deng Yunluo, her Juliet. "I believe my love for you is much deeper and will last longer than any man's love for you. . . . Can't you think of yourself as married to me?"[31] But Yunluo's family arranges a marriage for her, and although she cannot bear to lose Yingman, she feels she must obey. When Yingman learns that her love has married, she faints and sees a vision of Yunluo but is unable to tell if she is calling for help or smiling.

That schoolgirl romance was no well-kept and shameful secret is suggested by Xie Bingying's *Yige nübing de zizhuan* (*The Autobiography of a Woman Soldier*), the tale of a schoolgirl-turned-soldier who fought to liberate the Chinese masses. In the 1920s, at a women's college, Xie encountered the "troubles of same-sex love" when five classmates fell in love with her and fought for her attention.[32] Without embarrassment, Xie admitted to being "born with a male personality" that attracted such attention. Her unselfconsciousness about her past, even if superseded by heterosexual love and commitment to social revolution, makes clear how much stories of girls in love at school had filtered into public consciousness.

Whether newly scrutinized from the perspective of sexology or accepted as a natural consequence of sex segregation, passionate relationships at girls' schools and women's colleges spread word about the possibilities of love between women. From the United States to Europe to China to Japan, the education of women opened up the possibility of a professional and personal life without marriage to a man. As the stories of Lu Yin and Ding Ling suggest, for at least some women the relationships they formed in school had a lingering impact on their desires and ambitions. And the kind of community of women of which Lu Yin's heroine Lusha dreamed did, in fact, become a reality for some women in some places.

An Eye on the Women's Movement

The economic, social, and cultural developments that undergirded the emergence of communities of women in the early twentieth century tended to facilitate a breakdown of barriers between women and men, making heterosocial and heterosexual interactions more public while casting increasing suspicion on homosocial ties. Nowhere was this dynamic more in evidence than in feminist movements, where solidarity among women fostered not only intimate relationships but also antifeminist attacks from the outside. Havelock Ellis blamed the women's movement for an increase in lesbianism by bringing more women into contact with "congenital inverts" in colleges, settlement houses, and political organizations, and other experts followed suit. The French sexologist Julien Chevalier thought that homosexuality was congenital but also insisted that the number of lesbians was increasing as women became more emancipated.[33] A U.S. doctor wrote in the *New York Medical Journal* in 1900 that "the female possessed of masculine ideas of independence, the virago who would sit in the public highways and lift up her pseudo-virile voice, . . . and that disgusting antisocial being, the female sexual pervert, are simply different degrees of the same class—degenerates."[34] Following Havelock Ellis, Japanese physician Ōtsuka Shinzō denounced the "new women" of feminist circles as masculine "perverts."[35] Such attacks called attention to the bonds that women formed within the women's movement.

In Japan, the feminist Bluestocking Society (*Seitōsha*), founded in 1911, attracted negative attention for allegedly fostering same-sex eroticism. Most members had graduated from the Japanese Women's College, founded in 1901, whose students the media denounced as "sexual degenerates" from the outset.[36] Newspapers in Tokyo reported in 1912 that members had gone to a brothel district, hired a geisha (who had graduated from a girls' school—more of the schoolgirl taint), and spent the night with her in a teahouse.[37] One of the founders of the organization, Hiratsuka Raichō, formed an intimate relationship with a younger member, the artist Otake Kōkichi, and wrote about their mutual affection in the organization's journal. Both women wore male clothing and smoked and drank like men. They used the term *shōnen*, literally "boy" but in the slang of boys' schools a term for the younger member of a male couple, to describe Otake. She was indeed younger, tall, and unconventional in her dress and moved and spoke in an unrestrained way, all of which evoked masculinity. The press reported that Hiratsuka was a bisexual and sex addict and that Otake was a lesbian.[38] When Hiratsuka wrote her autobiography in 1971, long after both women had entered into relationships with men, she denied that her relationship with Otake had anything to do with "same-sex love." Their subsequent passion for men she put forth as proof that there was nothing "pathological" about their relationship.

The Bluestocking Society also brought together Tamura Toshiko, a novelist, and Naganuma (later Takamura) Chieko, an artist. Tamura was married but wrote about love between women. When Naganuma left her to marry a man, Tamura wrote in her novel *Samuke* (*Chills*), "I would like to let this man have a modest wife, a lovely and obedient woman to live with him. However, every time this thought strikes me, I cannot help crying out. . . . Every time I recall that we can live the women-only life without 'man,' I feel so happy, as though my body were sailing out over the wide open sea."[39] Tamura later expressed strong feelings for Hiratsuka Raichō but could not get around her masculinity. But the gender and sexual fluidity that marked members of the Bluestocking Society brought into public a challenge to both the Japanese expectations that women would be "good wives, wise mothers" and the pathologizing of relationships between women. The press pinned the label *garuson* (from the French word for "boy," *garçon*) on women considered "new," "modern," and/or "Western."[40]

In China, too, the "New Women" of the May Fourth movement negotiated between the "modern" emphasis on freer relations between women and men, on the one hand, and bonds of solidarity between women, on the other. Lu Yin, the author whose stories depicted girls wrenched apart in the interest of marriage, experienced her own conflict between her relationships with men and what literary scholar Tze-lan Sang persuasively argues was Lu Yin's erotic attraction to women.[41] This conflict played out on a trip to Japan with her second husband. Apparently freed both by travel and her marriage, she admitted to a fascination with prostitution and a desire to visit a brothel. "When I was still in China, I had often daydreamed about masquerading as a man so that I could visit a brothel to have a look at prostitutes' flirtatious smiles and luxurious, dissipated lives."[42] This she never dared do in China, out of fear that if she were discovered, "people might have dreadful suspicions" about her.[43] But in Japan, she was anonymous, so she dressed in Western clothes to pass herself off as a Japanese New Woman and found a guide to take her and her husband to a district where lower-class prostitutes worked. She started out excited about the adventure, but ended up repulsed and afraid, both of the prostitutes and of the men who buy sex from them.

Lu Yin's other experience of same-sex eroticism came in her first visit to a bathhouse, where she discovered that the Japanese were less modest than the Chinese and enjoyed communal bathing. Disrobing, she hurried into the bath and hid her body in the water. But after bathing and dressing, she began to look around in admiration of the women's bodies and beauty: "The other women were lovely and languorous after their bath.

And how natural they looked! Facing the glossy mirror, they combed their hair and applied powder and rouge to their faces, all the while without a stitch of clothing on. . . . I feasted on the sight. . . . I admired their bodies as I put on my socks."[44] Lu Yin's fascination with the sexuality of the brothel, reminiscent of the Bluestocking Society's night with a geisha, and her erotic attraction to the bodies of Japanese women suggest that the feminist concerns of May Fourth women writers helped to make public the possibilities of desire between women.

In the Western world, relationships between feminist women were much more private and less eroticized in public, although sometimes just as controversial within the movement. In the United States, the lingering acceptance of romantic friendship shielded women who were prominent in the women's movement from suspicion of sexual deviance. The women's movement provided a comfortable space for women such as Anna Howard Shaw, a suffrage leader and star orator of the movement, who fell in love with women throughout her life. Her long-term relationship with Lucy Anthony, suffrage great Susan B. Anthony's niece, was a marriage in which Anthony played wife to Shaw's husband. But Shaw also had flings with other women in her suffrage travels. Carrie Chapman Catt, Shaw's rival in the women's movement, responded to gossip about Shaw's advances by writing, "I think AS is too old for that sort of thing now. It used to happen often—about every *two years*."[45] Catt herself, despite her two marriages, made a life with another woman, Mary Garrett Hay, even before the death of her second husband. When another suffragist, Mary Peck, declared her attraction to Catt in the first decade of the twentieth century, Catt warned her that Hay's "affection, although never the A.S. [Anna Shaw] kind, is masculine as far as ownership goes."[46] Shaw's grandmotherly persona and Catt's marital status protected them from external denunciation, although gossip about their intimate connections circulated within the women's movement.

In other places, too, the women's movement provided a hospitable environment for women in relationships with other women. In 1904, in a speech to the pioneering German homosexual-rights group, the Scientific Humanitarian Committee, Anna Rühling commented that "the homosexual woman is particularly capable of playing a leading role in the international women's rights movement for equality. And indeed, from the beginning of the women's movement until the present day, a significant number of homosexual women assumed the leadership in the numerous struggles."[47] She was probably referring to German couples Käthe

Schirmacher and Klara Schleker, and Anita Augspurg and Lida Gustava Heymann.[48] We have already met Augspurg and Heymann boldly turning down proposals from neighboring Bavarian farmers. They were accepted as a couple in the German and transnational women's movement. When Heymann planned a trip to Geneva for a meeting of the Women's International League for Peace and Freedom in 1930, a staff member reported, "she is coming without Dr. Augspurg which is scarcely believable!"[49] Colleagues noticed that they died within two weeks of each other, having been left homeless and without country as pacifists and feminists when Hitler came to power in 1933.

Although such relationships—and this was true into the mid-twentieth century—were often accepted within the women's movement as life-partnerships in the Boston marriage sense, Anna Rühling's speech makes clear that homosexuality was also a label that could be applied both within and outside the movement. Members of transnational women's organizations used such terms as "queer," "perverse from a sexual point of view," and "Manly-Looking" to describe women, in one case commenting on women who "went about together at the Hague, hair cropped short and rather mannish in dress."[50] Doris Stevens, a U.S. militant feminist and early-twentieth-century sex radical who took a sharp turn to the political right by the 1940s, referred in her diary to Alice Paul, founder of the U.S. National Woman's Party, as a "devotee of Lesbos" and thanked a friend for recognizing that, despite the fact she was a feminist, she was "not a queerie."[51]

So women's movements, along with girls' schools, both facilitated love between women and made that love visible. Some claimed their love— or the love of other women—proudly, some named it pathological, some lived their lives in marriage-like relationships blithely ignoring the new science of homosexuality. However they responded, women in women's movements in places around the world helped make public the possibilities of love between women long before the lesbian feminism of the 1970s and 1980s.

Going Public in Private Spaces

Outside the women's movement, education and increasing access to employment and public space opened up other opportunities for women to forgo a traditional home-centered life of marriage and childbearing. What was different by the early twentieth century was the formation of communities of women, not just couples. Often these communities grew out of moments of intellectual and cultural ferment, as we have already seen in the case of the May Fourth movement in China. Women writers, artists, musicians, and performers—like Charlotte Cushman before them—took advantage of progressive movements to lead unconventional lives. Through their lives, often still lived in private spaces, and their cultural products, they also helped bring love between women into the public eye.

Perhaps the most famous community of women whose cultural productions publicized love between women gathered around Natalie Clifford Barney in Paris from the last decade of the nineteenth century into the mid-twentieth.[52] Barney was an extremely wealthy and flamboyant American heiress who spoke and wrote French as if born to the tongue. When her parents' marriage fell apart, she and her sister and mother moved to Paris. Barney's mother, a bit of a free spirit herself, was an accomplished portrait painter whose later subjects included many of Barney's lovers, although she denied knowing about Natalie's nature until her published writing made it impossible to avoid. Barney made Paris her home until her death at the age of ninety-five. It was there that she founded a salon that became the hallmark of elite and artistic lesbian life in the early twentieth century.

Protected by her wealth and influence, she rejected the negativity of the sexologists and, especially, the association of lesbianism with masculinity. Not only was she open about her love for women—as well as famous for her multiple conquests through a long life—but she embraced both femininity and feminism. Djuna Barnes, like Barney a lesbian American in Paris in the 1920s, described the heroine of her *Ladies Almanack*, a modern Amazon modeled on Barney, as a female who was "developed in the Womb of her most gentle Mother to be a Boy" but who "came forth an Inch or so less than this [yet] paid no Heed to the Error."[53] Barney had experienced same-sex desire at a young age, learning with something of a shock while still in her teens that others considered such tastes perverted. She described her desires as entirely natural, or sometimes "naturally unnatural": "I considered myself without shame: albinos aren't reproached for having pink eyes and whitish hair, why should they [society] hold it against me for being a lesbian? It's a question of nature: my queerness isn't a vice, isn't 'deliberate,' and harms no one."[54]

Barney's private-yet-public lesbian world had its origins in 1902 with the production of theatricals with and for a group of women friends, but when her experiences in both high society and the sexual underworld (she had an affair with the most famous courtesan in Paris) left her wanting more, she founded her salon. "I therefore have to find or found a milieu that fits my aspirations: a society composed of all those who seek to focus and improve their lives through an art that can give them pure presence," she recollected at the end of her life about the decision to make art out of conversation.[55] Both men and women gathered on Fridays for two months in the fall and two in the spring from 1909 to 1968, interrupted only by the Second World War. To some of her events she invited only women, although she liked men and did not mind even if they came as voyeurs to watch women together. In 1927, she founded what she called the Académie des Femmes, intended as an alternative to the elite Académie Française, which did not admit women. There she honored women writers, including Gertrude Stein, with whom she became good friends in the 1920s.

As in all great salons, intelligent conversation among talented writers and artists was the order of the day. But what was special about Barney's salon was the prominence of lesbian and bisexual women, many of them her lovers or ex-lovers. By the count of her longtime servant, Barney had more than forty serious affairs and many more casual ones during her long life. Eventually she formed a partnership with the painter Romaine Brooks that lasted more than forty-five years, although the relationship did nothing to slow down her conquests, causing Brooks much unhappiness.

Perhaps nothing gives a better sense of the impact of Barney's salon— from both the creativity it nurtured and its legacy—than the number of novels in which a character is modeled on Barney. In Liane de Pougy's *Idylle saphique*, written by the former courtesan whom Barney seduced and attempted to save, Barney appears as Emily Florence Temple Bradford, watching Sarah Bernhardt play Hamlet and raging against the tyranny of men. The actress and writer Collette, briefly Barney's lover and long a member of her circle, used the name by which Barney courted de Pougy as her Natalie character in her novel *Claudine s'en va*. Renée Vivien, one of Barney's serious lovers, who died young of anorexia and alcoholism, presented Natalie as Vally in *Une Femme m'apparut* (*A Woman Appeared to Me*); Vally asserts that "to be as different as possible from Nature is the true function of art."[56] (See figure 21 for a famous portrait of Vivien and Barney.)

And there were others. F. Scott Fitzgerald, no admirer of lesbians or feminists, depicted Barney in *Tender as the Night* as someone whom his hero, Dick Diver, had to go see because she wanted to buy some pictures from a

Figure 21. Renée Vivien and Natalie Barney, ca. 1900. Bibliothèque Littéraire Jacques Doucet, Paris. From Martha Vicinus, *Intimate Friends* (Chicago: University of Chicago Press, 2004).

friend of his who needed the money. "You're not going to like these people," he warned Rosemary, the young American friend falling in love with him. And inside, Rosemary is besieged by a "neat, slick girl with a lovely boy's face" until drawn into conversation with "the hostess," "another tall rich American girl, promenading insouciantly upon the national prosperity."[57]

But no doubt Natalie Barney's most famous literary incarnation is as Valérie Seymour in Radclyffe Hall's *The Well of Loneliness*. When Stephen Gordon is first taken to her salon, she describes Valérie: "Her face was humorous, placid and worldly; her eyes very kind, very blue, very lustrous. She was dressed all in white, and a large white fox skin was clasped round her slender and shapely shoulders. For the rest she had masses of thick fair hair, which was busily ridding itself of its hairpins; one could see at a glance that she hated restraint."[58] At first Stephen is angry, thinking that Valérie approves of her solely because she is a lesbian. But then Valérie smiles at her and begins to talk about work, books, and life. Then "Stephen began to understand better the charm that many had found in this woman; a charm that lay less in physical attraction than in a great courtesy and understanding, a great will to please, a great impulse towards beauty in all its forms. . . . And as they talked on it dawned upon Stephen that here was no mere libertine in love's garden, but rather a creature born out of her epoch, a pagan chained to an age that was Christian."[59]

And in fact Barney took on the name "Amazon," bestowed on her by Remy de Gourmont, a major French intellectual who became Barney's good friend, despite or because of the fact that he fell hopelessly in love with her. When he published a series of letters, later a book called *Lettres à l'Amazone*, her fame spread. Her mother wrote to her, "Tell me, my dear child, what did you do, since you've known this old gentleman, to be talked about this way all over Europe?"[60] Barney took up the challenge, publishing *Thoughts of an Amazon* and then *More Thoughts of the Amazon*, the change in the article telling.

Barney and her circle also claimed a history connecting them to Sappho. A hostile review of Barney's first book, responding to poems extolling the beauty of women, took the title "Sapho [*sic*] Sings in Washington," suggesting how readily the comparison between contemporary lesbians and Sappho came to mind.[61] Barney and Renée Vivien learned Greek in order to read the fragments in the original, visited Lesbos, where Vivien kept a villa, and sought out Pierre Louÿs, author of *Les Chansons de Bilitis* (*Songs of Bilitis*), billed as love poems written by one of Sappho's lovers. Louÿs took a shine to Barney and gave her and Vivien autographed copies of his book. Vivien evoked Sappho in her writing, in one poem imagining herself both as one of Sappho's lovers and also as a Sappho to future generations of women.[62] Barney associated her own regular infidelities with Sappho's, much to Vivien's chagrin. Sappho was a favorite subject for Barney's theatricals; in one, she (like Erica Jong so long after her) changed the story of Sappho's suicide, but in this case, Sappho leapt into the sea for love of a woman.

The fascination with Sappho suggests not only a longing for a history of women who loved women but also a recognition of the importance of community. Natalie Barney's private-world-made-public, through audacious self-presentation and immortalization in literature, represents an important development in the early twentieth century. Although her salon was a place for elite and often expatriate women to gather, its longevity and fame made it emblematic of the new spaces where women who desired women could gather without shame.

Going Out

More public and more accessible places for women to meet women emerged in the big cities of the industrialized world in the early twentieth century, perhaps reaching their zenith in Berlin in the 1920s and early 1930s. Places to go out were not entirely new: by the mid-nineteenth century in Paris, women seeking women found public places to meet, and in the 1880s and 1890s, according to a U.S. physician, "perverts of both sexes maintained a sort of social set-up in New York City, [and] had their places of meeting," including beer gardens and dance halls. In contrast to male "fairies," however, the women, as "mannishly dressed as the styles of that time would permit," were not as flamboyant in public.[63]

By the 1920s, some urban areas throughout western Europe and the United States spawned commercial establishments catering to women who desired women. In London, an observer in 1922 described the Café Royale as a place where "things in women's clothes . . . slide cunning eyes upon other women" and "hard-featured ambassadors from Lesbos" gathered.[64] In Soho and the West End, Radclyffe Hall and other wealthy lesbians, along with gay men, frequented the kind of bohemian and artistic clubs that could be found in Greenwich Village. Yet London was still a place where, in part because the latest fashions for young New Women in the 1920s were decidedly masculine, lesbians were both visible and invisible, at least until after the trial of *The Well of Loneliness*.[65] And there was no public lesbian culture comparable to that of Paris and Berlin. In fact, Radclyffe Hall had her heroine do the nightlife in Paris, and one real-life British lesbian booked a trip to Paris with the intention of finding a lesbian club. When she finally found her way to Le Monocle, one of the first lesbian nightclubs, she remembered, "Well it was wonderland. . . . In my wildest imagination I didn't know such a thing existed."[66] The mother of a masculine lesbian daughter who was friends with Radclyffe Hall could still insist that lesbianism "can carry on in Paris but certainly not here."[67] So the delightful scene in Sarah Waters's picaresque 1998 lesbian novel *Tipping the Velvet*, portraying a basement "ladies room" in the 1890s where "toms" gather along with "gay girls" (that is, prostitutes) who giggle about "tipping the velvet" with one another for the pleasure of paying male customers, is pure fiction.[68] But in Paris, Berlin, and New York, curious heterosexual tourists and people seeking adventure mixed with lesbians and gay men in a variety of clubs and bars, further increasing the visibility of enclaves of women variously known as "lesbians," "girlfriends," or, in the African American community, "bulldaggers," "ladylovers," or "studs."

In Paris, known in some circles as "Paris-Lesbos," prostitutes or showgirls made up the main clientele in public lesbian spaces.[69] The table d'hôte of Louise Taillandier, a madam, attracted the attention of Émile Zola in the course of research for his novel *Nana*. His notes, transformed in the novel into a description of a lesbian restaurant called Chez Laure, provide an image of the place: "In couples the women. All of them kiss Louise on the mouth. . . . The girls dressed as a man. . . . The maid skinny, infirm dyke."[70] Taillandier's place, like another lesbian restaurant in the 1890s, appeared in a guidebook on the pleasures of Paris, attracting voyeurs as well as the desired clientele. A music hall drag queen described young pretty women in the front rows of the music halls as "almost always two by two," belonging "to that immense sect whose gracious priestesses serve the altar of Sappho. . . . They were the principal Tribades of Paris."[71] After the First World War, lesbians gathered in bars and cafés as well, sometimes mingling with artists and bohemians. At Le Monocle, women with bobbed hair dressed in tuxedos.[72] Other public spaces open to lesbians included fancy transvestite balls on holidays, brothels that attracted elite women clients, certain baths and swimming pools, and even the city boulevards. Natalie Barney, it should be noted, courted the courtesan Liane de Pougy on the street and in the brothel. So not only did lesbians in Paris move into public spaces, but literary and artistic productions introduced them to a broader public.

Not every lesbian who had access to public places, by virtue of life in a city and disposable income, found them welcoming. Both Natalie Barney and her lover Djuna Barnes found the lesbian bars repugnant.[73] Returning to Radclyffe Hall, who based a scene in her novel on a real outing in Paris in 1926, we find Valérie Seymour accompanying Stephen, Stephen's new love, Mary, and a few others on an evening on the town in Montmartre. Hall makes her own viewpoint clear as she describes "the garish and tragic night life of Paris that lies open to such people as Stephen Gordon."[74] Valérie, like her real-life counterpart, thinks "the whole world has grown very ugly, but no doubt to some people this represents pleasure."[75] Moving from café to café, the women drink, smoke, dance, and kiss. When Stephen and Mary get home early in the morning, and Stephen proclaims it an awful night, Mary responds, "Well, at least we could dance together without being thought freaks; there was something in that."[76] However sleazy the clubs, there was always that to be said for them.

As the image of "The Lavender Song" being performed in a cabaret makes clear, Berlin was also home in the 1920s to an amazingly vibrant public lesbian world. Even before the First World War, a tabloid paper, *Grosse Glocke* (*Great Bell*), published from 1906 to 1922, called attention to communities of female homosexuals through its salacious attacks. A 1908 article described a "sickening orgy" among seven women, complete with smoking and drinking, discovered by a shocked landlady investigating the noise.[77] One of the women named in the article responded not by denying that they were homosexual but by insisting that they had behaved respectably. The next year the paper reported on a "New Women's Community," describing the president of the club as an "Amazon who lives together with a girlfriend and has a somewhat extravagant taste for appearing in an elegant men's evening suit" and the club's activities as involving "effusive caresses."[78] Five members of the club, affronted by the story, which included the charge that one member allowed another to seduce her teen-aged daughter, sued the editor. A mainstream Berlin paper picked up on the story, noting that "Sappho" and "Aphrodite" served as passwords for club members. In court, members admitted that they were homosexual but denied the charges of immorality. They lost. In 1910, *Grosse Glocke* reported on an even more public presence of lesbians with a story about the Bavarian Quarter "gradually becoming a ghetto for homosexual women."[79] They wore men's clothes, met during the day, talked openly in streetcars, and confused children, who did not know if they were women or men. What especially disgusted the editor of the paper was the public visibility of women who desired women.

After the war and until the Nazi rise to power, a large number of lesbian clubs, bars, balls, groups, circles, and publications catered to women who desired women, and cabaret acts openly represented lesbian love, marking Berlin as what one participant called the "lesbian El Dorado."[80] (See figure 22 for a photograph of women in a Berlin club in the 1920s.)

A 1929 book, *Berlins lesbische Frauen* (*Berlin's Lesbian Women*), with a preface by Magnus Hirschfeld, listed fourteen bars and clubs specifically marketed to women. Another guidebook, published the next year, described the class-differentiated clientele populating a wide variety of places. In Café Domino the women were tasteful and elegant, whereas in Taverne the atmosphere was rough and raunchy. At some clubs, such as Café Prinzess, lesbian savings clubs, lottery clubs, or clubs devoted to card games met.[81] Chez Ma Belle-Soeur, with frescoes of Lesbos, attracted mostly curious foreigners. Topp and Eldorado were places to be

Figure 22. Berlin club, 1920s. From *Eldorado: Homosexuelle Frauen und Männer in Berlin, 1850–1950* (Berlin: Fröhlich & Kaufmann, 1984).

seen.[82] Claire Waldoff, a lesbian cabaret artist, described in her memoirs a night out at a lesbian club. A fascinating mixture of women populated the club: painters, models, elegant women eager to learn about the Berlin underworld, white-collar workers in love. Four musicians played wind instruments, women danced, petty jealousies erupted. "It was typical Berlin nightlife with its transgressions and color."[83] Another participant remembered "a feeling of freedom. . . . At that time it was chic to oppose the moral pressure of the Empire. It was chic to be gay, or to act as if you were."[84] Others, echoing the fictional Valérie Seymour, recalled the bars and clubs as depressing and more hidden from public view.

All of this came to an end, of course, when the Nazis came to power. In Berlin, the authorities closed down homosexual bars, organizations, and publications. Lesbians—declared "sexually decadent women"—along with emancipated women and feminists, symbolized everything the Nazis thought wrong with the modern world. Although Hitler's government never revised Paragraph 175, the law that outlawed homosexuality, to include women, that did not mean that lesbians lived under the radar. One Nazi lawyer called for the inclusion of lesbian women under the law, calling it incomprehensible that "same-sex intercourse between women, tribadism," was not against the law.[85] But the Nazis did not bother to criminalize lesbianism, and most lesbians who were sent to concentration camps, if they were not Jewish or socialist, wore the black triangle, denoting them as "asocial," a vague term that covered many bases.[86] Some lesbians, accused of "moral weakness" for their desires or gender nonconformity, ended up in other kinds of institutions, subjected to draconian conditions and sometimes sterilization.[87] Lesbian culture did not die out entirely, but how thoroughly the Nazis destroyed such an elaborate public lesbian culture is a sobering corrective to notions of inexorable progress.

The lesbian world of Weimar Berlin, because of the pioneering nature of German sexology and the vibrancy of Weimar culture in general, was extraordinary in its commercial venues. In addition to public places, periodicals sold on the streets and through the mail, literature, and art introduced the world to a wide range of women who loved women. How advanced this world was is suggested by a letter from Cecilia F. in Brooklyn to a lesbian periodical, penned in 1927. "In the 'Land of the Free' people are inexpressibly prudish about sexual matters. 'We' are made out to be degenerate, lascivious, and disreputable. No association of friendship federation of any kind exists here. . . . America is fifty years behind Germany."[88]

Yet New York, too, was home to commercial and private venues that catered to a crowd with same-sex desires, and not just elite women. By the 1920s, both Greenwich Village and Harlem had established reputations as welcoming places for lesbians as well as gay men. Like Paris and Berlin, both neighborhoods were also artistic and bohemian centers. In the 1920s and 1930s, Greenwich Village morphed from a primarily Italian immigrant neighborhood to a bohemian enclave. Lesbians and gay men found tolerance in an unconventional environment, and the Village gained a reputation as the home of "long-haired men" and "short-haired women."[89] A vice investigator in 1919 commented that Greenwich Village places attracted "all sorts of people, . . . many obviously prostitutes and perverts, especially the latter."[90] As a study published in the 1930s put it, "The Village became noted as the home of 'pansies' and 'Lesbians,' and dives of all sorts featured this type."[91]

Restaurants, speakeasies, tearooms, and clubs sprang up around the Village, some sponsoring poetry readings, musical performances, and discussion groups. An article in the magazine *Variety* in 1925 listed twenty establishments that catered to the "temperamental" set, meaning "fairies" and "lady lovers."[92] There residents mixed with tourists, some of them seeking the gay life themselves. One lesbian proprietor, a Polish Jewish immigrant named Eva Kotchever, who took the name Eve Addams, opened the Black Rabbit, a tearoom that sported a sign on the door reading "Men are admitted but are not welcome." A local Village paper described the place as one where "ladies prefer each other." Called the "queen of the third sex" and a "man-hater" by the press, Addams was arrested after a police raid and deported for having written an "obscene" book called *Lesbian Love*. She reportedly later opened a lesbian club in Paris.[93]

Harlem, too, especially at the height of the Harlem Renaissance from 1920 to the mid-1930s, was home to a lively nightlife, including speakeasies and a wide variety of clubs catering to people with same-sex desires. Gladys Bentley, a masculine, cross-dressed Black singer of suggestive songs who sported a white tuxedo and top hat, performed regularly at Harry Hansberry's Clam House. (See her famous photograph in figure 23.) As in Paris, show business fostered a culture open to same-sex sexuality. Costume balls attracted thousands of attendees, many of them men in drag, as well as voyeurs eager to see what was going on. White lesbian socialite Mercedes de Acosta remembered that people "rushed up to Harlem at night to sit around places thick with smoke and the smell of bad gin, where Negroes danced about with each other until the small hours of the morning."[94]

In addition to clubs where class and racially mixed audiences could dance, drink, and listen to jazz and the blues, semiprivate parties brought together lesbians and gay men in Harlem. A'Lelia Walker, daughter of Madame C. J. Walker, who made a fortune marketing hair-straightening products, hosted a salon and threw lavish parties at her home with her female lovers in attendance.[95] Mabel Hampton, a Black performer who in her teens lived in Harlem, described parties where women who desired women could meet: "The bulldykers used to come and bring their women with them, you know."[96] Although hosted in private residences, rent parties, where guests paid admission to help out the host with his or her monthly obligations, were open to the public and could last all night long. A Harlem newspaper in 1926 told the story of a rent party gone wrong when "one jealous woman cut the throat of another, because the two were rivals for the affections of a third woman."[97] In 1928, a vice investigator attended a "woman's party" in Harlem, noting that "the women were

Figure 23. Gladys Bentley, Harlem performer, ca. 1920s. Moorland-Spingarn Research Center, Howard University, Washington, D.C. From Leila J. Rupp, *A Desired Past: A Short History of Same-Sex Love in America* (Chicago: University of Chicago Press, 1999).

dancing with one another and going through the motions of copulation." When he asked one of the women whether she was normal, she replied forthrightly, "Everybody here is either a bull dagger or faggot and I am here."[98]

As in Paris, Berlin, and Greenwich Village, the artistic flowering of the Harlem Renaissance spread word of lesbian love through literature, art, and music. Bessie Smith sang of a "mannish-acting woman," Lucille Bogan of "B.D." (bulldagger) women "who drink up many a whiskey" and "sure can strut their stuff," and George Hanna's lyrics advised, "when you see two women walking hand in hand, just shake your head and try to understand."[99] Ma Rainey, who was married but had women lovers, in "Prove It on Me Blues" admitted to her masculine dress and female companionship while challenging her listeners to "prove it" on her.[100] Even if these references were not always laudatory, they made women's same-sex desire and gender transgression visible. And in fact many of the great women blues singers were themselves lesbian or bisexual.

By the early 1930s, the Great Depression had dimmed the glamour and wildness of Harlem and the Village, just as the Nazi rise to power shut down the nightlife of Berlin. But places for lesbians to go did not disappear altogether. One woman remembered in the 1930s and 1940s "many places in Harlem run by and for Black Lesbians and Gay Men, when we were still Bull Daggers and Faggots and only whites were lesbians and homosexuals."[101] In San Francisco, Mona's, the first lesbian nightclub in the city, opened in 1934, followed by a string of other clubs that catered to lesbians, gay men, and tourists together. A tourist guidebook, *Where to Sin in San Francisco*, noted that at Mona's "the little girl waitresses look like boys . . . and many of the little girl customers look like boys."[102] In the 1940s, Gladys Bentley headlined at Mona's, along with other performers of color, including the "Latin star" Tina Rubio.[103] Even in places as remote from urban gay life as Oklahoma City, there were places in the 1930s where women seeking women could find one another among the gamblers, prostitutes, and bootleggers.[104]

The outbreak of a new global war closed commercial establishments across Europe at the same time that it facilitated, in Europe and the United States, women's same-sex connections in the military, in semimilitarized institutions (including, ironically, the Women's Labor Service in Nazi Germany), and in war industries.[105] In countries at war, the kind of sex-segregated spaces that had long fostered love between women proved fertile ground once again.

And through it all, where possible, lesbian commercial establishments survived. In cities across the United States, the 1940s and 1950s proved to be the heyday of a working-class lesbian bar culture. The war had loosened social conventions, allowing women to wear pants in public, walk the streets without male escorts, and go to bars and clubs. The lesbian bar culture was primarily a white working-class world, although throughout the 1950s women of color began to feel more welcome in white bars and to establish their own places, while middle-class white women became less afraid of the bars, diversifying the crowds out in public. In Buffalo, New York, one patron remembers a 1940s gay and lesbian bar, Ralph Martin's, as "fabulous," "hopping" on weekends, with dancing and drag shows.[106] In the 1950s, lesbians traveled from Niagara Falls, Rochester, and Toronto to a variety of Buffalo bars, most located near one another and some of them very rough places where prostitutes, johns, and pimps mixed with the lesbians. Bars catering to lesbians also opened in the Black section of Buffalo. In Detroit, the Sweetheart Bar welcomed straight people from the neighborhood along with lesbians and gay men, all in separate sections of the establishment. Fred's bar, also in Detroit, opened in 1952, and with its location closer to the suburbs, its size and cleanliness, and its lesbian-only policy, it attracted middle-class lesbians. Lesbian bars provided the women who patronized them friends, lovers, acceptance, and a place to gather in public, if not quite as visibly as in the clubs of Berlin in earlier decades. (See figure 24 for a photograph of butches and fems in a U.S. bar.)

In Canadian cities, too, a lesbian bar culture emerged in the 1950s. In Toronto, "uptowners" who lived in the suburbs, held pink- or white-collar jobs, and lived a double life, keeping their homosexuality secret, mixed with "downtowners" whose lives centered on the bar and who lived what they called the "gay life."[107] But in contrast to the patrons of lesbian bars in other places, downtowners in the public houses of Toronto welcomed straight men as potential johns, buyers of drinks, or people they could pickpocket. Continuing the earlier connection between sex work and same-sex sexuality, some fems and butches would have sex with men for money, and in the mid-1950, the lesbian scene shifted to Toronto's

Figure 24. U.S. butches and fems, ca. 1945. The Buddy Kent Collection, copyright LHEF, Inc. Lesbian Herstory Archives, Brooklyn, New York. From Leila J. Rupp, *A Desired Past: A Short History of Same-Sex Love in America* (Chicago: University of Chicago Press, 1999).

Chinatown, the center of the sex trade. The "sapphic set" included Black as well as white Canadians, and they mixed with Chinese sex workers.[108] The French bars in Montreal, with a reputation as rough and dangerous, had the same kind of connection to the criminal and sexual underworld. In Ponts de Paris, lesbians, gay men, heterosexual couples, and single men would be directed to their own sections by the doorman as he sized them up.[109]

A lesbian bar culture also developed across the Atlantic in Brighton, Manchester, and especially London in the 1940s and 1950s. The center of this public world in London was the Gateways Club in Chelsea, which opened in 1931 as a bohemian place that attracted artists, actors, musicians, and lesbians and gay men.[110] The club was in a dark, dimly lit, smoky basement, with room for about two hundred people. The Gateways was not the only place that lesbians could go, but the other clubs were seedier and more part of the sexual and criminal underworld. Chelsea was, like Greenwich Village, a haven for the unconventional, including women who desired women. The Gateways got around restrictive licensing laws by functioning as a membership club, and word of mouth served as a means of recruitment. By 1966, it had thousands of members.[111] It had become less elite and more lesbian after the Second World War, attracting working-class women, women in the military, prostitutes, and Black men and women. One young couple found out about it in 1947 when an elderly man approached them on the street and asked if they had ever been there. They said no and asked what it was, and he replied, "It's a club you two girls might like. You two are very fond of each other, aren't you? Well, you will find other people down there who are very fond of each other."[112]

Across the Euroamerican world, the bar and club culture developed clear norms and modes of dress and behavior, emphasizing, in the tradition of earlier lesbian culture, "butch" or (the preferred African American term) "stud" masculinity and "fem" femininity. At the Paper Doll in San Francisco, a tourist review advised that one could "see gay women who walk and talk like men, . . . and often you'll find it hard to tell whether . . . a gay woman is a woman because sometimes a gay woman cuts her hair like a man's and puts on men's clothes and looks more like a gay man than a gay woman."[113] In Montreal, some butches claimed the masculine article (*un butch*) and pronoun (*il*) and would be addressed as mister (*Monsieur*).[114] By the 1950s, the "tough butch" in Buffalo, like the "downtowners" in Toronto, dressed in typical working-class male attire as much of the time as possible and frequented the bar every night of the week, setting herself apart from respectable middle-class society and declaring her erotic interests in public. At the Gateways, too, butches wore "shorts or casual sweaters; trousers; and jackets. . . . And the femme always but always wore skirts, blouses, high-heeled shoes. Always carried . . . a hand-bag—earrings, makeup. . . . So you never had any problem in those days because you always knew who to ask for a dance."[115]

Butch and fem roles structured intimate relationships between women, anointing the butch as the "doer" who gave sexual satisfaction to the fem. Carried to its furthest point, this sexual system produced the ideal of the untouchable or "stone" butch, who, like Anne Lister, did not want a lover to make love to her. "If I could give her satisfaction to the highest, that's what gave me satisfaction," as one self-identified stone butch put it.[116] As Joan Nestle, who came out as a fem in the 1950s, insists, "We knew what we wanted and that was no mean feat for young women of the 1950s, a time when the need for conformity, marriage and babies was being trumpeted at us by the government's policy makers."[117]

Butch and fem ways of being challenged mainstream gender roles and created a core identity, even if it was one that changed over time. In the bar culture of the 1940s in Buffalo, butches were "gay" because of their masculinity and sexual desire for women, whereas fems often saw their only difference from heterosexual women as their association with butches. So fems were not necessarily "lesbians." One British woman, newly married and visiting the United States with her husband, fell in love with an American woman she met. "I didn't see myself as a lesbian, or her, because I didn't look as I imagined they all did, nor did she. . . . I got that image from *The Well of Loneliness*, like we all did."[118] Another British woman has no memory of "words being used": "in fact I'm not sure they were. I don't think they were because gay hadn't been invented; homosexual was a thing in books; lesbian was like a derogatory term that you hardly ever heard. . . . I think there was just an expectation that there were people like us and there were other people."[119] As a Buffalo butch woman who came out in 1957 while still underage put it, "I knew, before I put a concept or a word to it that I was gay."[120]

Women in the lesbian bar culture made same-sex love and desire publicly visible, and in that way they engaged in a form of everyday resistance. Not only did butch-fem couples affirm women's autonomous sexuality to people who passed them on the streets or viewed them in the bars, but butches stood up for and even physically fought the straight men, sometimes johns interested in fems who turned tricks, for their right to "their" fems and to public space. One London butch remembers her reaction to being stared at on the Tube; she turned to the offenders and said, "'What are you fucking looking at then? Is there something funny about us?' What a statement, because there was! I was five foot two, flat-chested, dressed as a bloke, standing on my toes trying to hang on to this strap I could hardly reach. There were these women all glammed up, hanging on to us. Nobody ever dared say anything back."[121] A Toronto butch announced that living openly was "an indication of pride in the homosexual way of life."[122] Although fems could pass more easily, butch-fem couples on the streets embodied "sexual courage" in making visible their erotic desires.[123]

Women who frequented the bars and clubs assert how important those places were in affirming their desires and identities. As one Buffalo woman put it, remembering a friend's first visit to a bar, "And she said, 'Oh I'm home.' God what a homecoming that was."[124] Like a home, the Palais, in 1940s Detroit, hosted birthday parties, lesbian weddings, and even baby showers.[125] Lesbian weddings, with fem in wedding gown and butch in tuxedo, took place in bars in various cities in North America, including Toronto in the 1950s, where the tabloid newspapers got wind of the practice.[126] For Gateways regulars, whether they were living a double life hiding their sexuality most of the time or not, the club became a lifeline. "The Gates was like an oasis in a hostile world," one woman insisted.[127] "The Gateways was a world of its own where you could go and be yourself," another remembered. "It was like my life's blood at the time. You didn't have to explain yourself, they knew what you were."[128] Another regular reported, "because it was so difficult for me to be who I was within my own family, the women that I got to know in the Gates became my family."[129] Mary McIntosh, who wrote one of the earliest classic articles about homosexual identity, "just loved being at the Gateways": "it gave me a huge buzz to be there when it was crowded and there was just a sea of women like us."[130]

In the United States, Canada, and England, lesbian commercial establishments not only gave women who desired women a place to go but also attracted public attention. The police periodically raided establishments or revoked their licenses to sell alcohol. In 1954 in San Francisco, an investigation of a group of high school girls who "donned mannish clothes" led to a bar raid. A police officer explained that the "girls admitted frequenting a 'gay' bar—one catering to sexual deviates. . . . It started as a lark. Then some of the girls began wearing mannish clothing. . . . We found that the activity was centering on Tommy's Place."[131] In Buffalo, crackdowns

Figure 25. Cover of *The Well of Loneliness*, Pocket Book edition published December 1950, sixteenth printing, 1974.

by the State Liquor Authority led to the closing of bars in the 1960s. The Carousel lost its license for being "frequented by homosexuals and degenerates."[132] A Gateways regular remembered the police coming in looking for drugs and announcing, "fellas on one side, and ladies on the other."[133] Sensational newspaper reports of bar raids both fed into the negative public perceptions of homosexual life fostered by McCarthyite attacks in the United States and spread word among those who were interested that there were places to go.

Lesbian bars also played a starring role in the lesbian pulp novels that flourished in the United States in the 1950s and were exported to the United Kingdom. (Even *The Well of Loneliness* appeared with a pulp cover; see figure 25.) An Englishwoman touring in the United States noticed such books: "There were in the drug stores around the States, these pulp books, lurid stories about lesbians who smoked cigars and had orgies with young girls."[134] Most were penned by male authors for men's titillation, but some lesbian authors, constrained as they were by the publishers' requirement of unhappy endings as a way to evade censorship, still managed to advertise the joys of lesbian bars. Lesbian pulp novelist Ann Bannon, in one of her series of stories about a young woman who moved to Greenwich Village from the country, takes her heroine to a lesbian bar for the first time. She enters a "basement bar saturated with pink light, paneled with mirrors, and filled with girls. More girls, more sizes, types, and ages, than Beebo had ever seen collected together in one place. . . . For the first time in her life she was proud of her size, proud of her strength, even proud of her oddly boyish face. She could see interest, even admiration on the faces of many of the girls. . . . It exhilarated her."[135]

In 1968, the Gateways transformed its semisecret existence by appearing in the film *The Killing of Sister George*, with its regulars as extras. The lesbian main characters descend the steps to the club, where women dance cheek to cheek. It was a spectacular coming out, for both the club and the women who agreed to be filmed. And then, in 1979, the lesbian feminist

Figure 26. Cover of the British lesbian magazine *Sappho*, 1979. Kate Charlesworth. From Jill Gardiner, *From the Closet to the Screen: Women at the Gateways Club, 1945–85* (London: Pandora, 2003).

magazine *Sappho* featured a cover with Prime Minister Margaret Thatcher appealing to the primly dressed Queen, "Let's go to the Gates!"[136] (See figure 26). By then the lesbian world had changed dramatically, with the rise of the women's and gay liberation movements. And despite the tension between the world of butch-fem bars and clubs and a new lesbian feminist ideology and style, the sexual courage and everyday resistance of women who announced their identities and desires in public cannot be overlooked as an important force in the struggle for equality and acceptance.

From the heady years of the 1920s through the 1950s, lesbian culture took on a more public face than ever before in the big cities of the industrialized world. Not until later, as far as we know, did lesbian commercial establishments open in other parts of the world. A short story by Dale Gunthorp about her life in Johannesburg, South Africa, in the 1960s, when women were not allowed in bars, describes a place where, because of apartheid, "only the ponciest of African queens, only the butchest of Indian dykes, could appear."[137] The first lesbian space in São Paulo, Brazil, emerged when lesbians took over a restaurant in the 1970s.[138] The anonymity of urban life, the movement of women into the labor force, the proliferation of commercialized entertainment, and the openness fostered by cultural flowering made public lesbian space possible. Literature, art, and music—perhaps most spectacularly Radclyffe Hall's novel—introduced the public to lesbian worlds. Despite the persistence of various forms of repression directed against women who desired women, lesbian commercial establishments, where they flourished, gave the women who sought them out a new kind of public presence.

In Print and in Groups

Publishing and organizing represent another way that women who loved women stepped out in public. In addition to the proliferation of public venues catering to lesbians, Berlin in the 1920s witnessed the emergence of lesbian publications in which the bars and clubs regularly advertised. *Die Freundin* (*Girlfriend*), published from 1924 to 1933, directed its stories and articles to women described as "same-sex loving" (*gleichgeschlechtlichliebend*), "homosexual" (*homosexuell*), "homoerotic" (*homoerotisch*), or "lesbian" (*lesbisch*).[139] (See figure 27 for a cover from 1928.) A censorship board described it as "a harmless newsletter without literary ambitions," suggesting a nonelite readership.[140] The transnational aspect of lesbian culture is evident

Figure 27. Cover of *Die Freundin*, 1928. From *Eldorado: Homosexuelle Frauen und Männer in Berlin, 1850–1950* (Berlin: Fröhlich & Kaufmann, 1984).

in the title of another periodical published in Berlin in the 1930s: *Garçonne*, appearing from 1926 as *Frauenliebe* (*Woman Love*) and from 1930 to 1932 under the new name, took the French word for "boy" and added a feminine ending. *Garçonne* catered to a lesbian and male heterosexual transvestite audience.[141] The term "Garçonne-type" had come by the 1920s to apply to "new" or "emancipated" women who adopted a masculinized style of dress and behavior.

Both periodicals featured stories, poems, and articles about homosexuality, as well as photographs and illustrations of a variety of lesbians, some cross-dressed, some in masculine-feminine couples, some entirely feminine. As a censorship board described the content, "the stories and poems that make up most of the content glorify the love between women in a most effusive, sugary, sometimes passionate way."[142] The magazines also featured personal ads that openly named lesbian desire, including both masculine-feminine and feminine-feminine pairings: "Young woman seeks young butch"; "Lady, young, elegant, full-figured, seeks similar girlfriend."[143] One woman remembered the importance and danger of reading *Die Freundin*: "I bought it where I was not known, at a kiosk where nobody knew me. . . . You felt as if you had a bomb in your pocket. I tried to read it wherever I could. On the toilet! Where no one could disturb you, that's where I read it."[144]

The reach of these publications extended beyond Berlin. Women who lived in small cities and towns found them a lifeline. A reader from Karlsruhe wrote to *Garçonne* to say, "I cannot any longer do without this magazine 'Garçonne,'" and a contributor from Görlitz explained that for "lonely women" the publication was "their best friend," "a joy," "a greeting from the world that is also theirs."[145] And the magazines reported on developments across the German border as well. *Frauenliebe* took note of the successful founding of the Vienna club Violetta in 1927.[146] In 1931, *Garçonne* ran an article titled "A Voice from Switzerland," which asserted the importance of lesbian publications and organizations and bemoaned the lack of both in Switzerland, leading eventually to the formation of a lesbian group, Amicitia, later that year.[147]

Even before the Nazis came to power, such periodicals ran into legal troubles. *Die Freundin* was shut down from 1928 to 1929 under a law designed to protect youth from "trashy and obscene" (*Schund und Schmutz*) literature, so a new title, *Ledige Frauen* (*Single Women*), appeared in its stead.[148] When *Frauenliebe* ran afoul of the law, it changed its name to *Garçonne*.[149] Although the topic of homosexuality itself was not sufficient to declare a publication obscene, the ruling that shut down *Frauenliebe* in 1928 stated that the "literary portion of the issues is worthless" and thus qualified as trashy, and "the way the issues accumulate advertisements that apparently serve to facilitate sexual relationships has to be seen as obscene in the sense of the law."[150] The Berlin police targeted personal ads with sexual content, even answering ads themselves in order to entrap those who placed them.[151] In addition, the debate about whether Paragraph 175, the law against homosexuality that targeted only men, should be revised to include women continued during the Weimar years. (Germany was not unique in outlawing same-sex acts only between men; Austria, Sweden, Finland, and some Swiss cantons targeted women, but other countries did not.)[152]

In addition to a flourishing commercial culture, Weimar Germany sported the first homosexual-rights organizations, in which a small number of women joined the predominantly male membership to fight for legal change and social acceptance.[153] The two competing national organizations, the Bund für Menschenrecht (League for Human Rights) and Deutsche Freundschaftsverband (German Friendship Association), sponsored separate women's clubs, as well as, respectively, the periodicals *Die Freundin* and *Frauenliebe/Garçonne*. The women's group associated with the League for Human Rights and *Die Freundin* offered an alternative to the bars in the form of readings, performances, and discussions, and the German Friendship Association/*Garçonne* circle featured Friday-night dancing in a rented room and eventually regular balls, socials, dances, and lectures under the auspices of two clubs, Violetta and Monbijou. Violetta—where "The Lavender Song" was sung—later switched its affiliation to the League for Human Rights, solidifying the parallel institutions of the two groups.[154] What differentiated them was class, erotic culture, and politics. The *Garçonne* group was more elite, institutionalized gender differences between masculine and feminine women, excluded men, and engaged less in politics.[155] *Die Freundin* tended to criticize women for attending only to pleasure. An article in 1929 urged women, "Don't go to your entertainments while thousands of our sisters mourn their lives in gloomy despair."[156] The two groups attacked each other publicly over these differences in membership, politics, and style. But what is remarkable is their level of organization and political activity, unrivaled in the rest of the world at this time. Not until the 1950s, in some places, and even later in others, can we find publications and organizations specifically for women who loved women.

Ironically, perhaps, the longest lasting and most important gay publication in Europe in the mid-twentieth century owed a great deal to lesbians. *Der Kreis* emerged in Switzerland out of a series of predecessors, the first of which was published for a year in 1932 through a collaboration of the women of Amicitia with a men's group. In 1933, Anna Vock, known as "Mammina," took over the editorship and financial responsibility for the paper, carrying the burden for many years and staying involved until her death in 1962. From 1943 until 1967, the paper with lesbian origins took on the name *Der Kreis/Le Cercle* and continued as a decidedly gay male magazine.[157]

As other publications that were geared to gay men emerged across Europe and in the United States in the context of burgeoning movements that took the name "homophile," women, first in the United States and later in England, launched their own magazines. In 1956, the Daughters of Bilitis, the first U.S. lesbian organization, bravely started a newsletter, *The Ladder*, that lasted until 1972, eventually gathering a mailing list of almost four thousand names. Like *Garçonne* before it, *The Ladder* meant everything to subscribers across the country. "I have been receiving THE LADDER and have been a member of the Daughters of Bilitis for more than a year now," wrote a New Jersey woman. "The day my copy arrives I sit and read it from cover to cover."[158] From California, another woman wrote, "Like many another LADDER reader, I am always thoroughly delighted with your magazine. . . . I wish I were blessed with financial means, talents with writing ability, or in some other way qualified to make more of a contribution to DOB than I can, but as I am not I join the ranks of those quiet followers who find you a light in the dark night and a warm fire for alien souls."[159] Black playwright Lorraine Hansberry, an early subscriber and contributor, commented,

> I'm glad as heck that you exist. You are obviously serious people and I feel that women, without wishing to foster any strict separatist notions, homo or hetero, indeed have a need for their own publications and organizations. . . . Women, like other oppressed groups of one kind or another, have particularly had to pay a price for the intellectual impoverishment that the second class status imposed on us for centuries created and sustained.[160]

The first British lesbian periodical, *Arena Three*, emerged later than *The Ladder* and utilized the pages of the Daughters' magazine to spread word of its existence. Prompted by a hostile article about lesbians in a current-affairs journal, a lesbian journalist and author began to seek like-minded women to launch a journal, a dream that became a reality in 1964 under the auspices of the Minority Research Group, founded for that purpose.[161] By the magazine's demise in 1971, it had just six hundred subscribers, with another fourteen hundred copies for sale at bookstores and newsstands. Like *The Ladder*, *Arena Three* aimed to educate researchers, social workers, educators, and the media about homosexuality and, as the name of the sponsoring organization suggests, to provide a nonpatient population of lesbians for researchers. But it also served the purpose of connecting readers to one another and forging a collective identity as lesbian. As in *The Ladder*, readers expressed their delight at making contact with other lesbians. Since *Arena Three* preceded the formation in Britain of an organization like the Daughters of Bilitis in the United States, readers expressed hopes for the formation of some kind of social club. One reader sought something different from "the kind of meeting-places which are familiar in Paris," where lesbians "only want to dance, chat, smoke."[162]

As that reader's comment suggests, readers of *Arena Three*, along with *Ladder* readers, tended to distinguish themselves from the butch/fem women of the bar scene. Both periodicals featured debates over proper dress and respectability, offering sharp criticism of those who chose to wear men's clothing. With the emergence of lesbian feminism in the 1970s, which trumpeted a critique of men and masculine values, the butch became a despised symbol of an old-style lesbian life.

Outside Britain and the United States, lesbian publications did not appear until the 1970s and 1980s. Yet that does not mean that women who desired women had no access to print. In Japan, the postwar years witnessed a kind of sexual revolution in reaction against the repression of wartime, and that included the emergence of trashy newspapers and magazines focusing on sex.[163] An article published in 1948 discussed masculine tribades (*toribādo*) and feminine sapphists (*Safuisto*), the latter likely to have been drawn into same-sex sexual activity in the school room or factory dormitory. But what is more interesting is that some women readers wrote in to such magazines, making their desires public. In 1954, one reader requested, "Beautiful maidens please get in touch," and another complained, "it seems that you think that perverse love between women is extremely rare but in fact I think that it is very common." The next year, a woman lamented that there were no coffee shops or bars where women could meet, as existed for "male homos," and suggested that the magazine sponsor hiking trips or visits to the cinema and jazz clubs for women seeking other women. Although later Japanese sex publications offered representations of lesbians geared to male pornographic fantasy, and politicized lesbian feminists began to publish their own magazines in the 1970s, these voices from the 1950s should not be overlooked.

That things were stirring in the postwar decade is also clear from the 1951 founding in Amsterdam of a transnational homophile organization, the International Committee for Sexual Equality. Yet this group remained heavily male, as is clear from its report on the lack of lesbian organizing outside the United States and Sweden. Women made up only 13 percent of the Dutch homophile organization, the Cultuur en Ontspannings Centrum Nederland (COC, Dutch Cultural and Recreational Center), and according to one male member, women "do not show any particular form of activity" and "hardly feel ashamed about this situation."[164] A representative of a German group reported that women in some parts of the country were organized, in other places not, and that in Belgium, France, and Switzerland there were no women in the homophile groups.[165] The first specifically lesbian organization, if a transitory one, was the Alle for Een Klubben (All for One Club), founded in Copenhagen in 1954, a year before the formation of the Daughters of Bilitis.[166] The U.S. organization, taking a name that harked back to the mythical lover of Sappho, formed in San Francisco in 1955 as a place safer than the bars to socialize and dance.[167] From a secret lesbian social club beginning with four couples, it grew into a political organization determined to work along with the mostly male homophile groups, the Mattachine Society and ONE, to win legal and social acceptance for homosexuals.

Lesbian organizing, of course, changed by the 1970s, with the birth of a more radical form of gay liberation. Lesbian publications, organizations, and cultural institutions flowered in different countries across the globe, sometimes rigidly separatist—giving rise to Erica Jong's portrait of the Amazons in *Sappho's Leap*—and sometimes working in conjunction with gay men. Women left the Dutch COC to found a radical feminist group, Lavender September, calling lesbianism the epitome of feminism and warning women not to sleep with their oppressors.[168] The Col.lectiu de Lesbianes de Barcelona (Barcelona Lesbian Collective) in 1978 issued a manifesto asserting, "Our voice must be heard to keep watch over and reveal the common aspects of our reality as women and assert *our difference* as lesbians."[169] On the other side of the divide, Atobá, an organization founded in Brazil after a young man died in a gay-bashing incident, attracted lesbians and gay men from working-class areas of Rio de Janeiro; in 1995, thirty-one different groups formed the Brazilian Association of Gays, Lesbians and Transvestites.[170] In the Czech Republic, SOHO, the Association of Organizations of Homosexual Citizens, founded in 1991, allots women a vice-presidential slot.[171] And in the 1980s in South Africa, gay and lesbian organizations in both the Black and white communities aligned with the African National Congress's Freedom Charter, arguing for gay rights as human rights, a principle recognized when the constitution of 1996 became the first in the world to outlaw discrimination on the basis of sexual orientation.[172]

In Mexico, in the 1970s, lesbian women found their interests ignored in the women's movement, leading Yan María Castro and Luz María Medina to think they "were the only Mexican lesbians in the entire country."[173] They went on to found Lesbos, the first lesbian organization in Mexico, and when Nancy Cárdenas, during the First World Conference for Women on the International Women's Year in 1975, set up a meeting between foreign and Mexican lesbians, she brought "lesbians who felt they were trapped in women's bodies, those who were in their sixties and had not accepted gay militancy, and young girls of twenty": "I wanted them to see everything."[174]

As these few examples suggest, across the continents women who desired women, spurred by both women's movements and gay/lesbian movements, stepped out into public in a variety of ways. Whether women founded magazines or formed groups in the 1920s or 1950s or 1980s, that kind of activism made it possible for women to find others with similar desires and to know they were not alone.

In different ways in different places around the globe, love between women gained a new kind of public face in the twentieth century. No one wondered if the butches and fems at Ralph Martin's or the Gateways had sex with one another, as the experts did when pondering schoolgirls falling in love with their classmates in the early years of the twentieth century. The schoolgirls themselves—from Buenos Aires to Italy to China to Japan— might have been rendered speechless by the cabarets and clubs of Berlin, Paris, Buffalo, Toronto, Montreal, and London, but it is worth noting that as late as the mid-twentieth century in England, girls' schools were still full of "raves" and "pashes," and these sometimes still seemed a harmless part of girlish development and only sometimes a sign of lesbianism.[175] If Havelock Ellis and Julien Chevalier and Ōtsuka Shinzō associated feminism with lesbians, it is hard to imagine what the likes of Hiratsuka Raichō or Lu Yin or Anna Howard Shaw or Anita Augspurg would have made of a Berlin garçonne or a butch-fem couple at the Gateways. Natalie Barney did experience the commercialized arena of lesbian bars in Paris but found her own world, in which the public took part only through reading or viewing the creations of her circle, more enchanting. By the second half of the twentieth century, it was not only elite literary productions such as those that flowed out of Barney's circle that publicized the world of lesbian love. Following Die Freundin and Garçonne, The Ladder and Arena Three and then other publications and organizations affirmed lesbian visibility in new ways. How important visibility could be is suggested by the statement of an Indian state minister determined to censor the film Fire: "though lesbianism is one of the older forms of sexual activity . . . these things are not in the open. People do not know about it. So we must make sure that such films do not insult [read "inform"?] the public."[176]

Yet it is important to remember that being in the public eye or going out in public was just one way that women who loved women lived their lives in the twentieth century. Where there were no salons or clubs, women still managed to find one another. Two Canadian women, Frieda Fraser and Edith "Bud" Bickerton Williams, formed an intimate relationship as university students in the 1910s and left a legacy of passionate letters. They recognized other women with emotional ties but carefully guarded the nature of their relationship in public.[177] In Deadwood, South Dakota, in the 1920s and 1930s, Julia Boyer Reinstein, a teacher, had affairs with women and eventually settled down in a committed relationship. Her parents knew about her sexuality, and she suspected that people gossiped, but as long as she kept her intimate life private and respectable, she was not named a lesbian.[178] In rural Finland in the 1950s, thirty-two women faced prosecution for "with another person of the same sex fornication," including a mother of four children, a group of religious women running an orphanage, a housekeeper and her employer, and the employer's sister and her dairy-farming trainee. Persistent male conceptions are clear in the questions posed by the police: was money involved, were devices used, who was on top, who was active, who was passive.[179]

Yet, even if women did know how to find others with like desires in private places, the possibility of a public world may have been alluring to women living in different circumstances. Commercial establishments catering to lesbians did not emerge outside the industrialized Western world until after the 1970s, but just as English women traveled to Paris in the 1920s, elite women from countries without a lesbian public culture could find it elsewhere. One Gateways regular told of meeting "two beautiful ladies, professional women, from Persia. They came to London each year and spent time at the Gateways. Then they'd return to their husbands and children."[180] The existence of public spaces changed the lives of the women who frequented them. And perhaps they also had an impact in entirely different places where women who loved women found other ways to live their lives.

The economic, political, and social developments that made a public lesbian life possible included the emergence of educational institutions for women, increased employment opportunities, the rise of commercialized entertainment in urban areas, and the development of publications and organizations. All these developments came together in places such as Weimar Berlin, Greenwich Village, and Harlem in the 1920s and in smaller cities in the industrialized world in the 1950s and 1960s. But even one of these developments—the emergence of girls' schools, for example—could facilitate public awareness of and possibilities for love between women, as we see in the cases of Japan and China. What these new public worlds made visible was the potential of women's independence from male control, long feared and increasingly a reality.

9

A World of Difference

(1960–Present)

The moment I touched her breast, I felt a sweet shock. My heart beat disorderly. A wild horse broke off its reins. She whispered something I could not hear. She was melting snow. I did not know what role I was playing anymore: her imagined man or myself. I was drawn to her. The horse kept running wild. I went where the sun rose. . . . I was spellbound by desire. I wanted to be touched. . . . I heard a little voice rising in the back of my head demanding me to stop. As I hesitated, she caught my lips and kissed me fervently. The little voice disappeared. I lost myself in the caresses.[1]

THIS IS A scene from Anchee Min's powerful novel *Red Azalea*. During the Cultural Revolution in China, Min was working at a labor collective when recruiters spotted her and sent her to work in the Shanghai film industry. After coming to the United States in the 1980s, she published this novel about a young woman working on a collective farm who falls in love with her woman commander, Yan. They are both Red Guards able to recite from Mao's teachings at will. When Yan is ordered to a new assignment far away, they lie in bed together and then make love. It is a reminder that in the late twentieth century, in societies that made no place for love between women, there were still unlikely spaces in which women could find one another.

We come to the end of this centuries-long story of women who loved, desired, and had sex with other women, recognizing that there is a world of difference out there. Berlin in the 1920s conjures one image of the contemporary world of women who love women: places to go, publications to read, organizations to join. We tend to think of this kind of world as rising out of the gay and lesbian liberation movements of the late 1960s and 1970s, even though from a long historical perspective, the early twentieth century represents a more striking departure, at least in some places around the globe. But there are other images that jostle for space in a vision of the contemporary world: women finding one another in sex-segregated spaces, women in love with their co-wives, women marrying one another, women crossing the gender line, women in love with their friends, women carrying on secret affairs, women with no name for their desires. In considering the incredibly complex contemporary world of women who love women, it is the range of options that we would do well to keep in mind.

Love and Desire in Sex-Segregated Spaces

In a scene in *The Almond*, a novel set in present-day Morocco and penned by the pseudonymously named Muslim woman Nedjma, the heroine, Badra, remembers when, as a child, she was introduced to sex play by her cousin Noura. Four girl cousins and schoolmates came to Badra's room, had tea, and pretended to be grown-up ladies visiting one another. Suddenly they began to press against one another two by two, and then Noura turned to Badra:

> I closed my thighs, but her hand quickly found my private parts and began to titillate my bud under my dress. As if to take revenge for the delicious sensations her caresses were providing me, I shoved my hand between her legs and did the same to her. There wasn't a sound to be heard, but hands were playing a delirious score on consenting bodies. A sweet and dizzying warmth flowed down my legs. My pussy was rising beneath the active hand rubbing it, kneading the little snail hidden away at the top. I tried not to slow down the movement of my finger so that Noura would go on rolling her eyes, wild, mouth open, her forehead covered in sweat. . . . For almost a year, a kind of frenzy overtook us, urging Noura and me to rub against each other at the least opportunity, alone or in the presence of the other little girls.[2]

Badra grows up to be a sexual woman, but heterosexual. This incident is part of her story of discovering desire and pleasure in a supposedly sexually repressive society.

That the fictional—or autobiographical—Badra is not the only one satisfying her desire with another girl in a society that does not acknowledge such activity as acceptable is suggested by a report in the Saudi press about "endemic" same-sex activities among schoolgirls. According to the story, girls have sex in the school bathrooms, shun those who reject their advances, and refuse to change their behavior.[3] As Syrian scholar Iman Al-Ghafari explains, "it is quite easy for Arab lesbians to deprive their emotional and physical intimacies of their lesbian connotations because it is common in a conservative Arab culture that advocates separation between the sexes to find intimate relations among members of the same sex, without having to call such relations homosexual."[4]

And the Saudi girls are not the only schoolgirls evoking the relationships found in so many other places at earlier points in time. In Lesotho, a small poor country in southern Africa where men tend to migrate to South Africa for employment, young women at school routinely form intimate and sexual bonds. Similar relationships exist among schoolgirls in Kenya and among Venda and Zulu schoolgirls in South Africa.[5] Slightly younger girls take on the role of "babies" to older girls' "mummies."[6] In a context in which bonds between men and women are fragile because of lengthy male absences and in which there is a taboo on discussion of sexuality between a woman who has borne a child and one who has not, mummy-baby relationships provide socialization into adult roles of domesticity, intimacy, and sexuality. The roles have roots in traditional cultural forms, including initiation ceremonies for girls and the practice of labia lengthening alone or in small groups, which provides an opportunity for autoerotic or mutual stimulation. But, as suggested by the use of the English words *mummy* and *baby* and the importance of schools in the formation of these relationships, they are also connected to the rise of a modern educational system. Some women maintain their relationships after school when they go to work in towns, and some young married women form new intimate ties after their marriages.

A mummy-baby relationship begins when one girl is attracted to another by looks, clothes, or behavior and asks her to be her mummy or her baby, depending on their relative ages. A mummy may have more than one baby, but a baby cannot have more than one mummy at a time, although a young woman can simultaneously be both a baby and a mummy. Plans to meet and do something together are initiated by the mummy. Mummies provide gifts of candy, cosmetics, head ties, or articles of clothing, and babies may reciprocate with small offerings. And mummies also offer advice on love and sex that a girl's mother would withhold. But what differentiates the relationship from other kinds of friendship is the element of love and sensuality. As one informant explained, "Friends may visit, love each other, even give gifts now and then. But between mummies and babies it is like an affair, a romance, and being alone together to hug and kiss each other is always a part of it."[7]

Mummies and babies kiss, embrace each other, lie in bed together, and sometimes engage in genital activity, although that is not much discussed. There is an element of secrecy about the intimacy, although mummy-baby relationships are accepted. Labia lengthening and other genital stimulation are not considered sex; as one woman explained, "You can't have sex unless somebody has a *koai* [penis]."[8] Adult women—domestic workers, university students, secretaries—sometimes engage in passionate kissing, tribadism, fondling, cunnilingus, and digital penetration without considering any of it sexual. Rather, they are "loving each other," "staying together nicely," "holding each other," or "having a nice time together."[9] Even if mummy-baby and other special friendships in Lesotho serve the purpose of socializing young women into heterosexuality and providing affection and intimacy for unmarried women or for married women who are not finding those things in their marriages, they must also be understood as a way that women find love in a society that has no concept of lesbianism.

And it is not only schoolgirls who continue to love one another in sex-segregated spaces. Women in prison, women sex workers, and nuns, among others, have found love and sexual satisfaction in institutions designed for entirely other purposes. In examples from China, a scholar writes of meeting a woman in 1985 who had been repeatedly jailed in Shanghai for heterosexual delinquency. During one sentence, her cellmate, charged with lesbian behavior, "treated Za as her lover, touching her, petting her, and opening up to her the possibilities of sex between women."[10] Two prostitutes in Guangzhou, hired to engage in a threesome with a male client, enjoyed it so much that they became lovers. And two nuns in a Buddhist convent, denounced to the authorities for their relationship, confessed that the older nuns had introduced them to love between women. In all these ways, love and sex in sex-segregated spaces continues.

Sita and Radha Redux

We have already met the fictional Sita and Radha, sisters-in-law in the film *Fire* who fall in love with each other. Deepa Mehta, the director of the film, based it loosely on an Urdu story, "The Quilt," written in 1941 by Ismat Chughtai, the headmistress of a girls' school.[11] In Chughtai's tale, which the government denounced as obscene, a young girl comes to live in a wealthy Muslim household, where she is witness to the relationship between Begum Jan, the lady of the house, and her servant Rabbo. Begum Jan is ignored by her husband, who prefers to spend his time with "boy-students," with their "slim waists, fair ankles, and gossamer shirts."[12] She wastes away until Rabbo arrives with her special oil massage that goes on hour after hour. The young girl, who narrates the story as an adult, is herself "quite enamored" of Begum Jan, but she is both drawn to and repulsed by her body and the constant touching.[13] And she resents Rabbo and is frightened in the night when awakened by Begum Jan's quilt "shaking vigorously as if an elephant was struggling beneath it," Rabbo's sobbing, and the "sounds of a cat slobbering in the saucer."[14] The story ends when, one night, the child turns on the light, the "elephant somersaulted beneath the quilt and dug in," and the quilt flies into the air. Chughtai ends the story with, "What I saw when the quilt was lifted, I will never tell anyone, not even if they give me a lakh of rupees."[15] It would seem that in the film Mehta transforms the notion of not telling into the lack of language to describe "what we are, what we feel for each other." Although Rabbo is not a co-wife, both the story and the film imagine the possibilities of love between women in the spaces of heterosexual marriage.

That such possibilities are not just historical or fictional is suggested by some contemporary accounts. An Indian woman who takes the pseudonym Supriya, at sixteen the second wife of an alcoholic husband whose first wife, Lakshmi, could bear no children, writes of the loving relationship that developed between the two women. Lakshmi had suggested that her husband take another wife, and Lakshmi took care of Supriya's children while their mother worked as a servant to support the family. She also protected Supriya from their husband's advances, since he had sex with prostitutes and Supriya was afraid of contracting a venereal disease. The two women slept together near the children, who considered both women their mothers, and their loving friendship became sexual as well.[16] Another Indian woman, interviewed when she was almost seventy, told of her relationship with her co-wife: "Gradually a friendship between us started to flourish. Inside the four walls of the home, we would rub each other's back and look at each other's bodies. We slept in the same bed with our feet locked together."[17]

An Indian lesbian living in the United States reports that when she was first involved with another girl as a teenager in India, she suggested to the other girl, "we should find a pair of brothers to marry so that we could live in the same house and continue our relationship. It seemed the closest thing to what we viewed as normal."[18] In a case reported in the Indian press in 1997, police arrested a young man and woman whom they suspected of having eloped under age, only to find that the young man was a woman. Like the Ladies of Llangollen so long before them, this was not the first time they had run off together, so their parents did not want them to come home. The families had already suggested that the girls marry two brothers, "which would ensure that they live in the same house."[19] And a documentary film made in New Delhi in 2003 tells the story of two women, one of them masculine, who announce that if they have to marry, they want to marry brothers so they can live together.[20]

Whether or not such negotiations go on in other societies with polygynous marriage or joint-family households—and there are suggestions that they do in the Islamic Arab world as well—it is clear that some women continue to make space for their love within the constraints of compulsory heterosexuality.[21]

Marrying Women

In 1996, the press in Malaysia reported that Azizah Abdul Rahman, a Malay woman, presented herself as a man and married another woman, Rohana. Reports focused on Azizah's looking "like a teenage boy" and wearing "a chocolate-colored pair of slacks and a purple t-shirt." Although it was Rohana's father who exposed Azizah, and Azizah claimed that they married only when Rohana threatened to end their relationship, Rohana told the press, "I did not marry Azizah because I am a lesbian." Although they had had intercourse, Rohana denied knowing that Azizah had a female body. While in prison for a *zina*, a sex-related crime, Azizah, according to the press, returned "to womanhood." She claimed that she had married Rohana out of love and to prevent her from "slipping through her hands into somebody else's."[22]

A Thai woman in her late seventies recalled a female couple who married in her rural village in the 1980s. "They got married formally. They married like a man and a woman." Although the Thai government encourages people to register marriages, not everyone does so. And since weddings are not regulated by Buddhism either, same-sex marriages do occur. In this case, villagers helped with and attended the wedding between what they called "the woman" and "the woman who was a man." "The 'woman' was very beautiful. Both of their parents had the 'woman who was a man' move into the woman's family house" (as is customary for ethnic Thais). "Nobody said anything negative or mean to them."[23]

In the 1990s in a very poor rural region of India, Geeta, a woman from a *dalit*, or "untouchable," family who was married to an abusive husband, met Manju, an older woman whose masculinity had won her a great deal of respect and power in her village. They became friends at a residential school run by a women's organization devoted to equality and empowerment, and then they fell in love. As Geeta put it, "I do not know what happened to me when I met Manju but I forgot my man. I forgot that I had been married. We were so attracted to each other that we immediately felt like husband and wife. . . . After that, we did not leave each other. . . . I knew I could lose my job. But I also knew it was impossible for me to stop. . . . I was in the grip of magic."[24] Geeta accepted Manju as her husband at a Shiva temple, Manju's family welcomed Geeta as a daughter-in-law, and Manju became both a second mother and a father to Geeta's daughter. Interviewed in 1999, Manju reported that she and Geeta had eagerly anticipated seeing the film *Fire* because it was about two Indian women in love, but "there was nothing in it that spoke to our experience," suggesting how differently women can live their lives, even in a similar cultural context.

Indian society does not condone same-sex relations, but the Hindu Marriage Act allows diverse communities to define marriage, making space for some same-sex marriages.[25] Elsewhere in the contemporary world, same-sex marriages have gained formal legal status. Beginning with the Netherlands in 2001, then Belgium in 2003, Canada, Spain, and South Africa in 2005, and Norway in 2008, diverse countries have changed their laws to allow women to marry women and men to marry men. Within the United States, individual states began to allow same-sex marriage, beginning with Massachusetts in 2004. In California, the first legal marriage, before a voter initiative overturned the state Supreme Court decision allowing same-sex marriage, joined longtime partners and activists Del Martin and Phyllis Lyon, two of the founders and the mainstays of the Daughters of Bilitis.

The right to marry has become a bitterly contested issue in the contemporary queer movement in the United States, with some people seeing it as a mimicking of heterosexuality, others as a fundamental right, and still others as a diversion from a proper critique of both the state's involvement in marriage and the tying of a whole host of legal rights to the institution of marriage. The issues are clear in the differing statements of women who married in San Francisco in 2004. One admitted that she married entirely to make a "political statement": "I was against the institution. I didn't want to be the same as straight people." Another remembered, "At first it was a rather spontaneous decision—to participate in part of history, but quickly it became something much more significant for us emotionally and politically." And yet another expressed a profound sense of shame turning to pride: "I felt less, I don't know if sinful is the right word, less of an outsider. I felt like I have nothing to be ashamed of. And I think up to that point, I felt somewhere inside that I had done something wrong."[26]

As in San Francisco, women around the world are choosing to marry their female lovers for a whole host of reasons. In some places, they just dream about it. In Uganda, where some women identify as lesbians and others as "tommy boys," Vivica, a lesbian, tells an interviewer that she and her lover plan to get married in the future. "We can't do it in public, but we have hopes that in time the government will accept it."[27] Whether marrying or dreaming of it, some women continue the tradition of women marrying women, whether they present as men, as romantic friends, or as two women proudly in love.

Still Crossing the Gender Line

We have already encountered female-bodied women who secretly dressed as men and married women. But it is important to add that, even in societies in which a lesbian life in public became possible, some women continued to cross the gender line and marry women. In 1945 in New Zealand, Mr. X, as the newspapers called him, was arrested for marrying a woman, and unlike in the earlier twentieth-century case of Percy Carol Redwood, the question of sexual deviance came into play.[28] Mr. X told reporters that life as a woman had been difficult because of his masculinity and that he had successfully passed and worked as a man for twelve years, even having his breasts removed and registering for the armed forces during the Second World War. Since he felt and acted like a man, the relationship with his wife seemed normal, and both were happy with the situation. The media focused on his masculinity, not just in appearance—"tall, robust, broad-shouldered and husky-looking, with a mop of unruly black hair and a virile mien"—but also in behavior. His conversation was "frank and fearless," his room was messy, and he worked as a laborer and enjoyed male sports, including boxing.[29] Yet both Mr. X and his wife admitted to the police during the investigation that they were "of the Lesbian type."[30] Although Mr. X insisted that his feelings and actions were "natural and normal," the legal system and the media thought differently.[31] A Methodist minister proclaimed that Mr. X's "sexual maladjustment" demanded "some form of skilled psychological treatment," and the judge denounced the marriage as "an extraordinary perversion."[32] The couple was ordered to separate and seek psychiatric treatment.

Then there is the case of Billy Tipton, who inspired the fictional tale of Joss Moody. Born Dorothy Lucille Tipton in Oklahoma City in 1914, at the age of nineteen Billy donned a man's suit for the first time in order to get hired as a jazz musician, something that had proven difficult as a woman.[33] Over time, he began to dress and present as a man more and more consistently, and although there were always some people from his past who knew his secret, and some who read him as a woman when they met him, it was not until after his death in 1991 that most of the world found out about the body beneath Billy Tipton's immaculate clothing.

Like Edward De Lacy Evans before him, Billy had a series of relationships and marriages with women, some of whom knew his secret and others of whom did not. With his last wife, he adopted and raised three sons, one of whom was with him when he died and witnessed paramedics opening his father's shirt to expose a woman's breasts. Billy had always wrapped his chest, explaining that his ribs needed support after injuries sustained in a terrible car accident, and he wore some kind of genital gear that gave him a realistic crotch. None of his lovers or children had ever seen him naked because he was a very private person and always bathed and dressed in a locked bathroom. He made love to most of his wives, who never suspected a thing. One wife, Betty, described their lovemaking: "Billy always wore a rubber he would strip off and toss away after we made love. So that's what it felt like, a man wearing a rubber."[34] She speculated that Billy's satisfaction must have come from kissing and fondling.

Billy was careful, as he had to be, so we can never really know how he viewed himself. He did tell one of the cousins who continued to know him as Dorothy that he considered himself a "normal person," not "a freak or a hermaphrodite," but what did that mean?[35] One of his wives, after they split up, called him a hermaphrodite. While still presenting as Dorothy, he had had a romantic friendship with another woman, suggesting that erotic interest in women had always been part of the picture, and while he began to turn into Billy, he lived with and eventually said he was married to a flamboyant older woman who sometimes dressed in trousers and clearly knew Billy was female bodied. When he moved entirely into a male persona, he fell for beautiful and sexy women, one a call girl and his last wife, Kitty, a stripper. It seems he felt strong desire for feminine women. Although few of Billy's letters have survived, Kitty kept some, and when she left him and threw them out, he salvaged and saved them in a locked filing cabinet. When she was hospitalized for an ulcer, he had written to her about his feelings: "I have loved you with all my heart for these past seven years. . . . You are instilled so deep in my heart that you have become a part of me. . . . You are my life, my life—Your husband, Billy."[36]

What is striking about Billy's story is the gradual move into manhood, the fact that in some sense he led a double life, keeping contact with those who knew he had a female body, and that he apparently considered going back into womanhood when his sons had grown up, at least according to a relative. Was he transgendered in a modern sense? A butch lesbian who found this the best way to be in the world? Or something else altogether? It is tantalizing that we will never really know.

In the twenty-first century, in at least some places in the world, it is possible, if not safe, to be openly transgendered. Manel is a biologically female transman from Sri Lanka who dresses, works, behaves, and identifies himself as a man. Manel described his family's reaction to him as he was growing up as a masculine girl: "My family is confounded by my behavior. My sisters could not bring me into our village society as a girl because of my manner of speech and behavior. The society I grew up in drew back in fear—is this a girl, is this a boy?"[37] His family explored the possibility of sex-reassignment surgery for him, and although Manel was not accepted by the doctors, he sees this as a positive move on his family's part. Manel found support through the Women's Support Group, the only lesbian, bisexual, and transgender organization in Sri Lanka. He said, "I only realized that homosexuality exists in Sri Lanka when I came here [to the Women's Support Group]. Because of this, the mentality I had about hospitals and wanting operations has gone away. I don't feel alone anymore." Although he was fascinated by lesbians in the Women's Support Group, he made clear that he could not live as a woman. "I am not homosexual. I don't know how to live as a homosexual, I don't understand it. I can't do women-with-women. I have my own unique method of sexual practice which suits the pleasures of my body."[38]

In contrast, Shanthi—who also grew up in Sri Lanka, dressed and behaved as a boy, and recognized her attraction to girls—has moved from wanting sex-reassignment surgery to embracing a lesbian identity. "I was told that the process involved constructing a penis from flesh taken from my body. I was told that it would be like a piece of meat. They do not construct testicles. I think this would be more mentally troublesome than my present state. I wouldn't be able to enjoy sex either. I have now reconciled myself to my choices as Buddhism has taught us to do."[39] Through exercise and weight training she developed a muscular frame with less body fat, and her relationship with a lesbian who perceives her as a woman has led her to accept that identity. "I will live as a lesbian and choose another lesbian as my partner."[40] Manel and Shanthi represent different possibilities for masculine female-bodied persons in the contemporary world.

The transgender movement in the United States makes clear how complicated the relationship can be between gender identities—whether one perceives oneself as male or female—and sexual identities—whether one identifies as homosexual, bisexual, or heterosexual. Oscar, a gay-identified transman from the San Francisco Bay Area who has had "top surgery" (the removal of breasts) and takes testosterone, explained the difference for him between his approach and the old model of erasing one's history as a woman: "So glad to have that behind us now, change the birth certificate, burn the photos, make up lies about when you were in the Boy Scouts, don't talk about it, don't show anybody the pictures. . . . I'm very grateful that in the last few years, a number of people have really seriously challenged all of the above: That you don't have to, necessarily, identify as a man."[41] And his sexual identity is not based on the gender of the person he is involved with sexually or on his own body's vagina (since he has not, like many female-to-male transsexuals, had "bottom surgery," creation of a penis from the vagina). So neither dating a fem woman nor having penis-in-vagina sex with a man would make him heterosexual.

Likewise Charlie, who is also from the Bay Area and queer-identified and who takes testosterone but has had no surgery, explains, "It doesn't work for me to be sexual with a straight identified man. It does work being with a woman and FtMs [female-to-male transsexuals] because I can relate to a woman as a man and FtMs as a fag."[42] What the transgender movement is fighting to make possible is the kind of life that would not constrain people like Billy Tipton to guard the secrets of their bodies so assiduously or Manel and Shanthi to struggle to find an identity and place to be safe and happy. But there remain many ways to be transgendered in the world, even when the concept of a transgender identity does not exist.

Female Masculinity Continued

If we consider the "troubling" rather than just the crossing of the gender line, we find a whole range of expressions of female masculinity in the contemporary world. Although the emergence of lesbian feminism throughout the "First World" in the 1970s and 1980s fostered the creation of a supposedly androgynous aesthetic along with the celebration of female values and a critique of masculinity, female masculinity remained and remains a central feature of many of the worlds in which women love women.

In a contemporary Thai nightclub, for example, Kot, with short hair and wearing men's pants and a button-down shirt over a white undershirt, explained what it means to be a *tom* (from the English word *tomboy*): "I always wanted to be a boy and even knew how to pee standing up."[43] When an old girlfriend slept with Kot's brother and then went back to Kot, the brother angrily called Kot a *kathoey*, a term meaning transgender or third sex. Kot's mother joked that since he was not using his penis much, he should give it to Kot. Kot's new girlfriend, a *dee* (from the English word *lady*) named Tee, also had boyfriends. With Kot, she would have sex only when she wanted it and the way she wanted it. For Kot, that is just how women are. (See the masculinity of a Thai *tom* in figure 28.)

Sex between women is not new in Thai society, and in fact improper heterosexual encounters are considered far more deviant than sex between women, which is often considered innocent.[44] But until the creation of *tom*/*dee* categories, there was no notion of women who have sex with women as a particular kind of person.[45] Even more novel is the concept of a *dee*, for a *dee* fits in the category *woman* and is only a *dee* when she is with a *tom*. Because most *dees* consider themselves ordinary women, they often expect to marry men. Says one *dee*, "I feel I am normal, but she is abnormal. . . . Sometimes I think she is like a man. . . . I just want her to be a real man, so I could be with her all our lives."[46] Some *dees*, however, are interested only in *toms*, not in men, and so see themselves as "born this way" or as "real *dees*."[47] One *dee*, Chang, even sees "real *dees*" as more "misgendered" than *toms* because they could be with men but prefer *toms*.[48]

Toms are defined by masculinity, but they differ from men and, ironically, fit into Thai concepts of femininity by making their goal serving their *dees*, both emotionally and sexually. Um, a *dee*, describes this ethic: "If I have a tom, she will take care of me and be worried about me. She will find nice presents for me and pay a lot of attention to me. . . . Toms

Figure 28. A Thai *tom*. From Megan J. Sinnott, *Toms and Dees: Transgender Identity and Female Same-Sex Relationships in Thailand* (Honolulu: University of Hawaii Press, 2004).

will take me out, take care of me, that's fun."[49] The relationship of service to *dees* extends to sexual relationships, as Kot's comment quoted earlier suggests. At least in theory, *toms*, like stone butches in the 1950s in the United States and England, are not touched sexually by their *dees*. *Toms* provide oral or manual stimulation so that their girlfriends have orgasms, but their own satisfaction comes through pleasuring their *dees*. A *dee* described in a newsletter how it should be: "I can't accept a tom that lets a dee do it for her. . . . Normally when I have sex with my girlfriend, she will do it for me always, which she has said that she enjoys. Just to see me enjoy myself and she is happy already."[50] A *tom*, Cuk, explains that if she keeps her clothes on and is not touched by her girlfriend, neither one of them will have to think about her being a woman. "If I take all my clothes off, I'll look like a woman, and I won't be confident in myself. I'll feel embarrassed."[51] Yet some *toms* criticize *dees* as selfish in asserting their right to sexual pleasure in a way they could not with a man.

Dees are like masculine men who have sex with men but are not homosexual or gay. The insistence of some *dees* that they are "real *dees*" suggests an incipient redrawing of categories, placing both *toms* and *dees* outside the boundaries of "ordinary women" and in the same slot. There is also the category of *les,* from *lesbian,* embraced by (usually feminine) women who desire women but do not embrace the gendered distinction between *toms* and *dees.*[52] The lesbian organization Anjaree, founded in 1986, introduced the term *ying-rak-ying,* "women who love women," to cover both *toms* and *dees,* but the differences remain important.[53]

Similar gender dynamics can be seen in Hong Kong, where "TBs" (tomboys) go with "TBGs" (tomboys' girls).[54] The term *TB* originated in girls' schools, where masculine girls with crushes on other students were an accepted part of the social scene. The terms spread to the lesbian community, which emerged in the 1990s out of private gatherings in earlier decades. The use of *TB* avoided negative terms in circulation and could be used in public without alerting others to its meaning. Like *toms,* TBs cut their hair short, wear men's clothes, and take care of their girlfriends in ways they perceive as masculine. In lesbian pubs, they drink beer and sing karaoke, choosing male pop songs. As Yin-shing, a TB, put it, "A TB must take care of her girlfriend; otherwise what's the point for her to keep a masculine appearance? . . . A masculine appearance means nothing if this TB does not take care of her girlfriend and cannot afford her girlfriend's daily expenses."[55] And in Hong Kong there is also the identity of "pure," which means "pure lesbian" and not TB or TBG. Hong Kong's integration into global society means that the Western notion of a non-gender-differentiated lesbian identity coexists with the gendered identities of TB and TBG.

In Taiwan, too, masculine and feminine identities structure women's relationships. Here they are called "T," for *tomboy,* and "*Po,*" from the Chinese word for "wife."[56] In the 1960s, masculine women who frequented gay bars earned the designation "tomboy" from gay men, and they considered themselves real men and often passed as men. Contemporary Ts, in contrast, think of themselves simply as Ts, not men. T-bars, which began to open in the major cities of Taiwan in the mid-1980s, are the spaces in which young women learn how to be proper Ts and *Pos.* Through elaborate toasting and karaoke and storytelling, Ts make clear that they are Ts, not "real men." For example, they might uncork a bottle of champagne held between their thighs, suggesting ejaculation, yet a T who underwent sex-change surgery and came back to the bar was rejected as not a real T any-more. In the same way, Ts bind their breasts to make them small, but, as one T put it, "not completely flat—otherwise they would look like man's chest, very *biantai* [abnormal, sickening]."[57] Like Thai *toms*, Ts do not want to take off their clothes when having sex with their *Pos*. One T told of a new *Po* who ripped open her shirt and exclaimed how cute her breasts were. They broke up as a result. Ts and *Pos* are not in the same conceptual category, although, as Anjaree has done in Thailand, a Taiwanese feminist group proposed a unifying term, *bu-fen*, to cover both Ts and *Pos*.[58]

The term *tomboy* (along with *t-bird*, *tibo*, and *third sex*) and the mas-culine-feminine dynamic can also be found in the Philippines. More re-cently, the terms *mars* (from the Spanish *madres*) and *pars* (from *padres*) have come into vogue. As in other Asian contexts, *pars* consider them-selves men who are responsible for making love and giving pleasure to their *mars*. There are also Filipinas who identify as lesbians.[59]

To take another case, in different parts of Indonesia masculine women also make a place for themselves in an Islamic society with clear expecta-tions for women's proper behavior. In South Sulawesi, masculine women are known as *calalai*, a term meaning literally "false man."[60] They do not identify as women and do not want to be men. Such women prefer the term *calalai* or *tomboi* to the term *lesbi*, which has negative connotations linked to Western sexology. *Calalai* wear men's clothes, engage in male be-havior and mannerisms, and gravitate to men's jobs such as taxi driving or working as DJs in nightclubs. They are less restrained than men in their re-lationships with women because they are recognized as female bodied, if masculine. As a result, they can enter a girlfriend's house even if no man is present, which a biologically male boyfriend could not. They are also able to move between groups of women and groups of men. In this sense, they inhabit a kind of space between male and female genders.

In the city of Padang in Indonesia, a more cosmopolitan place, mas-culine women call themselves *tomboi* or *lesbi*. Like *toms* in Thailand, they wear men's clothes and short hair and engage in male behavior such as smoking. Said one, "Tombois are pretty tough. They don't talk a lot, un-less it's important."[61] They both are and are not viewed as women: they claim the privileges of men, engaging in male activities and escaping the strictures imposed on women, but it is understood that they have female bodies. Their girlfriends are feminine, expect to be protected, and keep their relationships secret even from family members and friends. "I am the same as other women," said one girlfriend.[62] But unlike *dees* in Thailand, *tomboi* girlfriends are in the same conceptual category as *lesbi*, at least while they are with a *tomboi*.

In Japan, male-identified female-born *onabe* serve as sex workers in bars where they service heterosexually identified women. Featured in a documentary film, *Shinjuku Boys*, an *onabe* named Gaish described his/her sense of self: "I cannot make myself more feminine. I don't want to be a real man. If people think I'm in between, that's OK with me. I don't feel like a woman in my mind. . . . I've always been like this, it is natural to me." They dress and behave as men, some taking hormones to grow a beard and lower their voices. They make love to clients, keeping their clothes on. Said Tatsu, another *onabe* in the film, "I have heard lesbians take their clothes off, but we *onabe*, we hate that."[63]

Masculine-feminine dynamics have also been central in Lima, Peru. In the bar Ferretería, a Dutch lesbian scholar describes dynamics familiar to her from Jakarta:

> When I looked up I saw a woman approaching me from the other side of the room. . . . For a Latin woman she was rather tall and dark. . . . Swinging her hips she crossed straight to our table, ignoring the dancing couples. After the usual introductions she asked me "what I was."
>
> "*Soy una mujer.*" [I'm a woman.]
>
> She kept me at arm's length and looked me up and down with a quick glance.
>
> "No," she said decisively. "You're a *chita*." OK, a butch then.[64]

Here, too, masculine/feminine identifications are an essential part of relationships between women.

And, finally, consider the story of Phakamile and Cora, Black South African lesbians.[65] Phakamile is a working-class butch woman who lives in a small room attached to her parents' house in Soweto. She considers herself very masculine, despite her small size. She plays soccer and smokes tobacco and marijuana, all expressions of masculinity. Most lesbians in Soweto are butches who have relationships with women who identify as straight. (See figure 29, an African butch woman binding her breasts.) Phakamile is in love with Cora, a middle-class woman who lives with her family in a house that has running water and electricity. Cora identifies as a "lesbian woman" but is not open with her family about her identity, although Phakamile spends the night with her often enough that her mother confronted them about being lovers yet has accepted Phakamile as a family member. Cora is unusual in criticizing the butch-fem dynamic, a contentious issue between them. Phakamile says she proposed to Cora at a soccer game, where she was one of the star players, but Cora laughingly disagrees: "You know what . . . Phakamile, as butch as she is, I proposed to her. Really, really. Well, I could see that . . . she was interested and she was afraid, and so I thought let me make things easier for her, you know and propose."[66]

As all these examples suggest, there are both similarities and differences between *toms* and *dees* or TBs and TBGs or *calalai* or *tombois* and their girlfriends, on the one hand, and butches and fems in Western culture, on the other. Although dominant Western notions of lesbian identities have spread through the Internet, transnational gatherings, and personal contact through travel, local concepts of gender and sexual identities have by no means been erased by processes of globalization. Rather, local ideas of what it means to love and desire someone with a biologically alike body intertwine with Western concepts, and the product becomes local,

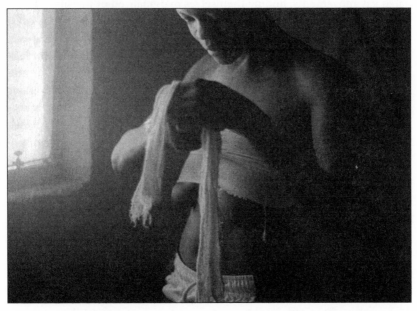

Figure 29. An African woman binds her breasts. Photograph by Zanele Muholi. From Ruth Morgan and Saskia Wieringa, *Tommy Boys, Lesbian Men and Ancestral Wives: Female Same-Sex Practices in Africa* (Johannesburg: Jacana Media, 2005).

in a metaphor developed by Tom Boellstorff, like a dubbed film.[67] The dynamic of female masculinity runs through all these stories, but how it operates in each case is shaped by the particular historical and social circumstances. These possibilities put contemporary U.S. notions of "lipstick lesbians," "bois," drag kings, transmen, and "gender-queer" in a broader transnational perspective.

Friends in Love

Of the women who loved women whom we have encountered across time and place, some did not differentiate themselves as masculine and feminine. Co-wives, female monastics, romantic friends, and sometimes schoolgirls seem instead to have eroticized sameness, not difference. We find the phenomenon of falling in love with someone just like oneself in lesbian feminism as it emerged in the United States, in Canada, in England, in parts of Europe, and elsewhere in the 1970s and 1980s.

Lesbians involved in both women's movements and early male-dominated gay movements, finding themselves marginalized or invisible, began to form their own groups and alternative institutions, such as bookstores, publishing and recording companies, support groups, and coffeehouses and restaurants.[68] Lesbian feminists claimed a heritage going back to Sappho and the Amazons, as indicated by the prominence of Sappho's name in book and magazine titles and by the double-bladed Amazon ax that became a prominent lesbian feminist symbol. Separatism from both heterosexual women and from men—sometimes situational, sometimes absolute, as in the formation of lesbian feminist communes—along with the celebration of "female values," became the hallmark of lesbian feminism. As one U.S. lesbian feminist put it, "We've been acculturated into two cultures, the male and the female culture. And luckily we've been able to preserve the ways of nurturing by being in this alternative culture."[69] A British lesbian feminist who was a separatist in the 1970s explained, somewhat cynically, "The rules are simple: whatever your race or class, provided you are a woman, you are a potential separatist. Whatever your race or class, if you are a man you are irredeemably the enemy." And, bringing to mind Elizabeth Gould Davis and her argument about the mutant origins of men, she added, "That Y chromosome, that mutated afterthought, was the cause of it all."[70]

Within lesbian feminism, sexual desire for women and resistance to male domination almost equally defined what it meant to be a "woman-identified woman." Women who did not want to have sex with women but identified with the lesbian feminist community came to be known as "political lesbians," described by an English group called the Leeds Revolutionary Feminists as "a woman-identified woman who does not fuck men. It does not mean compulsory sexual activity with women."[71] In Mexico, too, as women involved in the movement explained, "there were also lesbians who said 'I have come to be a lesbian through a political decision,' textbook lesbians."[72] Women came to lesbian feminism in different ways, sometimes out of their sexual desires and sometimes out of politics, which then led to new desires and a new identity.

Three women's stories from the United States illustrate these differences.[73] Barb Herman, from a lower-middle-class New York Italian family, was a tomboy growing up and knew she was attracted to girls at the age of eight, even though she did not have a name for her desires. She had her first sexual experience with another girl when she was fifteen; what she felt was a "mixture of fear and exhilaration."[74] "I always knew I was a lesbian, but I distanced myself from the word. It was too scary to consider."[75] Not until she went to a meeting of a radical lesbian group in 1971 did she adopt the identity of lesbian feminist. "It was like the messiah had come. There were all these people who were like me. . . . They were lesbians."[76] Like the "real *dees*," she considered herself a "real" lesbian because she was a "born" lesbian.[77]

In contrast, Margaret Berg, the daughter of Jewish leftist activists from New England, came to lesbianism through feminism. Finding the women's movement in 1969 was "the most exciting and validating thing."[78] Although she was involved in an intimate relationship with a man, her immersion in the women's movement took her further and further into all-female worlds. She had her first sexual relationship with a woman out of an interest in sexual experimentation rather than out of desire. "There was a certain reflection of myself I found in her," she said. She joined a consciousness-raising group focused on sexuality, and there she came out, calling herself a lesbian. But she differentiated herself from butch/fem culture. She described her emotions at her first women's dance: "I was very scared by a number of older women dressed sort of mannishly. Not scared that they'd do anything to me, but wary of being identified with them."[79] For Margaret, it was possible to choose lesbianism.

Ara Jones, an African American woman who grew up working class in the South, saw her lesbianism as "a changeable thing."[80] Her first woman lover was a white woman with whom she fell "madly in love."[81] She began to identify both as a lesbian and as a feminist, but not as a lesbian feminist, because she saw that world as mostly white. Bisexual in behavior if not identity, she liked the sex she had with men better but had deeper emotional commitments to women, so she defined lesbianism as "a relationship in which two women's strongest emotions and affections are directed toward each other."[82] Yet sexual passion with women was important to her. After marrying and divorcing a man, she fell in love with a woman again. She saw herself as choosing lesbianism but also said, "I'm not straight," meaning she could choose to deny her desire for women but did not.[83]

The aspect of lesbian feminism that garnered the most criticism was its rigidity about how to dress, live, and love. Rejecting traditional femininity but also critical of masculinity, the proper uniform consisted of tee-shirts, jeans, and flannel shirts, short hair, and no makeup. The requirements of lesbian feminist antistyle turned off many working-class women, who rejected the downward mobility inherent in lesbian feminist anticonsumerism, and women of color, who felt that their own cultural styles were rejected as politically incorrect. One working-class woman who visited the lesbian feminist center in Toronto, where the Lesbian Organization of Toronto (LOOT) shared space with a lesbian feminist newspaper and coffeehouse, remembered her first reaction: "You had to dress down at LOOT—all the women looked like they were ready to paint a barn. I thought to myself, I was in the army and I had to wear a uniform, I was a femme at home and I had to wear a uniform, and now these assholes have a uniform and it's not even pretty. I can't wear my polyester, I can't wear my lipstick, I can't wear my eye make-up, I had to exchange my purse for a knapsack."[84] The rules had to do with more than just dress. As a lesbian from Britain explained cynically, a lesbian feminist "must abandon all relationships with men, lovers, fathers and brothers. Sexually she is either celibate or lesbian. Politically and socially, her contact is confined to women. The music she listens to must be composed and played by women, the books she reads must have a woman author."[85]

Lesbian feminism also devised a proper way to have sex. *The Other Woman*, a lesbian feminist paper published in Toronto in the 1970s, instructed readers that "loving women is a gentle sensual thing and it's not something confined to genitals. It involves our whole selves," and a "woman knows best the desires, pace, mood of another woman and is best able to satisfy her."[86] A lesbian feminist quoted in an article in the *Toronto Star* in 1979 explained, "We're trying to forge relationships that aren't based on power but on mutual love and nurturing. Men are conditioned to take, emotionally, but women are conditioned to give." And another LOOT member, in a brief for gay rights sent to the Ontario legislature, described lesbian sex as "anything that makes caressing, whispering, stroking breasts, running fingers through her hair, nuzzling, more fun."[87]

The demand for political correctness in dress, behavior, and sex that developed within lesbian feminism never translated into complete conformity, and by the 1980s and 1990s it came under attack from working-class women, women of color, and what became known as "pro-sex" feminists, who emphasized the pleasures rather than just the dangers of a wide variety of sexual activities. It was in that context that an embrace of both femininity and masculinity came back into the lesbian scene, now with all sorts of modifiers such as "butchy fems" and "femmy butches." But what is important about the sexual ideology of lesbian feminism from a long historical perspective is the denial of the centrality of difference to sexual interactions and the eroticizing of intimacy with "someone just like me," even if that was more an ideal than a reality.

Still Other Ways of Loving Women

And all the preceding examples are just some of the ways that women or female-bodied individuals continue to love women. Makeda Silvera, an Afro-Caribbean Canadian, remembers a friend of her mother telling her about "man royals" in Jamaica, her country of birth: "Now with women, nobody really suspected. . . . I grew up seeing women holding hands, hugging-up, sleeping together in one bed and there was no question. . . . It wasn't a thing you would go out and broadcast."[88] Likewise, a Shoshoni (Native American) man remembered his grandmother, a two-spirited person, living on the reservation: "There's another woman that always hung around her. . . . But these women also had children, got married. . . . But they had their women friends and were always respected for that and everything else. But it was nothing overt, they didn't hold it out to the community. But everybody knew what was going on."[89] A lesbian from Beirut, whose mother found out about her interest in women when she was sixteen or seventeen, "re-closeted" herself and "started going out with a guy" as a way to remain invisible.[90]

Working-class Creole (Afro-Surinamese) women in Paramaribo, Suriname, form sexual relationships with other women while maintaining ties with men, sometimes husbands. This is called "*mati* work," meaning that it is not an identity but a form of activity. The relationship involves emotional and financial support, as well as sexual obligation. A thirty-seven-year-old mother of five, married to the father of two of her children, explained *mati* this way: "love between two women is stronger than between a man and a woman. . . . With a woman, you know what you like sexually and so does she."[91] Such relationships are accepted within the community without their having any special significance for women's sexual identities or intimate relationships with men.

In Carriacou, the Caribbean island made famous by Audre Lorde's autobiographical *Zami: A New Spelling of My Name*, women who love and have sex with other women are called *madivine* or *zami*, the word Lorde adopted. Lorde wrote, "How Carriacou women love each other is legend in Grenada, and so is their strength and their beauty."[92] An anthropologist writing in the 1960s explained that the strict taboo on extramarital affairs for women and the frequency with which married men worked overseas for long periods of time led to women having sexual relationships with other women. He also reported that "once developed, these Lesbian appetites may reduce the woman's interest in men considerably." Unmarried young women might also have sex with older married women, who could, if they had sufficient resources to provide gifts to their younger partners, have more than one. Men in Carriacou reported that "women are hotter than men" so that only women can really satisfy one another.[93]

Some women continue to have secret affairs: in one small southern U.S. city, housewives get together in the afternoon and make love while their husbands are at work.[94] Rokiah, a divorced poor Malay cabaret dancer, and Susan, a middle-class European woman, have been together for sixteen years in Malaysia, but they must hide their relationship from Rokiah's children.[95] In contemporary Egypt, women with female lovers also seem to lead normative heterosexual lives, and that may be true in other societies that deny the existence of sex between women.[96] One young Egyptian lesbian's mother asked her if she liked women—"I mean, do you *really* like women? Don't you want to get married and have children?"—but that was the only time the subject came up.[97] This woman uses the Internet to meet other women, many of whom are married. Syrian dissident Ammar Abdulhamid's novel *Menstruation*, written in English and not translated into Arabic, tells the story of a woman, Batul, who is married but has affairs with women. She tells her first lover, "Some of the married women have wonderful husbands, by their own admission. I mean, husbands who perfectly satisfy them sexually, still they go for me, they turn to putty in my hands."[98] In Japan, the women who play male parts in the Takarazuka Revue, who according to the founder are "more suave, more affectionate, more courageous, more charming, more handsome and more fascinating than a real male," are the subject of intense crushes from their women fans, and when they retire, sometimes they marry quickly to hide their lesbian relationships and then divorce and return to their lovers.[99]

Some women discover an identity when they are exposed to different ways of thinking. In Zimbabwe, a Black woman named Shikaye was a tomboy as a girl and saw that the life of men was better than that of women, causing her to want to become a man. She was also attracted to women, but the only way she could make sense of that was to think of wanting to be a man. She came to understand her desires differently on a visit to Europe, where she went to lesbian sex shows with an expatriate friend and "understood what [she] was," knowing that she was not the only woman in the world with such desires.[100]

In Chile, self-identified feminist lesbian Consuelo Rivera Fuentes when she was twelve years old began having lesbian fantasies about a popular singer rumored to be a lesbian. "I did not have a clear idea of what the term meant . . . but somehow I knew it was something I secretly liked and feared for the sexual desire it aroused in me."[101] She fell in love with her friends but went out with men and eventually married. Involved in the progressive political struggle after the 1973 coup, she felt that some of her *compañeras* touched her with more than comradely feelings, but she suppressed all of that until she finally met the woman who turned her "silent dreams into concrete Lesbian love."[102]

Then there are those who have been traditionally thought of as "maiden aunts," who make their lives with other women in societies that have a concept of lesbians, but no one questions their identities. Having read the story in my book *A Desired Past* about my Aunt Leila, who lived with and loved another schoolteacher, Diantha, Swedish scholar of same-sex sexuality Jens Rydström sent me the story of his Aunt Greta.[103] Growing up in the southern Swedish town of Höganäs, she went to horticultural school and started a market garden with her schoolmate, Elsa Niklasson, always known as "Niklasson." They stayed together all their lives. Niklasson wore a brown beret and smoked a pipe and never said much. Nobody in the family ever talked about them as anything other than friends. Once Greta told Jens that Niklasson should have been born a man, that when she was young she played softball with the sailors near the naval yard in Stockholm and they called her "Niklas." And, perhaps like Aunt Leila, who left me her teacher's insurance policy after Diantha died, Greta gave everything to charity after Niklasson died except for a silver vase that she willed to Jens because of some sense of kinship beyond family connection.[104]

There does, indeed, seem to be nothing, or nothing much, new under the sun. Throughout our journey through time and around the globe, we have seen many and various ways that women love other women. Some find spaces in which their love can flourish, some cross the gender line to marry their lovers, some form intimate friendships or marriage-like relationships, some embrace gender blurring, some embrace femininity, some express their love in passionate language, some simply make love to one another with hands, objects, tongues, or vulvas.

In all these spaces, indigenous practices and understandings merge in a variety of ways with globalized concepts of what it means to be "gay" or "lesbian" or "bisexual" or "transgendered." Processes of development that open up the possibility of economic independence for women, increased access to education, urbanization and social mobility, loosening of political and religious regulation of women's lives—all these developments have an impact on the ways that societies conceptualize love between women and the possibilities for women's lives. And the result is a world of difference.

10

Conclusion

WHAT CAN WE take away from this history, besides the ingenuity and creativity of women and social males with women's bodies who desired, loved, and made love to women across time and space? Without imposing too linear a trajectory or confining an admittedly sprawling history in a narrative straitjacket, some general observations are possible.

We have seen that, from the very earliest societies, the possibility of love between women has been acknowledged, even if it is feared, ignored, or denied. From myths of births out of the union of two female bodies to tales of two formerly whole, now half, humans seeking to reunite, we can see that heterosexuality was never the only conceptual option. Societies that valued sexuality tended to be more open to the possibility of love between women, and in some contexts same-sex love coexisted easily with heterosexual arrangements. It was female masculinity and independence from male control that made love between women threatening to the social order.

Everywhere women's subordination to men of the same social group shaped the possibilities for same-sex love and desire in a variety of ways. Being less important, women were often left out of religious prohibitions and legal codes specifying punishment for sex between men. Compulsory heterosexuality, marriage, and reproduction in most societies ensured that whatever women might do with one another, most of them they would still marry and have sex with men and reproduce heirs. The exceptions, at first primarily female monastics, fell under the control of male-dominated religious institutions, which, ironically, made space for love between women at the same time that they prohibited it. Other sex-segregated spaces—women's quarters, brothels, prisons, schools—also facilitated love and sex between women. The very lack of access of women to public space until recent times, which made the kind of world in which men with same-sex desires could move, created a different way for women to be together. And throughout time, prohibitions and tales and pornographic images and scurrilous attacks ensured the circulation of information about the possibilities of love between women.

The processes of economic development and urbanization, accompanied by women's access to education and employment, facilitated both the long-feared possibility of independence from male control and the emergence of more public worlds for women. As these processes unfolded in different places, we see similar consequences for the patterns of female same-sex sexuality. In the European context, women at both ends of the social scale—women of the urban underworld and aristocratic women—found possibilities to meet one another and, as a result, earned denunciation in bawdy street songs and political pornography. In China, commentators singled out factory workers, on the one hand, and co-wives in wealthy households and female members of the intellectual elite, on the other, for their same-sex desires. Class differences played out through greater access to public worlds such as the streets and factories for non-elite women, while wealthy women moved in more private spaces.

The creation of the category *lesbian,* and the tendency to treat male and female homosexuality as conceptually the same, spread around much of the globe as a way to view love between women that sometimes clashed with and sometimes merged with local practices. If the sexological category *lesbian* facilitated the embrace of an identity and the formation of communities in some places, in others it tainted love between women as a Western import.

As schoolgirls in love, romantic friends who chose not to marry men, feminists, and women who frequented commercial establishments catering to same-sex love came out from domestic and private spaces, they made the possibilities of love between women more visible and more worrisome. The bars and clubs and magazines and organizations that proliferated in industrialized Western countries in the twentieth century characterized one kind of lesbian life. But even in places where a public lesbian culture emerged, and certainly in parts of the world without commercial establishments or social-movement institutions, women continued to love in private spaces as well.

The wide variety of ways that women have desired, loved, and made love to other women throughout time and around the globe—and the variety of ways they continue to do so in the twenty-first century—makes clear how religions, family structures, legal codes, institutions, economic structures, political ideologies, intellectual trends, and social movements have the potential to shape the expressions and understandings of female same-sex sexuality. There is indeed a world of difference in the ways women love and have loved other women.

Yet despite the multitude of ways that women have found to act on their desires, we have seen the persistence of basic conceptions of women who love women: that they are masculine, that their bodies mark them as different from other women, that they are wanton, that they are deprived of access to men, that they hate men. And we have seen two dominant patterns in women's relationships, those that are gender differentiated—masculine-feminine pairings—and those that are based in eroticized friendship. From the Aztec *patlācheh* to the Mohave *hwame* Sahaykwisa to Catharina Linck to Moll Cutpurse to 1950s butches to Thai *toms* and Indonesian *tombois*, masculinity and attraction to masculinity has played a starring role in the history of female same-sex desire. Is this pattern an imitation of a heterosexual model that exists, if differently, in all societies? Or is it a sign of some essential transgenderism? I argue that the variety of female-bodied individuals who have claimed male gender or rejected female gender or created something altogether different from either male or female remind us that the varieties of ways women have loved one another are not limitless. But at the same time, we can see how differently societies have constructed genders and sexualities. That is, we cannot deny the persistence of a transgender impulse across time and place; but we can recognize the multitude of ways that individuals and societies have confronted, accommodated, resisted, or ignored the possibilities of crossing or troubling the lines of gender.

Alongside the pairing of masculine women or social males with feminine women throughout history and around the world, we find the eroticization of sameness rather than difference. Although not entirely overlooked in the scholarship on male same-sex sexuality, eroticized same-sex friendship between people of the same age, gender, and class, I suggest, is more persistent in the history of love between women.[1] From female monastics to Chinese co-wives to the *doganas* of Urdu poetry to romantic friends to schoolgirls to lesbian feminists, relationships between non-gender-differentiated women have coexisted with masculine-feminine couples. Sometimes we find elements of both sameness and difference in the same relationships, as between teachers and students or "mummies" and "babies" or when one schoolgirl presents herself as somewhat masculine. Perhaps the best example of such a mixture of sameness and difference is the romantic and sexual relationship between Katharine Bradley and her niece, Edith Cooper, English poets who wrote jointly under the pen name "Michael Field." Although Katharine was fifteen years older than Edith and originally took a maternal role with her, the two women bonded so entirely that they kept a diary together and united under a single name.[2]

The importance of nondifferentiated intimate connections between women suggests the need to think about the different patterns of male and female erotic attraction and to ponder what conditions—such as women's confinement to sex-segregated space and lack of access to the heterogeneity of public places—may be responsible for the prominence of the eroticization of sameness in the history of female same-sex sexuality. We might also consider what lies behind the long history of the eroticization of difference in male same-sex sexuality.

In another way, too, we can see that paying as much attention to women as to men leads to a different view of the broad sweep of the history of same-sex sexuality. Based on the U.S. and European experience, scholars have argued that into at least the early twentieth century, men who played the insertive role in sex did not warrant labeling as homosexual, and in fact, such sexual activity could enhance a man's masculinity. Still today in some cultures and subcultures, notably in much of Latin America and in Latino and African American cultures within the United States, as long as men do not play the enclosing role, their sexual activity has no meaning for their sexual identities. But at different points in different times and places, heterosexuality for men came to be defined as never participating in same-sex acts, no matter the sexual role. This is the story of the creation of homosexuality and heterosexuality.

But this tale has nothing to do with women. Women who enclosed other women's fingers or dildos or tongues along with men's penises were not perceived as more feminine than women who did not, even if they were sometimes seen as more "normal" than the women who made love to them. But penetrating or enclosing was not the heart of the story. Recognizing that women could be sexual with one another and then confronting the fact that economic and social change loosened the bonds of compulsory marriage for women and created the possibility for women to choose one another have more to do with the creation of "lesbianism" than the sexual acts in which women engaged.

Finally, what we have seen across time and place undermines a Western-dominated narrative of progress. A global view makes clear that both private and public spaces are important for love between women, that erotic love between women has sometimes fit nicely into all sorts of heterosexual societal arrangements, and that the emergence of an identity based on sexual object choice is a minor part of the story of sapphistries. That is not to deny the value of societies that make a more welcoming place for open avowal of same-sex love, but we need to recognize that acceptance can take many forms and that women have been creative in making space for their love and desire.

Perhaps nothing illustrates the need to think beyond the traditional Western narrative more than the history of finger-pointing about the cultural origins of female same-sex sexuality. As we have seen, there is a long tradition in European history of associating female same-sex sexuality with Asia, Africa, and the Middle East. There women grew large clitorises, there women engaged in all sorts of shameful acts with one another, hidden away in harems or polygynous households. But now the tables are turned, and lesbianism is perceived as a Western phenomenon in countries around the world and as a white perversion by many communities of color in white-dominated societies such as the United States. The rise of sexology in Europe and later in the United States, as we know, has a great deal to do with this shift in perspective. As a narrative of homosexuality spread across the globe, and later lesbian and gay movements transmitted a notion of a lesbian identity, loving and desiring women came to seem something imported, something that undermined national or ethnic strength and solidarity. So in Thailand, it is the educated urban classes that have absorbed the sexological concepts of homosexuality and the government's attack on same-sex sexuality as anti-Thai, while in rural villages there remains some acceptance of masculine women and marriage between two women.[3] In the Society Islands of French Polynesia, where there are female *māhū* (half-man, half-woman) who make love to women, *lesbiennes* are French or foreign but definitely not "truly Polynesian."[4] Throughout Africa, people believe that same-sex sexuality does not exist in their countries except where it was imposed by foreigners.[5] According to the minister for women's affairs in Indonesia, "lesbianism is not part of Indonesia culture or state ideology."[6] In Jamaica, loving women is "a white people ting."[7] An Indian critic of *Fire* proclaimed that it was unfair "to show such things which are not part of Indian culture," calling the film "sort of a social AIDS."[8] Throughout the Arab-Islamic world, homosexuality is often seen as a disease that can be caught from foreigners and passed on to others. When a group of Egyptian men was arrested at the Queen Boat nightclub in 2001, the press reported that they "imported the perverse ideas from a European group."[9] When Mahmoud Ahmadinejad, the president of Iran, spoke at Columbia University in 2007, he announced that there were no homosexuals in Iran, not even one.[10]

Women around the world challenge the notion that desire, sex, and love between women is foreign to their cultures. An Australian Aboriginal lesbian rejects the idea that same-sex sexuality was imported into her country: "I get that all the time. . . . As far as I know, homosexuality has existed here for a long time, it's not a white man's disease—it's probably the only thing we didn't catch off the white man!"[11] Lesbians in India work to counteract the notions that lesbianism is Western, that the term *lesbian* has no meaning in an Indian context, and that because there is no vocabulary for lesbianism, it does not exist.[12] In fact, what societies in many different places did import from Western colonial powers was institutionalized homophobia, since Christian doctrine and history played such a major role in denouncing homosexuality.[13] But it is important to see that both the development of the concept of the homosexual as a kind of person and the growth of gay and lesbian movements transnationally have had consequences in shifting global notions of the source of same-sex sexuality.

Despite the continuing long history of oppression and murderous violence directed at some times and in some places toward women who desired women, let us end on a hopeful, a utopian, note. First of all, there are groups of women all around the world who are resisting oppression, sometimes in explicit recognition of the past we have explored here. Sappho continues to echo in the names of organizations and publications, and in Johannesburg, South Africa, a building occupied by lesbians and gay men took the name "Radclyffe Hall."[14]

So let us reinvent the fanciful tale with which we started in order to imagine not only a beginning we cannot know but a future toward which we must work:

For a long period of time, things did not go so well with the goddesses' children. Some of them acquired more than they needed and set themselves above the others. Those who could not give birth turned that disability into superiority and lorded it over those who could. Some proclaimed their own color and physical characteristics better than all others. And some decided that only one kind of pleasure was right. They fought and stole and enslaved and raped and murdered and waged war as a result of these differences. And they nearly laid waste to the lovely Earth.

But then—and how we do not know—the goddesses turned things around again. They restored the flowers and trees and plants, the fish and birds and insects, the animals that swim or fly or crawl or walk. Once again people found what they needed to eat to sustain themselves and did not long for more. Once again they honored the goddesses by creating beautiful things and inventing

*fanciful tales and making pleasure in diverse ways with their bodies. They rec-
ognized that their differences were nothing to kill over, that they were all in
everything together. So once again, every time they created beauty or understanding or pleasure, of whatever kind, the goddesses smiled.*

Notes

Chapter 1

1. Pat (now Patrick) Califia (1980) wrote a book about lesbian sexuality called *Sapphistry*. Margaret Reynolds (2000) titles a chapter of her edited collection, *The Sappho Companion*, "Sapphistories."
2. S. Murray 1997, 99.
3. Robertson 1999, 9.
4. Sang 2003, 128.
5. Kizinska 1999.
6. "Court Rules Lesbians Are Not Just from Lesbos," July 22, 2008, Reuters website, http://www.reuters.com/article/OddlyEnoughNews/idUSN2231197820080722/ (accessed April 29, 2009); I am grateful to Birgitte Søland for this reference.
7. Malti-Douglas 2001, 124.
8. Brooten 1996, 66.
9. Ruan and Bullough 1992, 218.
10. Kendall 1998, 230.
11. Vanita 2004b, 17.
12. Arguelles and Rich 1984, 687.
13. Quoted in Bonnet 1981, 23 (my translation).
14. Quoted in Gowing 2006, 126.
15. See, for example, M. Sharma 2007; Thadani 1996.
16. Rich 1980; see discussion of the issues surrounding Rich's original work in Rich et al. 2003.
17. Blanche Cook, in a pioneering article, argued that "women who love women, who choose women to nurture and support and to create a living environment in which to work creatively and independently, are lesbians" (Cook 1977: 48). Lillian Faderman's *Surpassing the Love of Men* defines *lesbian* as "a relationship in which two women's strongest emotions and affections are directed toward each other" (Faderman 1981: 17–18). In my earlier work (Rupp 1989), I attempted to navigate between the poles of proclaiming all women who in some way loved women *lesbians* and denying the desire and eroticism of relationships between women who would not have claimed the identity. Martha Vicinus, in her recent

study, argues for the importance of sexual desire in determining what women are part of "lesbian" history (Vicinus 2004), and Arlene Stein, in a study of U.S. lesbian feminism in the 1980s, problematizes the relationship between sexual desire and acts, on the one hand, and lesbian identity, on the other (Stein 1997). Terry Castle, in her introduction to her monumental collection *The Literature of Lesbianism*, eschews the idea that we can know who was a "lesbian writer" because we do not know if writing another woman a romantic poem, fantasizing about making love to a woman, sharing a bed with a woman, living with a woman for fifty years, or even bringing a woman to orgasm means that one is a lesbian (Castle 2003, 3).

18. Bennett 2000.

19. Smith-Rosenberg 1976.

20. Faderman 1981, 17.

21. Vicinus 2004; Marcus 2007.

22. Quoted in Wieringa and Blackwood 1999, 6.

23. Halberstam 1998, 54.

24. Jones 2007 is a study of gay and lesbian historical fiction that argues for its importance in understanding gay and lesbian history.

25. Quoted in Holoch and Nestle 1999, xvii.

26. Vance 1989.

27. Traub 2007, 125. In her words, "recurrent explanatory meta-logics" give a "sense of consistency" to lesbian history over time. These meta-logics "draw their specific content from perennial axes of social definition" that periodically come into play, and we can identify "cycles of salience" in which meanings reappear, configured somewhat differently, over time.

28. Traub 2007, 127.

29. See, for example, Greenberg 1988, Spencer 1995, S. Murray 2000, and Halperin 2002. The latter offers four "pre-homosexual categories of male sex and gender deviance" (109): effeminacy, "active" sodomy with a male of lesser status, friendship, and passivity or inversion.

30. Halperin 2002, 79.

31. On globalization and sexuality and a critique of Western-dominated narratives, see especially Thadani 1996; Povinelli and Chauncey 1999; Vanita and Kidwai 2000; Grewal and Kaplan 2001; Cruz-Malavé and Manalansan 2002; King 2002; Vanita 2002; Manalansan 2003; Boellstorff 2005; Wieringa, Blackwood, and Bhaiya 2007.

32. The most comprehensive syntheses of the history of same-sex sexuality are Greenberg 1988, Spencer 1995, S. Murray 2000, and Crompton 2003, although all include more material on men than women. Duberman, Vicinus, and Chauncey 1989 and Aldrich 2006b are anthologies that cover a broad sweep of time. Studies devoted to women mostly either concentrate on a specific period, as does Brooten 1996; or a particular country, for example, Donoghue 1993 and Sang 2003; or both, as is the case with Faderman 1991.

Chapter 2

1. Davis 1971.
2. Cavin 1985, 24i.
3. See Bachofen 1967 and Engels 1972.
4. Moraga 2000 and Anzaldúa 2002. I am grateful to Sharon Doetsch (Doetsch 2004) for her discussion of this reinterpretation.
5. Lessing 2007, ix.
6. Lessing 2007, 27.
7. Lessing 2007, 144.
8. Lessing 2007, 32.
9. Lessing 2007, 41, 62.
10. Stone 1976.
11. Gimbutas 1982, 1989, 1991.
12. See, for example, the discussion of Gimbutas in Talalay 1994 and Ruether 2005. See also the eloquent argument against matriarchal origins in Eller 2000.
13. "Origin Tale (1931)," in Elledge 2002.
14. Van Over 1980, 68.
15. Vanita and Kidwai 2000, 12–13.
16. Quoted in Thadani 1996, 25.
17. Wieringa 2007, 28.
18. Diamant, 1997. I am grateful to April Bible for giving me a copy of this book, one of her favorites.
19. Diamant 1997, 15.
20. Diamant 1997, 186.
21. Diamant 1997, 188.
22. Hamilton 1942, 287.
23. Wilde 1999, 28. The following account comes from Wilde as well.
24. Wilde 1999, 39–40.
25. Quoted in Wilde 1999, 43.
26. Cavin 1985, 65.
27. Quoted in Wilde 1999, 159.
28. See Pöllauer 2002.
29. Quoted in Cavin 1985, 250.
30. Quoted in Cavin 1985, 248.
31. Wilde 1999, 173.
32. Blackwood and Wieringa 1999, 43.
33. Natarajan 2007.
34. Quoted in Penrose 2001, 19.
35. Sobol 1972, 145.
36. Sobol 1972, 146.
37. Pöllauer 2002, 138.

38. Quoted in Cavin 1985, 75–76.

39. Quoted in Wilde 1999, 174.

40. Jong 2003.

41. Jong 2003, 164.

42. Jong 2003, 170.

43. For a psychoanalytical interpretation, see Slater 1968; see also Keuls 1985.

44. See Patai 1967, 209–11.

45. Van Over 1980, 214–16; see also Halperin 1989. For a detailed discussion of evidence of goddess worship during the Neolithic period, see the controversial work of Gimbutas 1991.

46. See Downing 1997.

47. Downing 1997, 424–25.

48. See Rehak 2002.

49. Blackwood and Wieringa 1999, 49.

50. Blackwood 1986, 10–13.

51. Shostak 1981.

52. Quoted in S. Murray 2000, 361.

53. Blackwood 1986, 11.

54. Rich 1980.

Chapter 3

1. "He is more than a hero," in Sappho 1958, 39.

2. Brooten 1996, 61, citing Olyan 1995.

3. Greenberg 1988, 124–83.

4. Kimball 1993, 16.

5. Quoted in Goldin 2002, 127–28.

6. Ruan 1991, 135–36.

7. See Goldin 2002, 6–7.

8. Vanita and Kidwai 2000, 24–25.

9. Thadani 1996, 59.

10. Sweet and Zwilling 1993, 597.

11. Sweet and Zwilling 1993, 597.

12. Vanita and Kidwai 2000.

13. See Pomeroy 1975. On Plutarch, see Cantarella 1992, 84.

14. Cited in S. Murray 2000, 204.

15. Pomeroy 1975, 55.

16. See Pomeroy 1975 and Dover 1978.

17. Rabinowitz 2002.

18. Cantarella 1992, 92; and Brooten 1996, 41.

19. See Brooten 1996, 42; and Halperin 2002, 51. I should add that through most of the history I consider here, tribadism does not seem to assume any kind of penetration, just rubbing.

20. Cantarella 1992, 92–93.

21. See the discussion of the controversy over the translation and interpretation of this song in Cantarella 1992, 86–87.

22. Brooten 1996, 4–5.

23. Cantarella 1992, 78–84. See also Snyder 1995, a short book intended for young adults that is a very accessible yet also sophisticated analysis of Sappho's life and lyrics; and Snyder 1997.

24. Quoted in Cantarella 1992, 80.

25. See Hallett 1979.

26. Pomeroy 1975, 54.

27. Cantarella 1992, 87. See also Brooten 1996, 22; and Halperin 2002, 50.

28. Quoted in Snyder 1997, 8.

29. See Klinck 2005.

30. Quoted in Snyder 1997, 56.

31. Quoted in Downing 1997, 439.

32. Winkler 1993.

33. Quoted in Skinner 2002, 70.

34. Quoted in Klinck 2005, 194–95.

35. Jong 1973.

36. Jong 2003, xvi.

37. The following discussion is based on Brooten 1996.

38. Brooten here bases her discussion on Hallett 1989.

39. Quoted in Brooten 1996, 46–47.

40. Quoted in Brooten 1996, 47.

41. Quoted in Brooten 1996, 63. The following discussion of Jewish practices is based on Brooten as well.

42. Brooten 1996.

43. One of Brooten's most vociferous critics is Halperin 2002. See also the forum Castelli et al. 1998.

44. Boswell 1980.

45. Brooten 1996, 86, 87.

46. Quoted in Brooten 1996, 87.

47. Quoted in Brooten 1996, 121, 123.

48. Brooten 1996, 150, 162–63, 166. Brennan 1997 questions the connection between clitoridectomy and *tribades* on the basis of the texts.

49. Brooten 1996, chap. 6.

50. Quoted in Manniche 1987, 22.

51. Brooten 1996, 322, 332, 139. See also Brennan 1997, 6–7; and Cameron 1998, 141, 150.

52. See especially Cameron 1998.

53. See D'Angelo 1990.

54. Jong 2003, 314–15.

Chapter 4

1. Quoted in Boswell 1980, 220.

2. Jong 2003, 66.

3. Boswell 1980 and 1994.

4. See Kuefler 2006, a collection of essays titled *The Boswell Thesis.*

5. Boswell 1980, xv.

6. Brooten 1996, 362.

7. Quoted in Boswell 1980, 158.

8. Boswell 1980, 265.

9. Romans 1:26.

10. Brooten 1996, 301.

11. See Brennan 1997, 7.

12. Brooten 1996, 61. Brooten relies on Olyan 1994.

13. Quoted in Brooten 1996, 66.

14. Duran 1993, 181–97.

15. Quoted in S. Murray 1997, 97; Murray cites Bellamy 1979, 37.

16. See Wafer 1997.

17. Quoted in Duran 1993, 182.

18. Quoted in Crompton 1997, 150. El-Rouayheb 2005 analyzes the acceptance of male-male erotic love but the condemnation of sexual relations.

19. Roth 1996, 322. S. Murray (1997, 99) uses the term "Arab Sappho."

20. Quoted in AbuKhalil 1993, 34.

21. Quoted in AbuKhalil 1993, 34.

22. The following discussion is based on A. Sharma 1993, quotation on 77.

23. A. Sharma 1993, 52.

24. A. Sharma 1993, 52, 53; the term *kanya* comes from Thadani 1996, who also discusses these laws.

25. Vanita 2005a, 558.

26. Thadani 1996, 54.

27. Quoted in A. Sharma 1993, 68.

28. The following discussion is based on Cabezón 1993.

29. Quoted in S. Murray 1997, 98.

30. Quoted in Traub 2002, 200.

31. Quoted in S. Murray 1997, 97.

32. S. Murray 1997, 100.

33. Quoted in S. Murray 1997, 98.

34. Blackwood 2000, 354.

35. Quoted in Malti-Douglas 2001, 128.

36. Malti-Douglas 2001, 129.

37. Doniger and Kakar 2002, 125–26; on the use of the term *Oriental,* see the editors' introduction, xxxv.

38. Vanita 2004b, 34.

39. Quoted in Vanita 2005a, 552, 553, 554; see also Vanita 2001, 244.

40. Quoted in Vanita 2005a, 566.

41. Thadani 1996, 66.

42. Quoted in Sinnott 2004, 49.

43. Penrose 2001, 26–27.

44. Pflugfelder 1999, 23.

45. Quoted in Hinsch 1990, 175; see also Ruan and Bullough 1992.

46. Quoted in Hinsch 1990, 174.

47. Quoted in Ruan and Bullough 1992, 220.

48. Cabezón 1993, 84.

49. Quoted in Sang 2003, 49.

50. Hatem 1986.

51. All quotations from Wawrytko 1993, 202–3, 213–14.

52. Quoted in Blackwood and Wieringa 1999, 41–42.

53. Baum 1993, 23; see also Morgan and Wieringa 2005.

54. Evans-Pritchard 1970, 1431–32.

55. Zwilling 1992.

56. Zwilling 1992.

57. Quoted in Wieringa 2007, 32.

58. Wawrytko 1993, 203.

59. Levin 1996, 341.

60. Quoted in Brown 1986, 6.

61. Quoted in Brown 1986, 7.

62. Quoted in Brown 1986, 7.

63. All quoted in J. Murray 1996, 198.

64. Quoted in J. Murray 1996, 196.

65. This discussion is based on Wilfong 2002.

66. Quoted in Wilfong 2002, 310, 316, 317.

67. The following discussion is based on Brown 1986.

68. Quoted in Brown 1986, 117–18, 120, 125.

69. Santos 1984. I am grateful to José Ramos-Rebollo for calling my attention to this novel.

70. Santos 1984, quotations from 33, 31, 44.

71. Quoted in the appendix to J. Murray 1996, 211.

72. Quoted in Matter 1986, 85.

73. Quoted in Schibanoff 2001, 51.

74. Quoted in Schibanoff 2001, 54–55, 51, 49.

75. Quoted in Lochrie 1997, 188.

76. Bynum 1987 takes the nursing position; Lochrie 1997 argues for the wound as vulva. The additional evidence I cite is from Lochrie.

77. This discussion is based on Holsinger 1993.

78. Quoted in Holsinger 1993, 101, 117.

79. Quoted in J. Murray 1996, 199.

80. Quoted in Wiethaus 2003, 309.

81. The following discussion is based on Lavezzo 1996.

82. Quoted in Lavezzo 1996, 181, 182, 187, 190.

83. Quoted in Vanita 2001, 240.

84. See Richards 1990.

85. Quoted in J. Murray 1996, 216–17.

86. Quoted in Holler 1999, 224.

87. Quoted in Tortorici 2007, 365.

88. McNally 2001.

89. Le Fanu 1973; see McNally 2001.

90. Brooks 2000.

91. Quoted in Richards 1990, 143.

92. Quoted in Evans 1978, 76.

93. Quoted in Richards 1990, 75.

94. Quoted by Brooten 1996, 317.

95. Heinrich Krämer and Jacob Sprenger, "The *Malleus Maleficarum*," in Kors and Peters 1972, 151.

96. See Zika 2003.

97. Quoted in Mello e Souza 2003, 74.

98. See M. Murray 1921; Russell 1972; Evans 1978.

99. Levin 1989, 204.

100. Dworkin 1974.

101. Daly 1978.

102. See Adler 1979.

103. Quoted in Maitland 1996, 75, 76, 77, 78, 79.

104. Quoted in Crompton 1980–81, 13.

105. Benkov 2001, 110.

106. Quoted in Hinds 2001, 27.

107. Levin 1989, 203–4.

108. Quoted in Bennett 2000, 18; this account is based also on Benkov 2001 and J. Murray 1996.

109. Quoted in J. Murray 1996, 202.

110. Quoted in Benkov 2001, 114.

111. Quoted in Benkov 2001, 115.

112. Puff 2000, 44.

113. Puff 2000, 43.

114. Puff 2000, 44.

115. Puff 2000, 46, 45.

116. Quoted in Monter 1980–81, 46–47.

117. Quoted in J. Murray 1996, 200.

118. Quoted in J. Murray 1996, 200–201.

119. Quoted in Malti-Douglas 2001, 134.

120. Quoted in J. Murray 1996, 200.

121. Quoted in S. Murray 1997, 147.

122. Quoted in R. Clark 2001, 166–67.

123. Quoted in Amer 2001, 185, 186, 186–87, 192.

124. See J. Murray 1996, 205–6.

125. Quoted in Bogin 1976, 133.

126. Esquibel 2006.

127. "Don't Go, My Darling. I Don't Want This to End Yet," in De la Cruz 1997, 35. For a fictionalized version of Sor Juana's life, see Gaspar de Alba 1999.

Chapter 5

1. Ramet 1996, 4.

2. Penrose 2001.

3. Quoted in Bullough 1974, 1383.

4. Roscoe 1997, 67.

5. Quoted in Sweet and Zwilling 1993, 601.

6. See Nanda 1990 and Reddy 2005.

7. Quoted in Penrose 2001, 16. There is debate about the translation of this passage; see Vanita and Kidwai 2000, 49–50, and Doniger and Kakar 2002.

8. Ruan and Bullough 1992, 219.

9. Quoted in Penrose 2001, 16.

10. Penrose (2001) thinks they do, as does Wilhelm (2007), who describes the *svairini* as part of *tritiya-prakriti*, or the third sex, in an article on the website of the Gay and Lesbian Vaishnava Association.

11. Callender and Kochems 1983 reports 113 cultures recognizing what they call the "berdache" status, with only 30 of them including female berdaches. The term *berdache*, a French word derived from the Arabic word for a boy slave used for sexual purposes, is the term used by Europeans.

12. See Blackwood 1984.

13. Blackwood 1986 argues for "cross-gender"; Callender and Kochems 1983, Roscoe 1996, and Whitehead 1981 opt for "mixed" or "third" and "fourth gender"; and Lang 1997 and Williams 1986 use the term "two-spirit."

14. Devereux 1937, 515.

15. Blackwood 1984.

16. Schaeffer 1965.

17. Schaeffer 1965; see also Williams 1986.

18. Quoted in Schaeffer 1965, 202.

19. Quoted in Schaeffer 1965, 203, 196.

20. Quoted in Schaeffer 1965, 206.

21. Schaeffer 1965.

22. Quoted in Devereux 1937, 519

23. Quoted in Devereux 1937, 523.

24. Quoted in Devereux 1937, 525.

25. Quoted in Fur 2006, 496.

26. Westphal-Hellbusch 1997.

27. Grémaux 1993.

28. Quoted in Grémaux 1993, 262.

29. Phillimore 1991.

30. Oboler 1980.

31. Quoted in Carrier and Murray 1998, 259.

32. Quoted in Carrier and Murray 1998, 263.

33. Lorde 1984, 49–50.

34. Krige 1974; Oboler 1980; Tietmeyer 1985; Amadiume 1987. For a full discussion of this issue, see Wieringa 2005.

35. Amadiume 1987, 7.

36. Herskovits 1937, 338; see Blackwood and Wieringa 1999.

37. Oboler 1980; see also Carrier and Murray 1998.

38. Quoted in Donoghue 1993, 66.

39. Quoted in Donoghue 1993, 67.

40. Quoted in Rupp 1999, 42.

41. Quoted in Donoghue 1993, 81.

42. Quoted in Donoghue 1993, 84.

43. The transcript of the trial has been translated and published; see Eriksson 1980–81, 28. All of the following quotations are from Eriksson.

44. All in Crompton 1980–81, 17.

45. Crompton 1980–81.

46. The following account is based on Burshatin 1996.

47. Quoted in Burshatin 1996, 111.

48. Quoted in Burshatin 1996, 111.

49. Quoted in Burshatin 1996, 106.

50. Quoted in Burshatin 1996, 106.

51. Quoted in Burshatin 1996, 108.

52. Quoted in Burshatin 1996, 107.

53. Quoted in Burshatin 1996, 119.

54. Quoted in Dekker and van de Pol 1989, xv.

55. Quoted in Dekker and van de Pol 1989, 15.

56. De Erauso 1996, 17, 28.

57. Quoted in Donoghue 1993, 79.

58. Lyons 2007.

59. Quoted in Dekker and van de Pol 1989, 26.

60. Quoted in Dekker and van de Pol 1989, 68.

61. Quoted in Dekker and van de Pol 1989, 52.

62. Quoted in Dekker and van de Pol 1989, 59.

63. Quoted in Dekker and van de Pol 1989, 51.

64. Quoted in Dekker and van de Pol 1989, 53.

65. Quoted in Dekker and van de Pol 1989, 67.

66. Chesser 1998; see also Chesser 2008.

67. Quoted in Chesser 1998, 60.

68. Coleman 2001.

69. Kay 1998. On Billy Tipton, see Middlebrook 1998.

70. Kay 1998, 18–19.

71. Kay 1998, 21.

72. Kay 1998, 35.

73. Kay 1998, 22.

74. Kay 1998, 40.

75. Kay 1998, 95.

76. Kay 1998, 251–52.

77. Kay 1998, 198.

Chapter 6

1. Galford 1985, quotation on back cover.

2. Galford 1985, 221.

3. Galford 1985, 37.

4. Galford 1985, 41.

5. Galford 1985, 46–47.

6. Quoted in Orgel 1992, 20–21.

7. Quoted in Faderman 1981, 57.

8. Quoted in Krantz 1995, 6.

9. Quoted in Krantz 1995, 16.

10. Quoted in Krantz 1995, 14.

11. Gowing 2006, 140.

12. Everard 1994. Van der Meer 1991 says that *lollen* sometimes referred specifically to same-sex acts and that, by the twentieth century at the least, *lollepot* had come to mean "lesbian."

13. Van der Meer 1991, 428, 433.

14. Van der Meer 1991, 429, 434.

15. Dekker and van de Pol 1989, 37–38.

16. The following account is based on Norton 2000.

17. Quoted in Donoghue 1993, 96.

18. Quoted in Donoghue 1993, 97.

19. Norton 2000.

20. Wieringa 2007, 33.

21. Quoted in Miller 2000, 70.

22. Everard 1986.

23. Quoted in Sautman 1996, 191.

24. Quoted in Sautman 1996, 190.

25. Quoted in San Francisco Lesbian and Gay History Project 1989, 188.

26. Quotation from Miller 2000, 67; on Lucknow courtesans, see Vanita 2004b, 17, citing Oldenberg 1997, 149. See also Nestle 1987.

27. Quoted in Gowing 2006, 140.

28. Quoted in Gowing 2006, 140.

29. Quoted in Sautman 1996, 191–92.

30. Quoted in Pflugfelder 1999, 189–90.

31. Quoted in Epprecht 2004, 99.

32. See Kunzel 2008 and Freedman 1996a and 1996b.

33. Quoted in Katz 1983, 85–86.

34. Quoted in Sautman 1996, 183.

35. Van der Meer 1991, 432.

36. Van der Meer 1991, 433.

37. Quoted in Wieringa 2007, 34.

38. Mustola and Rydström 2007, 44.

39. Quoted in Sautman 1996, 195.

40. Kunzel 2008; see also Freedman 1996b.

41. Quoted in Traub 2002, 54.

42. Quoted in Traub 2002, 157.

43. Quoted in Robinson 2006, 98.

44. Quoted in Donoghue 1993, 233; see also Robinson 2006.

45. Quoted in Elfenbein 1999, 101.

46. Quoted in Donoghue 1993, 146.

47. Quoted in Donoghue 1993, 147.

48. Quoted in Robinson 2001, 53, 54.

49. Quoted in Blanc 2001, 76.

50. Quoted in Merrick 1996, 41; see also Bonnet 1981.

51. Quoted in Merrick 1996, 41.

52. Quoted in Merrick 1996, 44.

53. Quoted in Merrick and Ragan 2001, 208.

54. Merrick 1996; Colwill 1996.

55. Quoted in Colwill 1996, 54.

56. Quoted in Colwill 1996, 63.

57. Quoted in Bonnet 1981, 162 (my translation).

58. Quoted in Merrick 1996, 45.

59. Quoted in Donoghue 2004, 593 (italics in the original).

60. See Lanser 2001, which analyzes the writings that represented tribades as members of communities and secret societies.

61. Topley 1975. See also Sankar 1986.

62. Sang 2003, 52.

63. Sang 2003, 53.

64. Hinsch 1990; Ruan and Bullough 1992.

65. Topley 1975; Barnes 1987.

66. Ruan and Bullough 1992, 219–20.

67. Quoted in Hinsch 1990, 178.

68. Topley 1975, 76.

69. Sang 2003, 59.

70. Sang 2003, 59.

71. Quoted in Sang 2003, 60–61.

72. Sang 2003, 61.

73. See Petievich 2002. Petievich and Vanita have different takes on *Rekhti*; Petievich downplays the same-sex eroticism, focusing on its male creation and suppression by Urdu literary critics. My analysis is based heavily on Vanita 2004b.

74. Petievich 2002; quotation from Vanita 2004b, 18.

75. Quoted in Vanita 2004b, 19.

76. Quoted in Vanita 2004b, 20.

77. Quoted in Vanita 2004b, 48.

78. Quoted in Vanita 2004b, 24.

79. Quoted in Vanita 2004b, 28.

80. Quoted in Vanita 2004b, 28.

81. Quoted in Vanita 2004b, 27.

82. Quoted in Vanita 2004b, 28.

83. Quoted in Vanita 2004b, 29. Vanita does not interpret this poem any differently than the others, but it strikes me as more designed to titillate.

84. Quoted in Vanita 2004b, 47.

85. Quoted in Vanita and Kidwai 2000, 222; the title of the poem is translated as "Tribad Testimonials" in Petievich 2002.

86. There is an enormous literature on romantic friendship. The classic works are Smith-Rosenberg 1976 and Faderman 1981; see also Moore 1992, Stanley 1992, Vicinus 1992 and 2004, Martin 1994, Diggs 1995, Rupp 2001. More recently, scholarship based on a combination of literary texts and historical documents has shifted the debate. Traub 2002 argues for a "renaissance" of lesbianism in seventeenth-century England, placing growing suspicion about intimate friendships between women in the late seventeenth century, a result of

the rediscovery of the clitoris and the reemergence of the figure of the tribade. Marcus 2007 argues for the existence of different phenomena in nineteenth-century England: female friendship, which involved the eroticization of femininity; unrequited love of one woman for another; and marriages between women, which were understood to include sex. All, she argues, were central to the sex, gender, and marriage systems of Victorian England rather than an alternative to heteronormativity.

87. Vicinus 1984.
88. Quoted in Lützen 1990, 97 (my translation).
89. Quoted in Vicinus 1984, 613.
90. Quoted in Faderman 1981, 79, 80.
91. Quoted in Smith-Rosenberg 1976, 4–5.
92. Everard 1986.
93. Quoted in Smith-Rosenberg 1976, 6, 7–8.
94. Quoted in Faderman 1981, 164, 165.
95. Quoted in D'Emilio and Freedman 1988, 126.
96. See Vicinus 2004.
97. Quoted in Vicinus 2004, 6.
98. Quoted in Vicinus 2004, 9.
99. Quoted in Marcus 2007, 46.
100. Quoted in Donoghue 1993, 265.
101. Quoted in Donoghue 1993, 150.
102. Quoted in Donoghue 1993, 148.
103. Lister 1988, 210.
104. Quoted in Vicinus 2004, 15.
105. Quoted in Vicinus 2004, 15.
106. Faderman 1981 and 1993.
107. Quoted in Knowlton 1997, 48.
108. Quoted in Frančíková 2000, 24.
109. Quoted in Hull 1987, 139.
110. See Frančíková 2000, 24.
111. Quoted in Hansen 1995, 159, 160.
112. Quoted in Hansen 1995, 160.
113. Quoted in Hansen 1995, 162, 164.
114. "Female rake" is the term used in Vicinus 2004.
115. Quoted in Vicinus 2004, 22.
116. Quoted in Vicinus 2004, 23.
117. On Lister's feelings for Walker, see A. Clark 1996.
118. Quoted in Vicinus 2004, 26.
119. Lister 1988, 105.
120. Quoted in Vicinus 2004, 21.
121. Lister 1992, 65.

122. Lister 1992, 85. Halberstam 1998 sees this passage as clear evidence of "an active and functional but preidentitarian female masculinity," 72.

123. Lister 1988, 164, 48–49.

124. Lister 1988, 145.

125. Lister 1988, 297.

126. Lister 1992, 49.

127. Lister 1988, 291.

128. For a different interpretation, see Halberstam, who thinks Lister may be referring to her own use of a dildo (1998, 67).

129. On Cushman's circle, see Vicinus 2004 and Marcus 2007; on Lewis, see Richardson 2002.

130. Quoted in Vicinus 2004, 36.

131. Quoted in Vicinus 2004, 39–40, 41.

132. Quoted in Vicinus 2004, 41.

133. Quoted in Vicinus 2004, 43.

134. Quoted in Marcus 2007, 201.

135. Quoted in Vicinus 2004, 43.

136. Quoted in Vicinus 2004, 39.

137. Quoted in Faderman 1993, 147.

138. Quoted in Faderman 1993, 281.

139. Quoted in Faderman 1993, 282.

140. See Faderman 1993, xiii–xiv.

141. Quoted in Vicinus 2004, 65.

142. Quoted in Faderman 1993, 82.

143. Faderman 1993, 153.

144. A. Clark 2005.

145. Lister 1988, 273.

Chapter 7

1. On *Fire,* see Gopinath 2005.

2. See Carton 2006, 310.

3. Furth 1999; see Sang 2003.

4. Laqueur 1990. Sang 2003 makes the comparison between Chinese and European conceptions. See Traub 2002 and Park 1997 for critiques of Laqueur's thesis.

5. A. Clark 1996, 40.

6. Traub 2002; see also Park 1997.

7. See Gowing 2006; Traub 2002; Park 1997.

8. Quoted in Gowing 2006, 127.

9. Quoted in Traub 2002, 194.

10. Quoted in Traub 2002, 200.

11. Trumbach 1993 has the English sapphist being classified as a separate gender at the end of the eighteenth century, following the model of the earlier sodomite.

12. This and the following text from Krafft-Ebing quoted in Smith-Rosenberg 1989, 269. See also Terry 1999 for a full discussion of sexology.

13. Quoted in Smith-Rosenberg 1989, 270.

14. Quoted in Vicinus 1984, 619.

15. Quoted in Newton 1989, 270.

16. This and the following quotations from Forel quoted in Terry 1999, 63–64.

17. Quoted in Chauncey 1982–83, 122.

18. Everard 1986.

19. Quoted in Chauncey 1982–83, 138.

20. On Japan, see Pflugfelder 1999 and 2005.

21. Quoted in Pflugfelder 1999, 176.

22. See Robertson 1999.

23. Quoted in Pflugfelder 2005, 150.

24. Pflugfelder 2005, 143.

25. Pflugfelder 2005, 144.

26. Quoted in Pflugfelder 2005, 144.

27. Sang 2003.

28. Sang 2003, 24.

29. Quoted in Sang 2003, 107, 108.

30. See Oram 2007.

31. See Duggan 2000.

32. Quoted in Duggan 2000, 202, 203.

33. Quoted in Duggan 2000, 100.

34. Quoted in Duggan 2000, 106.

35. Pflugfelder 1999, 176–77.

36. Quoted in Pflugfelder 1999, 177.

37. Quoted in Mak 2004, 54.

38. Quoted in Mak 2004, 56.

39. Quoted in Mak 2004, 59.

40. Quoted in Mak 2004, 61.

41. Quoted in Mak 2004, 62.

42. Quoted in Marcus 2007, 49.

43. Quoted in Vicinus 2004, 83.

44. Quoted in Vicinus 2004, 127.

45. Vicinus 2004, 134.

46. Quoted in Faderman 1991, 53.

47. Vicinus 2004.

48. Quoted in Sang 2003, 139.

49. Quoted in Sang 2003, 144.

50. Quoted in Faderman 1991, 54.

51. See Freedman 1996a.

52. Horowitz 1994.

53. Quoted in Rupp 1997, 582.

54. Quoted in Doan 2001, 138, 137.

55. Quoted in Smith-Rosenberg 1989, 273.

56. Quoted in Doan 2001, 144.

57. See Vicinus 2004, 217.

58. Quoted in Newton 1989, 291; see also Doan 2001.

59. See Terry 1999.

60. Quoted in Terry 1999, 227.

61. Quoted in Terry 1999, 242.

62. Quoted in Terry 1999, 243.

63. Quoted in Jennings 2007b, 34.

64. Hall 1950, 26.

65. Hall 1950, 106.

66. Hall 1950, 146.

67. Hall 1950, 154.

68. Hall 1950, 204.

69. Sang 2003, 128.

Chapter 8

1. Billing and Schwabach 1997; see Jelavich 1997.

2. Ellis 1920, 368.

3. Ellis 1920, 373.

4. Ellis 1920, 376.

5. Ellis 1920, 378.

6. Ellis, 1920, 381.

7. Ellis 1920, 383–84.

8. Ellis 1920, 374.

9. Quoted in Faderman 1991, 35.

10. Pflugfelder 2005. This discussion of Japanese schoolgirls is based on Plugfelder's chapter and on Wu 2007.

11. Quoted in Pflugfelder 2005, 147.

12. Quoted in Pflugfelder 2005, 148.

13. Quoted in Frühstück 2003, 70.

14. Quoted in Pflugfelder 2005, 145.

15. Pflugfelder 2005, 170.

16. Quoted in Pflugfelder 2005, 171.

17. Quoted in Pflugfelder 2005, 145.

18. Pflugfelder 2005, 153–54. See Vanita 2005b for a discussion of joint suicide as a rite of marriage.

19. Quoted in Robertson 1999, 28.

20. Quoted in Pflugfelder 2005, 159,

21. Quoted in Robertson 1999, 16.

22. The case is analyzed in Robertson 1999.

23. Quoted in Robertson 1999, 18.

24. Quoted in Robertson 1999, 21.

25. Robertson 1999, 20.

26. Quoted in Sang 2003, 108. This discussion of schoolgirls in China is based on Sang.

27. Sang 2003, 117.

28. Quoted in Sang 2003, 122.

29. Sang 2003, 134–38.

30. Quoted in Sang 2003, 151.

31. Quoted in Sang 2003, 150.

32. Quoted in Sang 2003, 157.

33. Faderman 1991, 46.

34. Quoted in Smith-Rosenberg 1989, 272.

35. Quoted in Pflugfelder 2005, 169–70.

36. Quoted in Wu 2007, 77.

37. Pflugfelder 2005, 165–67.

38. Wu 2007.

39. Quoted in Wu 2007, 87.

40. Robertson 2005, 198.

41. Sang 2003.

42. Quoted in Sang 2003, 144.

43. Quoted in Sang 2003, 144.

44. Quoted in Sang 2003, 146.

45. Quoted in Faderman 1999, 53.

46. Quoted in Faderman 1999, 72.

47. Rühling 1980, 88.

48. See Bosch 1990 and Kokula 1981.

49. Quoted in Rupp 1997, 583.

50. Quoted in Rupp 1997, 581.

51. Quoted in Rupp 1989, 304.

52. This discussion of Barney is based on Jay 1988, Latimer 2005, Rodriguez 2002, Vicinus 2004, and Wickes 1976.

53. Quoted in Latimer 2005, 15.

54. "Naturally unnatural" quoted in Jay 1988, 4; second quotation from Vicinus 2004, 189–90.

55. Quoted in Vicinus 2004, 185–86.

56. Quoted in Vicinus 2004, 193–94.

57. Fitzgerald 1933, 71, 72, 73.

58. Hall 1950, 244.

59. Hall 1950, 246.

60. Quoted in Rodriguez 2002, 201.

61. Quoted in Jay 1988, 4.

62. Jay 1988, 37.

63. On Paris, see Choquette 2000, 123; quotation from physician on the United States, quoted in Katz 1983, 218–22.

64. Quoted in Houlbrook 2005, 86.

65. Doan 2001. Oram 2007 also argues, on the basis of representations of women who passed as men in the mass-circulation press, that cross-dressing was not associated with lesbianism in Britain in the 1920s.

66. Quoted in Jivani 1997, 41.

67. Quoted in Jivani 1997, 40.

68. Waters 1998, 410–17. On the authenticity of Waters's portrayal, personal communication from Laura Doan, August 6, 2008.

69. "Paris-Lesbos" from Benstock 1986, 47; Choquette 2000.

70. Quoted in Choquette 2000, 124.

71. Quoted in Choquette 2000, 124.

72. Tamagne 2004, 68.

73. Choquette 2000.

74. Hall 1950, 378. Rodriguez 2002 notes that Hall based this incident on a real evening out.

75. Hall 1950, 382.

76. Hall 1950, 391.

77. Quoted in Lybeck 2007, 269.

78. Quoted in Lybeck 2007, 270.

79. Quoted in Lybeck 2007, 273.

80. Quoted in Lybeck 2007, 321. This discussion of Berlin is heavily indebted to Lybeck. See also Kokula 1984 and 1986, Tamagne 2004, Schader 2004, Schlierkamp 1984, and Vogel 1984.

81. Kokula 1984.

82. Tamagne 2004.

83. Quoted in Kokula 1984, 152 (my translation).

84. Quoted in Kokula 1986, 92.

85. Quoted in Kokula 1984, 155 (my translation).

86. Kokula 1984; Schoppmann 1996.

87. "Über Lesben gestolpert" 2008. I am grateful to Kerstin Bronner for calling my attention to this article.

88. Quoted in Lybeck 2007, 369.

89. Quoted in Chauncey 1994, 229.

90. Quoted in Chauncey 1994, 237.

91. Quoted in Chauncey 1994, 235.

92. Quoted in McGarry and Wasserman 1998, 63.

93. Quoted in Chauncey 1994, 240; see also McGarry and Wasserman 1998, 65.

94. Quoted in Garber 1989, 329.

95. McGarry and Wasserman 1998, 69.

96. Nestle 1993, 933.

97. Quoted in Garber 1989, 321.

98. Quoted in Chauncey 1994, 279, 280.

99. Quoted in Garber 1989, 320.

100. Quoted in Garber 1989, 326.

101. Quoted in Garber 1989, 331.

102. Quoted in Boyd 2003, 69.

103. Boyd 2003.

104. Middlebrook 1998, 72.

105. See Lybeck 2007; Schoppmann 1996; Bérubé 1990; Meyer 1996; Gluck 1987.

106. Quoted in Kennedy and Davis 1993, 48.

107. Chenier 2004. Some middle-class women in English Canada avoided the bars as seedy and dangerous, preferring private house parties. See K. Duder 2001 and, on the same phenomenon in Colorado, Gilmartin 1996.

108. Chenier 2004, 100.

109. Chamberland 1993.

110. On the Gateways, see Gardiner 2003 and Jennings 2007b.

111. Jennings 2007b, 115.

112. Quoted in Gardiner 2003, 6.

113. Quoted in Boyd 2003, 82.

114. Chamberland 1993.

115. Quoted in Jennings 2007b, 119.

116. Quoted in Kennedy and Davis 1993, 191.

117. Nestle 1984, 233.

118. Quoted in Gardiner 2003, 34.

119. Quoted in Jennings 2007b, 181.

120. Quoted in Kennedy and Davis 1993, 355.

121. Quoted in Gardiner 2003, 55–56.

122. Quoted in Chenier 2004, 107.

123. The term "sexual courage" comes from Nestle 1981.

124. Quoted in Kennedy and Davis 1993, 78.

125. Thorpe 1997, 170.

126. Chenier 2008 and forthcoming.

127. Quoted in Gardiner 2003, 83.

128. Quoted in Gardiner 2003, 78.

129. Quoted in Gardiner 2003, 79.

130. Quoted in Gardiner 2003, 79.

131. Quoted in Boyd 2003, 94, 95.

132. Quoted in Kennedy and Davis 1993, 146.

133. Quoted in Gardiner 2003, 54.

134. Quoted in Gardiner 2003, 78.

135. Bannon 1983, 40–41.

136. Quoted in Gardiner 2003, 226.

137. Gunthorp 1999, 86.

138. Green 1999a, 251.

139. Vogel 1984.

140. Quoted in Lybeck 2007, 354.

141. Schlierkamp 1984.

142. Quoted in Lybeck 2007, 304.

143. Quoted in Lybeck 2007, 292–93.

144. Quoted in Lybeck 2007, 350.

145. Quoted in Plötz 1999, 39, 40 (my translations).

146. Hacker 1987.

147. Kokula and Böhmer 1991.

148. Schader 2004, 44.

149. Schader 2004.

150. Quoted in Lybeck 2007, 303.

151. Lybeck 2007.

152. Tamagne 2006, 187.

153. Kokula 1984; Lybeck 2007.

154. On "The Lavender Song," see Tamagne 2004.

155. Lybeck 2007.

156. Quoted in Lybeck 2007, 392.

157. See Kokula and Böhmer 1991; H. Kennedy 1999.

158. Quoted in Gallo 2006, 40.

159. Quoted in Gallo 2006, 40.

160. Quoted in Gallo 2006, 21–22. On *The Ladder* and other lesbian magazines, see also Whitt 2001.

161. On *Arena Three*, see Jennings 2007b.

162. Quoted in Jennings 2007b, 157.

163. This discussion is based on McLelland 2007; see also McLelland 2005.

164. "The position of the women in the Dutch Homophile Movement COC," mimeographed document, 3, ICSE Papers, ONE National Gay and Lesbian Archives, Los Angeles.

165. "Protokoll der I.C.S.E.-Arbeitstagung in Bremen, v. 8/9," August 1959, ICSE Papers, ONE National Gay and Lesbian Archives.

166. Harriet Freyberg to International Committee for Sexual Equality, April 17, 1955, ICSE Papers, COC Papers, box 163, Nationaal Archief, The Hague.

167. On the Daughters of Bilitis and *The Ladder*, see Gallo 2006.

168. Schuyf and Krouwel 1999, 176.

169. Quoted in Llamas and Vila 1999, 217.

170. Green 1999b, 102.

171. Long 1999, 248.

172. Palmberg 1999, 272–73.

173. Quoted in Mogrovejo 1999, 311.

174. Quoted in Mogrovejo 1999, 320. On lesbian feminist organizing around the globe, see Reinfelder 1996.

175. Jennings 2007b.

176. Quoted in Bhaiya 2007, 205.

177. K. Duder 2001; see also C. Duder 2006.

178. E. Kennedy 1996.

179. Mustola and Rydström 2007, 54.

180. Quoted in Gardiner 2003, 157.

Chapter 9

1. Min 1994, 129.

2. Nedjma 2004, 133.

3. Whitaker 2006, 72–73.

4. Quoted in Whitaker 2006, 204.

5. Baraka 2005; Blacking 1978.

6. This discussion is based on Gay 1985 and Kendall 1998; see also Epprecht 2004.

7. Quoted in Gay 1985, 105.

8. Quoted in Kendall 1998, 228–29.

9. Quoted in Kendall 1998, 233.

10. Quoted in Ruan and Bullough 1992, 222. The following examples are from that article as well.

11. Chughtai 1994; see Gopinath 2005 on the relationship between "The Quilt" and *Fire*.

12. Chughtai 1994, 6.

13. Chughtai 1994, 8.

14. Chughtai 1994, 8, 9.

15. Chughtai 1994, 12.

16. Vanita 2005a, 564.

17. Quoted in Bhaiya 2007, 72.

18. Quoted in Vanita 2005a, 567.

19. Quoted in Vanita 2005a, 567.

20. Vanita 2005a, 567.
21. Najmabadi 2005, 251.
22. Quoted in Tan 1999, 290, 291.
23. Quoted in Sinnott 2004, 55–56.
24. Quoted in Swarr and Nagar 2004, 500.
25. Vanita 2004a; see also Vanita 2005b.
26. Quotations from Taylor, Kimport, and Andersen 2008.
27. Nagadya 2005, 74.
28. Glamuzina 2001.
29. Quoted in Glamuzina 2001, 70.
30. Quoted in Glamuzina 2001, 72.
31. Quoted in Glamuzina 2001, 75.
32. Quoted in Glamuzina 2001, 75, 77.
33. This discussion is based on Middlebrook 1998.
34. Quoted in Middlebrook 1998, 147.
35. Quoted in Middlebrook 1998, 278.
36. Quoted in Middlebrook 1998, 233.
37. Quoted in Wijewardene 2007, 106.
38. Quoted in Wijewardene 2007, 111.
39. Quoted in Wijewardene 2007, 113.
40. Quoted in Wijewardene 2007, 114.
41. Quoted in Vidal-Ortiz 2002, 203.
42. Quoted in Vidal-Ortiz 2002, 213.
43. Sinnott 2004, 76.
44. Sinnott 2004, 14.
45. Sinnott 2007, 122.
46. Quoted in Sinnott 2007, 131.
47. Quoted in Sinnott 2007, 132.
48. Quoted in Sinnott 2007, 133.
49. Quoted in Sinnott 2007, 128.
50. Quoted in Sinnott 2007, 129.
51. Quoted in Sinnott 2007, 129.
52. Hidalgo 2009.
53. Sinnott 2004, 165.
54. Lai 2007.
55. Quoted in Lai 2007, 170.
56. Chao 2001.
57. Quoted in Chao 2001, 191.
58. Sinnott 2004, 43.
59. Marin 1996.
60. Davies 2007, 142.
61. Quoted in Blackwood 2007, 184; see also Blackwood 2005.

62. Quoted in Blackwood 2007, 184.

63. Quoted in Wieringa 2007, 39, 40.

64. Quoted in Wieringa 1999, 219.

65. Swarr and Nagar 2004.

66. Quoted in Swarr and Nagar 2004, 508.

67. Boellstorff 2005. Boellstorff developed the concept of "dubbing culture" with regard to gay life in Indonesia.

68. There is a great deal of literature on lesbian feminism. See, for example, Ross 1995 and Nash 2001 on Canada; Echols 1989, Franzen 1993, Taylor and Rupp 1993, Whittier 1995, Stein 1997, Freeman 2000, and Enke 2007 on the United States. Willett 2000 includes material on Australia, and Jennings 2007a discusses Britain.

69. Quoted in Taylor and Rupp 1993, 42.

70. Quoted in Jennings 2007a, 175.

71. Quoted in Jennings 2007a, 177.

72. Mogrovejo 1999, 323.

73. From Stein 1997.

74. Quoted in Stein 1997, 49.

75. Quoted in Stein 1997, 50.

76. Quoted in Stein 1997, 51.

77. Quoted in Stein 1997, 53.

78. Quoted in Stein 1997, 53.

79. Quoted in Stein 1997, 56.

80. Quoted in Stein 1997, 57.

81. Quoted in Stein 1997, 58.

82. Quoted in Stein 1997, 58–59.

83. Quoted in Stein 1997, 59.

84. Quoted in Ross 1995, 106.

85. Quoted in Jennings 2007a, 176.

86. Quoted in Ross 1995, 121.

87. Quoted in Ross 1995, 122.

88. Quoted in Silvera 1992, 524.

89. Quoted in Lang 1999, 107.

90. Quoted in Whitaker 2006, 24.

91. Quoted in Wekker 1999, 128; see also Wekker 2006.

92. Lorde 1982, 14.

93. Smith 1962, 199.

94. Confidential personal communication.

95. Baba 2001.

96. Khayatt 2000.

97. Quoted in Whitaker 2006, 23.

98. Quoted in Whitaker 2006, 86.

99. Quoted in Wieringa 2007, 37, 38. On Takarazuka, see Robertson 1998.

100. Quoted in Aarmo 1999, 272.

101. Fuentes 1996, 139–40.

102. Fuentes 1996, 141.

103. Rupp 1999.

104. E-mail communication from Jens Rydström, August 26, 2000.

Chapter 10

1. Bray 2003 is a major exception, arguing that homosocial friendship is a specifically male form and that female friendship is "the silence between the lines" of male friendship. See also Traub 2004, in a special issue of *GLQ* devoted to Bray's work. Halperin 2002 includes friendship as a category in the history of same-sex sexuality, so I do not mean to overstate the lack of attention to this form of same-sex love. But the eroticization of difference plays a much stronger part in global histories of male same-sex sexuality. In scholarship on female same-sex sexuality, Traub 2002 contrasts the tribade to the friend, and obviously there has been a great deal of attention paid to romantic friendship among women. My point is that it has not often been thought about in terms of the eroticization of sameness.

2. Vicinus 2004, 98–108. On the "oneness" of Bradley and Cooper, as well as of the Ladies of Llangollen, see Vanita 1996.

3. Sinnott 2004.

4. Elliston 1999, 233, 240.

5. Aarmo 1999, 255.

6. Quoted in Blackwood 2007, 186.

7. Silvera 1992.

8. Quoted in Bachmann 2002, 238–39.

9. Quoted in Whitaker 2006, 71.

10. Cooper 2007. See King 2002 for a discussion of the global meaning of the phrase "There are no lesbians here."

11. Quoted in Aldrich 2006a, 19.

12. Thadani 1996, 115.

13. Epprecht 2004 makes this point strongly, as does Kendall 1998.

14. Wieringa 1999, 227.

References

Aarmo, Margrete. 1999. "How Homosexuality Became 'Un-African': The Case of Zimbabwe." In *Same-Sex Relations and Female Desires: Transgender Practices across Cultures,* edited by Evelyn Blackwood and Saskia E. Wieringa, 255–80. New York: Columbia University Press.

AbuKhalil, As'ad. 1993. "A Note on the Study of Homosexuality in the Arab/Islamic Civilization." *Arab Studies Journal* 1: 32–34.

Adler, Margot. 1979. *Drawing Down the Moon: Witches, Druids, Goddess-Worshippers, and Other Pagans in America Today.* Boston: Beacon.

Aldrich, Robert. 2006a. "Gay and Lesbian History." In *Gay Life and Culture: A World History,* edited by Robert Aldrich, 7–27. London: Thames & Hudson.

———, ed. 2006b. *Gay Life and Culture: A World History.* London: Thames & Hudson.

Amadiume, Ife. 1987. *Male Daughters, Female Husbands: Gender and Sex in an African Society.* London: Zed Books.

Amer, Sahar. 2001. "Lesbian Sex and the Military: From the Medieval Arabic Tradition to French Literature." In *Same Sex Love and Desire among Women in the Middle Ages,* edited by Francesca Canadé Sautman and Pamela Sheingorn, 179–98. New York: Palgrave.

Anzaldúa, Gloria. 2002. "now let us shift . . . the path of conocimiento . . . inner work, public acts." In *This Bridge We Call Home: Radical Visions for Transformation,* edited by Gloria Anzaldúa and Analouise Keating, 540–78. New York: Routledge.

Arguelles, Lourdes, and B. Ruby Rich. 1984. "Homosexuality, Homophobia, and Revolution: Notes toward an Understanding of the Cuban Lesbian and Gay Male Experience, Part I." *Signs: Journal of Women in Culture and Society* 9: 683–99.

Baba, Ismail. 2001. "Gay and Lesbian Couples in Malaysia." *Journal of Homosexuality* 40(3–4): 143–63.

Bachmann, Monica. 2002. "After the Fire." In *Queering India: Same-Sex Love and Eroticism in Indian Culture and Society,* edited by Ruth Vanita, 234–43. New York: Routledge.

Bachofen, Johann Jacob. 1967. *Myth, Religion, and Mother Right: Selected Writings.* Translated by Ralph Manheim. Princeton, NJ: Princeton University Press.

Bannon, Ann. 1983. *Beebo Brinker*. Tallahassee, FL: Volute Books.

Baraka, Nancy, with Ruth Morgan. 2005. "'I Want to Marry the Woman of My Choice without Fear of Being Stoned': Female Marriages and Bisexual Women in Kenya." In *Tommy Boys, Lesbian Men and Ancestral Wives: Female Same-Sex Practices in Africa*, edited by Ruth Morgan and Saskia Wieringa, 25–50. Johannesburg: Jacana Media.

Barnes, Nancy Schuster. 1987. "Buddhism." In *Women in World Religions*, edited by Arvind Sharma. Albany: State University of New York Press.

Baum, Robert M. 1993. "Homosexuality and the Traditional Religions of the Americas and Africa." In *Homosexuality and World Religions*, edited by Arlene Swidler, 1–46. Valley Forge, PA: Trinity.

Bellamy, James A. 1979. "Sex and Society in Islamic Popular Literature." In *Society and the Sexes in Medieval Islam*, edited by Afaf Lutfi al-Sayyid Marsot, 23–42. Malibu, CA: Undena.

Benkov, Edith. 2001. "The Erased Lesbian: Sodomy and the Legal Tradition in Medieval Europe." In *Same Sex Love and Desire among Women in the Middle Ages*, edited by Francesca Canadé Sautman and Pamela Sheingorn, 101–22. New York: Palgrave.

Bennett, Judith M. 2000. "'Lesbian-Like' and the Social History of Lesbianism." *Journal of the History of Sexuality* 9(1–2): 1–24.

Benstock, Shari. 1986. *Women of the Left Bank: Paris, 1900–1940*. Austin: University of Texas Press.

Bérubé, Allan. 1990. *Coming Out under Fire: The History of Gay Men and Women in World War II*. New York: Free Press.

Bhaiya, Abha. 2007. "The Spring That Flowers between Women." In *Women's Sexualities and Masculinities in a Globalizing Asia*, edited by Saskia E. Wieringa, Evelyn Blackwood, and Abha Bhaiya, 69–76. New York: Palgrave Macmillan.

Billing, Arno, and Kurt Schwabach. 1997. "The Lavender Song." English lyrics by Jeremy Lawrence, from a translation by Alan Lareau. Ute Lemper, *Berlin Cabaret Songs* CD booklet. London: Decca Record Company.

Blacking, John. 1978. "Uses of the Kinship Idiom in Friendships at Some Venda and Zulu Schools." In *Social System and Tradition in Southern Africa*, edited by John Argyle and Eleanor Preston-Whyte, 101–17. Cape Town: Oxford University Press.

Blackwood, Evelyn. 2007. "Transnational Sexualities in One Place: Indonesian Readings." In *Women's Sexualities and Masculinities in a Globalizing Asia*, edited by Saskia E. Wieringa, Evelyn Blackwood, and Abha Bhaiya, 181–99. New York: Palgrave Macmillan.

———. 2005. "*Tombois* in West Sumatra: Constructing Masculinity and Erotic Desire." In *Same-Sex Cultures and Sexualities: An Anthropological Reader*, edited by Jennifer Robertson, 232–60. Oxford, UK: Blackwell.

———. 2000. "Harems." In *Lesbian Histories and Cultures*, edited by Bonnie Zimmerman, 353–54. New York: Garland.

———. 1986. "Breaking the Mirror: The Construction of Lesbianism and the Anthropological Discourse on Homosexuality." In *Anthropology and Homosexual Behavior*, edited by Evelyn Blackwood, 1–17. New York: Haworth.

———. 1984. "Sexuality and Gender in Certain Native American Tribes: The Case of Cross-Gender Females." *Signs: Journal of Women in Culture and Society* 10: 27–42.

Blackwood, Evelyn, and Saskia E. Wieringa. 1999. "Sapphic Shadows: Challenging the Silence in the Study of Sexuality." In *Female Desires: Same-Sex Relations and Transgender Practices across Cultures*, edited by Evelyn Blackwood and Saskia E. Wieringa, 39–63. New York: Columbia University Press.

Blanc, Olivier. 2001. "The 'Italian Taste' in the Time of Louis XVI, 1774–92." *Journal of Homosexuality* 41(3–4): 69–84.

Boellstorff, Tom. 2005. *The Gay Archipelago*. Princeton, NJ: Princeton University Press.

Bogin, Meg. 1976. *The Women Troubadours*. New York: Norton.

Bonnet, Marie-Jo. 1981. *Un choix sans equivoque*. Paris: Éditions Denoël.

Bosch, Mineke, with Annemarie Kloosterman. 1990. *Politics and Friendship: Letters from the International Woman Suffrage Alliance, 1902–1942*. Columbus: Ohio State University Press.

Boswell, John. 1994. *Same-Sex Unions in Premodern Europe*. New York: Villard Books.

———. 1980. *Christianity, Social Tolerance, and Homosexuality: Gay People in Western Europe from the Beginning of the Christian Era to the Fourteenth Century*. Chicago: University of Chicago Press.

Boyd, Nan Alamilla. 2003. *Wide Open Town: A History of Queer San Francisco to 1965*. Berkeley: University of California Press.

Bray, Alan. 2003. *The Friend*. Chicago: University of Chicago Press.

Brennan, T. Corey. 1997. Review in *Bryn Mawr Classical Review* 97.5.7, http://bmcr.brynmawr.edu/.

Brooks, Carellin. 2000. "Vampires." In *Lesbian Histories and Cultures*, edited by Bonnie Zimmerman, 791–92. New York: Garland.

Brooten, Bernadette J. 1996. *Love between Women: Early Christian Responses to Female Homoeroticism*. Chicago: University of Chicago Press.

Brown, Judith C. 1986. *Immodest Acts: The Life of a Lesbian Nun in Renaissance Italy*. New York: Oxford University Press.

Bullough, Vern L. 1974. "Transvestites in the Middle Ages." *American Journal of Sociology* 79: 1381–94.

Burshatin, Israel. 1996. "Elena Alias Eleno: Genders, Sexualities, and 'Race' in the Mirror of Natural History in Sixteenth-Century Spain." In *Gender Reversals and Gender Cultures: Anthropological and Historical Perspectives*, edited by Sabrina Petra Ramet, 105–22. New York: Routledge.

Bynum, Caroline Walker. 1987. *Holy Feast and Holy Fast: The Religious Significance of Food to Medieval Women*. Berkeley: University of California Press.

Cabezón, José Ignacio. 1993. "Homosexuality and Buddhism." In *Homosexuality and World Religions*, edited by Arlene Swidler, 81–101. Valley Forge, PA: Trinity.

Califia, Pat. 1980. *Sapphistry: The Book of Lesbian Sexuality*. Tallahassee, FL: Naiad.

Callender, Charles, and Lee M. Kochems. 1983. "The North American Berdache." *Current Anthropology* 24: 443–56.

Cameron, Alan. 1998. "Love (and Marriage) between Women." *Greek, Roman, and Byzantine Studies* 39: 137–56.

Cantarella, Eva. 1992. *Bisexuality in the Ancient World*. New Haven, CT: Yale University Press.

Carrier, Josephe M., and Stephen O. Murray. "Woman-Woman Marriage in Africa." In *Boy-Wives and Female Husbands: Studies in African Homosexualities*, edited by Stephen O. Murray and Will Roscoe, 255–66. New York: Palgrave.

Carton, Adrian. 2006. "Desire and Same-Sex Intimacies in Asia." In *Gay Life and Culture: A World History*, edited by Robert Aldrich, 302–31. London: Thames & Hudson.

Castelli, Elizabeth A., David Halperin, Ann Pellegrini, et al. 1998. "Lesbian Historiography before the Name?" in "The GLQ Forum," *GLQ: A Journal of Lesbian and Gay Studies* 4: 557–630.

Castle, Terry, ed. 2003. *The Literature of Lesbianism: A Historical Anthology from Ariosto to Stonewall*. New York: Columbia University Press.

Cavin, Susan. 1985. *Lesbian Origins*. San Francisco: Ism.

Chamberland, Line. 1993. "Remembering Lesbian Bars: Montreal, 1955–1975." In *Gay Studies from the French Cultures: Voices from France, Belgium, Brazil, Canada, and The Netherlands*, edited by Rommel Mendès-Leite and Pierre-Olivier de Busscher, 231–69. New York: Harrington Park.

Chao, Y. Antonia. 2001. "Drink, Stories, Penis, and Breasts: Lesbian Tomboys in Taiwan from the 1960s to the 1990s." *Journal of Homosexuality* 40: 185–209.

Chauncey, George. 1994. *Gay New York: Gender, Culture, and the Making of the Gay Male World, 1890–1940*. New York: Basic Books.

———. 1982–83. "From Sexual Inversion to Homosexuality: Medicine and the Changing Conceptualization of Female Deviance." *Salmagundi* 58–59: 114–46.

Chenier, Elise. Forthcoming. "Freaking: Marriage as Postwar Lesbian Pleasure Practice." *Journal of the History of Sexuality*.

———. 2008. "Freak Wedding! Lesbian Marriage as a Pleasure Practice in Post–World War II Toronto." Paper presented at the Berkshire Conference on the History of Women, Minneapolis, MN.

————. 2004. "Rethinking Class in Lesbian Bar Culture: Living 'The Gay Life' in Toronto, 1955–1965." *Left History* 9(2): 85–118.

Chesser, Lucy. 2008. *Parting with My Sex: Cross-Dressing, Inversion and Sexuality in Australian Cultural Life.* Sydney: Sydney University Press.

————. 1998. "'A Woman Who Married Three Wives': Management of Disruptive Knowledge in the 1879 Australian Case of Edward De Lacy Evans." *Journal of Women's History* 9(4): 53–77.

Choquette, Leslie. 2000. "Paris-Lesbos: Lesbian Social Space in the Modern City, 1870–1940." In *Proceedings of the Western Society for French History*, edited by Barry Rothaus. Boulder: University Press of Colorado.

Chughtai, Ismat. 1994. *The Quilt and Other Stories.* Translated by Tahira Naqvi and Syeda S. Hameed. Riverdale-on-Hudson, NY: Shee Meadow.

Clark, Anna. 2005. "Twilight Moments." *Journal of the History of Sexuality* 14: 139–60.

————. 1996. "Anne Lister's Construction of Lesbian Identity." *Journal of the History of Sexuality* 7: 23–50.

Clark, Robert L. A. 2001. "Jousting without a Lance: The Condemnation of Female Homoeroticism in the *Livre des manières.*" In *Same Sex Love and Desire among Women in the Middle Ages*, edited by Francesca Canadé Sautman and Pamela Sheingorn, 143–78. New York: Palgrave.

Coleman, Jenny. 2001. "Unsettled Women: Deviant Genders in Late Nineteenth- and Early Twentieth-Century New Zealand." *Journal of Lesbian Studies* 5: 13–26.

Colwill, Elizabeth. 1996. "Pass as a Woman, Act like a Man: Marie-Antoinette as Tribade in the Pornography of the French Revolution." In *Homosexuality in Modern France*, edited by Jeffrey Merrick and Bryant T. Ragan, Jr., 54–79. New York: Oxford University Press.

Cook, Blanche Wiesen. 1977. "Female Support Networks and Political Activism." *Chrysalis* 3: 43–61.

Cooper, Helene. 2007, September 25. "Ahmadinejad, at Columbia, Parries and Puzzles." *New York Times.*

Crompton, Louis. 2003. *Homosexuality and Civilization.* Cambridge, MA: Belknap Press of Harvard University.

————. 1997. "Male Love and Islamic Law in Arab Spain." In *Islamic Homosexualities: Culture, History, and Literature*, edited by Stephen O. Murray and Will Roscoe, 142–57. New York: New York University Press.

————. 1980–81. "The Myth of Lesbian Impunity: Capital Laws from 1270 to 1791." *Journal of Homosexuality* 6(1–2): 11–25.

Cruz-Malavé, Arnaldo, and Martin F. Manalansan IV. 2002. *Queer Globalizations: Citizenship and the Afterlife of Colonialism.* New York: New York University Press.

Daly, Mary. 1978. *Gyn/Ecology: The Metaethics of Radical Feminism.* Boston: Beacon.

D'Angelo, Mary Rose. 1990. "Women Partners in the New Testament." *Journal of Feminist Studies in Religion* 6(1): 65–86.

Davies, Sharyn Graham. 2007. "Hunting Down Love: Female Masculinities in Bugis South Sulawesi." In *Women's Sexualities and Masculinities in a Globalizing Asia,* edited by Saskia E. Wieringa, Evelyn Blackwood, and Abha Bhaiya, 139–57. New York: Palgrave Macmillan.

Davis, Elizabeth Gould. 1971. *The First Sex.* New York: Penguin Books.

De Erauso, Catalina. 1996. *Lieutenant Nun: Memoir of a Basque Transvestite in the New World.* Translated by Michele Stepto and Gabriel Stepto. Boston: Beacon.

Dekker, Rudolf M., and Lotte C. van de Pol. 1989. *The Tradition of Female Transvestism in Early Modern Europe.* New York: St. Martin's.

De la Cruz, Sor Juana Inés. 1997. *Sor Juana's Love Poems.* Translated by Joan Larkin and Jaime Manrique. Madison: University of Wisconsin Press.

D'Emilio, John, and Estelle B. Freedman. 1988. *Intimate Matters: A History of Sexuality in America.* New York: Harper and Row.

Devereux, George. 1937. "Institutionalized Homosexuality of the Mohave Indians." *Human Biology* 9: 498–527.

Diamant, Anita. 1997. *The Red Tent.* New York: Pan Books.

Diggs, Marylynne. 1995. "Romantic Friends or a 'Different Race of Creatures'? The Representation of Lesbian Pathology in Nineteenth-Century America." *Feminist Studies* 21: 317–40.

Doan, Laura. 2001. *Fashioning Sapphism: The Origins of a Modern English Lesbian Culture.* New York: Columbia University Press.

Doetsch, Sharon. 2004. "'Feeding People in All Their Hungers': Spiritual Activism in Queer Chicana Feminist Writing." Unpublished paper in author's possession.

Doniger, Wendy, and Sudhir Kakar, trans. and eds. 2002. *Kamasutra.* Oxford: Oxford University Press.

Donoghue, Emma. 2004. *Life Mask.* New York: Harcourt.

———. 1993. *Passions between Women: British Lesbian Culture, 1668–1801.* New York: HarperCollins.

Dover, K. J. *Greek Homosexuality.* New York: Vintage Books.

Downing, Christine. 1997. "Lesbian Mythology." In *Que(e)rying Religion: A Critical Anthology,* edited by Gary David Comstock and Susan E. Henking, 415–40. New York: Continuum.

Duberman, Martin, Martha Vicinus, and George Chauncey, Jr., eds. 1989. *Hidden from History: Reclaiming the Gay and Lesbian Past.* New York: New American Library.

Duder, Cameron. 2006. "'Two Middle-Aged and Very Good-Looking Females That Spend All Their Week-Ends Together': Female Professors and Same-Sex

Relationships in Canada, 1910–1950." In *Historical Identities: The Professoriate in Canada*, edited by Paul Stortz and E. Lisa Panayotidis, 332–50. Toronto: University of Toronto Press.

Duder, Karen. 2001. "The Spreading Depths: Lesbian and Bisexual Women in English Canada, 1910–1965." Ph.D. diss., University of Victoria.

Duggan, Lisa. 2000. *Sapphic Slashers: Sex, Violence, and American Modernity*. Durham, NC: Duke University Press.

Duran, Khalid. 1993. "Homosexuality and Islam." In *Homosexuality and World Religions*, edited by Arlene Swidler, 181–97. Valley Forge, PA: Trinity.

Dworkin, Andrea. 1974. *Woman Hating*. New York. Dutton.

Echols, Alice. 1989. *Daring to Be Bad: Radical Feminism in America, 1967–1975*. Minneapolis: University of Minnesota Press.

Elfenbein, Andrew. 1999. *Romantic Genius: The Prehistory of a Homosexual Role*. New York: Columbia University Press.

Elledge, Jim, ed. 2002. *Gay, Lesbian, Bisexual, and Transgender Myths from the Arapaho to the Zuñi*. New York: Peter Lang.

Eller, Cynthia. 2000. *The Myth of Matriarchal Prehistory: Why an Invented Past Won't Give Women a Future*. Boston: Beacon.

Ellis, Havelock. 1920. "Appendix: The School-Friendships of Girls." In *Studies in the Psychology of Sex*, 3rd ed., vol. 2, 368–84. Philadelphia: F. B. Davis.

Elliston, Deborah A. 1999. "Negotiating Transnational Sexual Economies: Female *Māhū* and Same-Sex Sexuality in 'Tahiti and Her Islands.'" In *Same-Sex Relations and Female Desires: Transgender Practices across Cultures*, edited by Evelyn Blackwood and Saskia E. Wieringa, 232–52. New York: Columbia University Press.

el-Rouayheb, Khalid. 2005. *Before Homosexuality in the Arab-Islamic World, 1500–1800*. Chicago: University of Chicago Press.

Engels, Frederick. 1972. *The Origin of the Family, Private Property, and the State*. New York: International Publishers.

Enke, Anne. 2007. *Finding the Movement: Sexuality, Contested Space, and Feminist Activism*. Durham, NC: Duke University Press.

Epprecht, Marc. 2004. *Hungochani: The History of a Dissident Sexuality in Southern Africa*. Montreal: McGill-Queen's University Press.

Eriksson, Brigitte. 1980–81. "A Lesbian Execution in Germany, 1721: The Trial Records." *Journal of Homosexuality* 6: 27–40.

Esquibel, Catrióna Rueda. 2006. *With Her Machete in Her Hand: Reading Chicana Lesbians*. Austin: University of Texas Press.

Evans, Arthur. 1978. *Witchcraft and the Gay Counterculture*. Boston: Fag Rag Books.

Evans-Pritchard, E. E. 1970. "Sexual Inversion among the Azande." *American Anthropologist* 72: 1428–34.

Everard, Myriam. 1994. "Ziel en Zinnen: Over Liefde en Lust tussen Vrouwen in de Tweede Helft van de Achttiende Eeuw." Ph.D. diss., University of Groningen.

————. 1986. "Lesbian History: A History of Change and Disparity." In *Historical, Literary, and Erotic Aspects of Lesbianism*, edited by Monika Kehoe, 123–37. New York: Harrington Park.

Faderman, Lillian. 1999. *To Believe in Women: What Lesbians Have Done for America—A History*. Boston: Houghton Mifflin.

————. 1993. *Scotch Verdict*. New York: Columbia University Press.

————. 1991. *Odd Girls and Twilight Lovers: A History of Lesbian Life in Twentieth-Century America*. New York: Columbia University Press.

————. 1981. *Surpassing the Love of Men: Romantic Friendship and Love between Women from the Renaissance to the Present*. New York: William Morrow.

Fitzgerald, F. Scott. 1933. *Tender Is the Night*. New York: Scribner's Sons.

Frančíková, Dáša. 2000. "Female Friends in Nineteenth-Century Bohemia: Troubles with Affectionate Writing and 'Patriotic Relationships.'" *Journal of Women's History* 12(3): 23–28.

Franzen, Trisha. 1993. "Differences and Identities: Feminism and the Albuquerque Lesbian Community." *Signs: Journal of Women in Culture and Society* 18: 891–906.

Freedman, Estelle B. 1996a. *Maternal Justice: Miriam Van Waters and the Female Reform Tradition*. Chicago: University of Chicago Press.

————. 1996b. "The Prison Lesbian: Race, Class, and the Construction of the Aggressive Female Homosexual, 1915–1965." *Feminist Studies* 22: 397–423.

Freeman, Susan K. 2000. "From the Lesbian Nation to the Cincinnati Lesbian Community: Moving toward a Politics of Location." *Journal of the History of Sexuality* 9(1–2): 137–74.

Frühstück, Sabine. 2003. *Colonizing Sex: Sexology and Social Control in Modern Japan*. Berkeley: University of California Press.

Fuentes, Consuelo Rivera. 1996. "'Todas Locas, Todas Vivas, Todas Libres': Chilean Lesbians, 1980–95." In *Amazon to Zami: Towards a Global Lesbian Feminism*, edited by Monika Reinfelder, 138–51. London: Cassell.

Fur, Gunlög. 2006. "Reading Margins: Colonial Encounters in Sápmi and Lenapehoking in the Seventeenth and Eighteenth Centuries." *Feminist Studies* 32: 491–521.

Furth, Charlotte. 1999. *A Flourishing Yin: Gender in China's Medical History, 960–1665*. Berkeley: University of California Press.

Galford, Ellen. 1985. *Moll Cutpurse: Her True History*. Ithaca, NY: Firebrand Books.

Gallo, Marcia M. 2006. *Different Daughters: A History of the Daughters of Bilitis and the Rise of the Lesbian Rights Movement*. New York: Carroll & Graf.

Garber, Eric. 1989. "A Spectacle in Color: The Lesbian and Gay Subculture of Jazz Age Harlem." In *Hidden from History: Reclaiming the Gay and Lesbian Past*, edited by Martin Duberman, Martha Vicinus, and George Chauncey, Jr., 318–31. New York: New American Library.

Gardiner, Jill. 2003. *From the Closet to the Screen: Women at the Gateways Club, 1945–85*. London: Pandora.

Gaspar de Alba, Alicia. 1999. *Sor Juana's Second Dream*. Albuquerque: University of New Mexico Press.

Gay, Judith. 1985. "'Mummies and Babies' and Friends and Lovers in Lesotho." *Journal of Homosexuality* 11(3–4): 97–116.

Gilmartin, Katie. 1996. "'We Weren't Bar People': Middle-Class Lesbian Identities and Cultural Spaces." *Gay and Lesbian Quarterly* 3: 1–51.

Gimbutas, Marija. 1991. *The Civilization of the Goddess*. San Francisco: HarperSanFrancisco.

———. 1989. *The Language of the Goddess*. San Francisco: HarperSanFrancisco.

———. 1982. *Goddesses and Gods of Old Europe, 6500–4500 B.C.* Berkeley: University of California Press.

Glamuzina, Julie. 2001. "An Astounding Masquerade." *Journal of Lesbian Studies* 5: 63–84.

Gluck, Sherna B. 1987. *Rosie the Riveter Revisited: Women, the War, and Social Change*. Boston: Twayne.

Goldin, Paul Rakita. 2002. *The Culture of Sex in Ancient China*. Honolulu: University of Hawaii Press.

Gopinath, Gayatri. 2005. *Impossible Desires: Queer Diasporas and South Asian Public Cultures*. Durham, NC: Duke University Press.

Gowing, Laura. 2006. "Lesbians and Their Like in Early Modern Europe, 1500–1800." In *Gay Life and Culture: A World History*, edited by Robert Aldrich, 125–43. London: Thames & Hudson.

Green, James N. 1999a. *Beyond Carnival: Male Homosexuality in Twentieth-Century Brazil*. Chicago: University of Chicago Press.

———. 1999b. "'More Love and More Desire': The Building of a Brazilian Movement." In *The Global Emergence of Gay and Lesbian Politics: National Imprints of a Worldwide Movement*, edited by Barry D. Adam, Jan Willem Duyvendak, and André Krouwel, 91–109. Philadelphia: Temple University Press.

Greenberg, David. F. 1988. *The Construction of Homosexuality*. Chicago: University of Chicago Press.

Grémaux, René. 1993. "Woman Becomes Man in the Balkans." In *Third Sex, Third Gender: Beyond Sexual Dimorphism in Culture and History*, edited by Gilbert Herdt, 241–81. New York: Zone Books.

Grewal, Inderpal, and Caren Kaplan. 2001. "Global Identities: Theorizing Transnational Studies of Sexuality." *GLQ: A Journal of Lesbian and Gay Studies* 7(4): 663–79.

Gunthorp, Dale. 1999. "Gypsophila." In *The Vintage Book of International Lesbian Fiction*, edited by Naomi Holoch and Joan Nestle, 83–101. New York: Vintage Books.

Hacker, Hanna. 1987. *Frauen und Freundinnen: Studien zur 'weiblichen Homosexualität' am Beispiel Österreich, 1870–1938*. Weinheim: Beltz Verlag.

Halberstam, Judith. 1998. *Female Masculinity*. Durham, NC: Duke University Press.

Hall, Radclyffe. 1950. *The Well of Loneliness*. New York: Pocket Books.

Hallet, Judith P. 1989. "Female Homoeroticism and the Denial of Roman Reality in Latin Literature." *Yale Journal of Criticism* 3: 209–27.

———. 1979. "Sappho and Her Social Context." *Signs: Journal of Women in Culture and Society* 4: 460–71.

Halperin, David M. 2002. *How to Do the History of Homosexuality*. Chicago: University of Chicago Press.

———. 1989. "Sex before Sexuality: Pederasty, Politics, and Power in Classical Athens." In *Hidden from History: Reclaiming the Gay and Lesbian Past*, edited by Martin Duberman, Martha Vicinus, and George Chauncey, Jr., 37–53. New York: New American Library.

Hamilton, Edith. 1942. *Mythology*. New York: New American Library.

Hansen, Karen V. 1995. "'No *Kisses* Is like Youres': An Erotic Friendship between Two African-American Women during the Mid-Nineteenth Century." *Gender and History* 7: 153–82.

Hatem, Mervat. 1986. "The Politics of Sexuality and Gender in Segregated Patriarchal Systems: The Case of Eighteenth- and Nineteenth-Century Egypt." *Feminist Studies* 12: 250–74.

Herskovits, Melville J. 1937. "A Note on 'Woman Marriages' in Dahomey." *Africa* 10: 335–41.

Hidalgo, Danielle Antoinette. 2009. "Embodying *Krungtheep:* Geographies of Genders and Sexualities in Bangkok Nightclubbing." Ph.D. diss., University of California, Santa Barbara.

Hinds, Leonard. 2001. "Female Friendship as the Foundation of Love in Madeleine de Scudéry's 'Histoire de Sapho.'" *Journal of Homosexuality* 41(3–4): 23–35.

Hinsch, Bret. 1990. *Passions of the Cut Sleeve: The Male Homosexual Tradition in China*. Berkeley: University of California Press.

Holler, Jacqueline. 1999. "'More Sins than the Queen of England': Marina de San Miguel before the Mexican Inquisition." In *Women in the Inquisition: Spain and the New World*, edited by Mary E. Giles, 209–28. Baltimore: Johns Hopkins University Press.

Holoch, Naomi, and Joan Nestle. 1999. *The Vintage Book of International Lesbian Fiction*. New York: Vintage Books.

Holsinger, Bruce Wood. 1993. "The Flesh of the Voice: Embodiment and the Homoerotics of Devotion in the Music of Hildegard of Bingen (1098–1179)." *Signs: Journal of Women in Culture and Society* 19: 92–125.

Horowitz, Helen Lefkowitz. 1994. *The Power and Passion of M. Carey Thomas*. New York: Knopf.

Houlbrook, Matt. 2005. *Queer London: Perils and Pleasures in the Sexual Metropolis, 1918–1957.* Chicago: University of Chicago Press.

Hull, Gloria T. 1987. *Color, Sex, and Poetry: Three Women Writers of the Harlem Renaissance.* Bloomington: Indiana University Press.

Jay, Karla. 1988. *The Amazon and the Page: Natalie Clifford Barney and Renée Vivien.* Bloomington: Indiana University Press.

Jelavich, Peter. 1997. CD insert copy. *Berlin Cabaret Songs,* recorded by Ute Lemper. London: Decca Record Company.

Jennings, Rebecca. 2007a. *A Lesbian History of Britain: Love and Sex between Women since 1500.* Oxford, UK: Greenwood World.

———. 2007b. *Tomboys and Bachelor Girls: A Lesbian History of Post-war Britain, 1945–71.* Manchester: Manchester University Press.

Jivani, Alkarim. 1997. *It's Not Unusual: A History of Lesbian and Gay Britain in the Twentieth Century.* Bloomington: Indiana University Press.

Jones, Norman W. 2007. *Gay and Lesbian Historical Fiction: Sexual Mystery and Post-Secular Narrative.* New York: Palgrave Macmillan.

Jong, Erica. 2003. *Sappho's Leap: A Novel.* New York: Norton.

———. 1973. *Fear of Flying.* New York: American Library.

Katz, Jonathan Ned. 1983. *Gay/Lesbian Almanac: A New Documentary.* New York: Harper and Row.

Kay, Jackie. 1998. *Trumpet.* New York: Vintage Books.

Kimball, Geoffrey. 1993. "Aztec Homosexuality: The Textual Evidence." *Journal of Homosexuality* 26: 7–24.

Kendall. 1998. "'When a Woman Loves a Woman' in Lesotho: Love, Sex, and the (Western) Construction of Homophobia." In *Boy-Wives and Female Husbands: Studies in African Homosexualities,* edited by Stephen O. Murray and Will Roscoe, 223–41. New York: Palgrave.

Kennedy, Elizabeth Lapovsky. 1996. "'But We Would Never Talk about It': The Structures of Lesbian Discretion in South Dakota, 1928–1933." In *Inventing Lesbian Cultures in America,* edited by Ellen Lewin, 15–39. Boston: Beacon.

Kennedy, Elizabeth Lapovsky, and Madeline D. Davis. 1993. *Boots of Leather, Slippers of Gold: The History of a Lesbian Community.* New York: Routledge.

Kennedy, Hubert. 1999. *The Ideal Gay Man: The Story of Der Kreis.* New York: Harrington Park.

Keuls, Eva. 1985. *The Reign of the Phallus: Sexual Politics in Ancient Athens.* New York: Harper and Row.

Khayatt, Didi. 2000. "Egypt." In *Lesbian Histories and Cultures,* edited by Bonnie Zimmerman, 257–58. New York: Garland.

King, Katie. 2002. "'There Are No Lesbians Here': Lesbianisms, Feminism, and Global Gay Formations." In *Queer Globalizations: Citizenship and the Afterlife of Colonialism,* edited by Arnaldo Cruz-Malavé and Martin F. Manalansan IV, 33–45. New York: New York University Press.

Kizinska, Rose. 1999. "A Love Letter from NADIA (Non-Anglo Dykes in Austra-lia)." In *Multicultural Queer: Australian Narratives*, edited by Peter A. Jackson and Gerard Sullivan, 159–68. New York: Haworth.

Klinck, Anne L. 2005. "'Sleeping in the Bosom of a Tender Companion': Homo-erotic Attachments in Sappho." *Journal of Homosexuality* 49: 193–208.

Knowlton, Elizabeth W. 1997. "'Only a Woman like Yourself'—Rebecca Alice Baldy: Dutiful Daughter, Stalwart Sister, and Lesbian Lover of Nineteenth-Century Georgia." In *Carryin' On in the Lesbian and Gay South*, edited by John Howard, 34–53. New York: New York University Press.

Kokula, Ilse. 1986. *Jahre des Glücks, Jahre des Leids: Gespräche mit älteren lesbis-chen Frauen: Dokumente.* Kiel: Frühlings Erwachen.

———. 1984. "Lesbisch leben von Weimar bis zur Nachkriegszeit." In *Eldo-rado: Homosexuelle Frauen und Männer in Berlin 1850–1950,* 149–61. Berlin: Fröhlich & Kaufmann.

———. 1981. *Weibliche Homosexualität um 1900 in zeitgenösssischen Dokumenten.* Munich: Verlag Frauenoffensive.

Kokula, Ilse, and Ulrike Böhmer. 1991. *Die Welt gehört uns doch! Zusammen-schluss lesbischer Frauen in der Schweiz der 30er Jahre.* Zurich: eFeF-Verlag.

Kors, Alan C., and Edward Peters, eds. 1972. *Witchcraft in Europe, 1100–1700: A Documentary History.* Philadelphia: University of Pennsylvania Press.

Krantz, Susan E. 1995. "The Sexual Identities of Moll Cutpurse in Dekker and Middleton's *The Roaring Girl* and in London." *Renaissance and Reformation/ Renaissance et Réforme* 19(1): 5–20.

Krige, Eileen Jensen. 1974. "Woman-Marriage, with Special Reference to the Lovedu: Its Significance for the Definition of Marriage." *Africa* 44: 11–37.

Kuefler, Mathew, ed. 2006. *The Boswell Thesis: Essays on Christianity, Social Toler-ance, and Homosexuality.* Chicago: University of Chicago Press.

Kunzel, Regina. 2008. *Criminal Intimacy: Prison and the Uneven History of Modern American Sexuality.* Chicago: University of Chicago Press.

Lai, Franco. 2007. "Lesbian Masculinities: Identity and Body Construction among Tomboys in Hong Kong." In *Women's Sexualities and Masculinities in a Globalizing Asia*, edited by Saskia E. Wieringa, Evelyn Blackwood, and Abha Bhaiya, 159–79. New York: Palgrave Macmillan.

Lang, Sabine. 1999. "Lesbians, Men-Women and Two-Spirits: Homosexuality and Gender in Native American Cultures." In *Female Desires: Same-Sex Rela-tions and Transgender Practices across Cultures*, edited by Evelyn Blackwood and Saskia E. Wieringa, 91–116. New York: Columbia University Press.

———. 1997. "Various Kinds of Two-Spirit People: Gender Variance and Ho-mosexuality in Native American Communities." In *Two-Spirit People*, edited by Sue-Ellen Jacobs, Wesley Thomas, and Sabine Lang, 100–118. Urbana: University of Illinois Press.

Lanser, Susan. 2001. "'*Au sein de vos pareilles*': Sapphic Separatism in Late Eighteenth-Century France." *Journal of Homosexuality* 41(3–4): 105–16.

Laqueur, Thomas. 1990. *Making Sex: Body and Gender from the Greeks to Freud.* Cambridge, MA: Harvard University Press.

Latimer, Tirza True. 2005. *Women Together/Women Apart: Portraits of Lesbian Paris.* New Brunswick, NJ: Rutgers University Press.

Lavezzo, Kathy. 1996. "Sobs and Sighs between Women: The Homoerotics of Compassion in *The Book of Margery Kempe*." In *Premodern Sexualities*, edited by Louise Fradenburg and Carla Freccero, 175–98. New York: Routledge.

Le Fanu, Sheridan. 1973. "Carmilla." In *A Clutch of Vampires*, edited by Raymond McNally. New York: Graphic Society.

Lessing, Doris. 2007. *The Cleft.* London: Fourth Estate.

Levin, Eve. 1996. "Eastern Orthodox Christianity." In *Handbook of Medieval Sexuality*, edited by Vern L. Bullough and James A. Brundage, 329–43. New York: Garland.

———. 1989. *Sex and Society in the World of the Orthodox Slavs, 900–1700.* Ithaca, NY: Cornell University Press.

Lister, Anne. 1992. *No Priest but Love: The Journals of Anne Lister from 1824–1826.* Edited by Helena Whitbread. New York: New York University Press.

———. 1988. *I Know My Own Heart: The Diaries of Anne Lister, 1791–1840.* Edited by Helena Whitbread. New York: New York University Press.

Llamas, Ricardo, and Fefa Vila. 1999. "Passion for Life: A History of the Lesbian and Gay Movement in Spain." In *The Global Emergence of Gay and Lesbian Politics: National Imprints of a Worldwide Movement*, edited by Barry D. Adam, Jan Willem Duyvendak, and André Krouwel, 214–41. Philadelphia: Temple University Press.

Lochrie, Karma. 1997. "Mystical Acts, Queer Tendencies." In *Constructing Medieval Sexuality*, edited by Karma Lochrie, Peggy McCracken, and James A. Schultz, 180–200. Minneapolis: University of Minnesota Press.

Long, Scott. 1999. "Gay and Lesbian Movements in Eastern Europe: Romania, Hungary, and the Czech Republic." In *The Global Emergence of Gay and Lesbian Politics: National Imprints of a Worldwide Movement*, edited by Barry D. Adam, Jan Willem Duyvendak, and André Krouwel, 242–65. Philadelphia: Temple University Press.

Lorde, Audre. 1984. *Sister/Outsider.* Trumansburg, NY: Crossing.

———. 1982. *Zami: A New Spelling of My Name.* Watertown, MA: Persephone.

Lützen, Karin. 1990. *Was das Herz beherht: Liebe und Fruendschaft zwischen Frauen.* Translated from Danish by Gabriele Haefs. Hamburg: Ernst Kabel Verlag.

Lybeck, Marti. 2007. "Gender, Sexuality and Belonging: Female Homosexuality in Germany, 1890–1933." Ph.D. diss., University of Michigan.

Lyons, Clare A. 2007. "Mapping an Atlantic Sexual Culture: Homoeroticism in Eighteenth-Century Philadelphia." In *Long Before Stonewall: Histories of Same-Sex Sexuality in Early America*, edited by Thomas A. Foster, 164–203. New York: New York University Press.

Maitland, Sara. 1996. "The Burning Times." In *Angel Maker: The Short Stories of Sara Maitland*, 69–79. New York: Holt.

Mak, Geertje. 2004. "Sandor/Sarolta Vay: From Passing Woman to Invert." *Journal of Women's History* 16(1): 54–77.

Malti-Douglas, Fedwa. 2001. "Tribadism/Lesbianism and the Sexualized Body in Medieval Arabo-Islamic Narratives." In *Same Sex Love and Desire among Women in the Middle Ages*, edited by Francesca Canadé Sautman and Pamela Sheingorn, 123–41. New York: Palgrave.

Manalansan, Martin F., IV. 2003. *Global Divas: Filipino Gay Men in the Diaspora*. Durham, NC: Duke University Press.

Manniche, Lise. 1987. *Sexual Life in Ancient Egypt*. London: KPI.

Marcus, Sharon. 2007. *Between Women: Friendship, Desire, and Marriage in Victorian England*. Princeton, NJ: Princeton University Press.

Marin, Malu. 1996. "Stolen Strands: The In and Out Lives of Lesbians in the Philippines." In *Amazon to Zami: Towards a Global Lesbian Feminism*, edited by Monika Reinfelder, 30–55. London: Cassell.

Martin, Sylvia. 1994. "'These Walls of Flesh': The Problem of the Body in the Romantic Friendship/Lesbianism Debate." *Historical Reflections/Réflexions Historiques* 20: 243–66.

Matter, Ann E. 1986. "My Sister, My Spouse: Women-Identified Women in Medieval Christianity." *Journal of Feminist Studies in Religion* 2(2): 91–93.

McGarry, Molly, and Fred Wasserman. 1998. *Becoming Visible: An Illustrated History of Lesbian and Gay Life in Twentieth-Century America*. New York: Penguin Books.

McLelland, Mark. 2007. "'Homosexuality Is Not Just for Men. Even among Women It Is a Splendid Rage!' Representations of Women's Same-Sex Love in Early Postwar Japan." Unpublished manuscript in possession of the author.

———. 2005. *Queer Japan from the Pacific War to the Internet Age*. Lanham, MD: Rowman and Littlefield.

McNally, Raymond T. 2001. "In Search of the Lesbian Vampire: Barbara von Cilli, Le Fanu's 'Carmilla' and the Dragon Order." *Journal of Dracula Studies* 3. Available online at http://www.blooferland.com/drc/index.php?title=Journal_of_Dracula_Studies.

Mello e Souza, Lura. 2003. *The Devil and the Land of the Holy Cross: Witchcraft, Slavery, and Popular Religion in Colonial Brazil*. Translated by Diane Grosklau Whitty. Austin: University of Texas Press.

Merrick, Jeffrey. 1996. "The Marquis de Villette and Mademoiselle de Raucourt: Representations of Male and Female Sexual Deviance in Late Eighteenth-

Century France." In *Homosexuality in Modern France*, edited by Jeffrey Merrick and Bryant T. Ragan, Jr., 30–53. New York: Oxford University Press.

Merrick, Jeffrey, and Bryant T. Ragan, Jr. 2001. *Homosexuality in Early Modern France: A Documentary Collection.* Oxford: Oxford University Press.

Meyer, Leisa D. 1996. *Creating GI Jane: Sexuality and Power in the Women's Army Corps during World War II.* New York: Columbia University Press.

Middlebrook, Diane Wood. 1998. *Suits Me: The Double Life of Billy Tipton.* Boston: Houghton Mifflin.

Miller, Heather Lee. 2000. "Sexologists Examine Lesbians and Prostitutes in the United States, 1840–1940." *NWSA Journal* 12(3): 67–91.

Min, Anchee. 1994. *Red Azalea.* New York: Pantheon.

Mogrovejo, Norma. 1999. "Sexual Preference, the Ugly Duckling of Feminist Demands: The Lesbian Movement in Mexico." In *Female Desires: Same-Sex Relations and Transgender Practices across Cultures*, edited by Evelyn Blackwood and Saskia E. Wieringa, 308–35. New York: Columbia University Press.

Monter, E. William. 1980–81. "Sodomy and Heresy in Early Modern Switzerland." *Journal of Homosexuality* 6(1–2): 41–53.

Moore, Lisa. 1992. "'Something More Tender Still than Friendship': Romantic Friendship in Early-Nineteenth Century England." *Feminist Studies* 18: 499–520.

Moraga, Cherríe. 2000. *Loving in the War Years.* Expanded ed. Cambridge, MA: South End.

Morgan, Ruth, and Saskia Wieringa, eds. 2005. *Tommy Boys, Lesbian Men and Ancestral Wives: Female Same-Sex Practices in Africa.* Johannesburg: Jacana Media.

Murray, Jacqueline. 1996. "Twice Marginal and Twice Invisible: Lesbians in the Middle Ages." In *Handbook of Medieval Sexuality*, edited by Vern L. Bullough and James A. Brundage, 191–222. New York: Garland.

Murray, Margaret. 1921. *The Witch Cult in Western Europe.* New York: Oxford University Press.

Murray, Stephen O. 2000. *Homosexualities.* Chicago: University of Chicago Press.

———. 1997. "Woman-Woman Love in Islamic Societies." In *Islamic Homosexualities: Culture, History, and Literature*, edited by Stephen O. Murray and Will Roscoe, 97–104. New York: New York University Press.

Murray, Stephen O., and Will Roscoe, ed. 1997. *Islamic Homosexualities: Culture, History, and Literature.* New York: New York University Press.

Mustola, Kati, and Jens Rydström. 2007. "Women and the Laws on Same-Sex Sexuality." In *Criminally Queer: Homosexuality and Criminal Law in Scandinavia, 1842–1999*, edited by Jens Rydström and Kati Mustola, 41–60. Amsterdam: aksant.

Nagadya, Marie, with Ruth Morgan. 2005. "'Some Say I Am Hermaphrodite Just Because I Put on Trousers': Lesbians and Tommy Boys in Kampala, Uganda." In *Tommy Boys, Lesbian Men and Ancestral Wives: Female Same-Sex Practices in Africa*, edited by Ruth Morgan and Saskia Wieringa, 65–75. Johannesburg: Jacana Media.

Najmabadi, Afsaneh. 2005. *Women with Mustaches and Men without Beards: Gender and Sexual Anxieties of Iranian Modernity.* Berkeley: University of California Press.

Nanda, Serena. 1990. *Neither Man nor Woman: The Hijras of India.* Belmont, CA: Wadsworth.

Nash, Catherine. 2001. "Siting Lesbians: Urban Spaces and Sexuality." In *In a Queer Country: Gay and Lesbian Studies in the Canadian Context,* edited by Terry Goldie, 325–53. Vancouver: Arsenal Pulp.

Natarajan, Kanchana. 2007. "Desire and Deviance in Classical Indian Philosophy: A Study of Female Masculinity and Male Femininity in the Tamil Folk Legend *Alliyarasanimalai.*" In *Women's Sexualities and Masculinities in a Globalizing Asia,* edited by Saskia E. Wieringa, Evelyn Blackwood, and Abha Bhaiya. New York: Palgrave Macmillan.

Nedjma. 2004. *The Almond.* New York: Grove.

Nestle, Joan. 1993. "Excerpts from the Oral History of Mabel Hampton." *Signs: Journal of Women in Culture and Society* 18: 925–35.

———. 1987. "Lesbians and Prostitutes: A Historical Sisterhood." In *Sex Work: Writings by Women in the Sex Industry,* edited by Frédérique Delacoste and Priscilla Alexander, 231–47. San Francisco: Cleis.

———. 1984. "The Fem Question." In *Pleasure and Danger: Exploring Female Sexuality,* edited by Carole S. Vance, 232–41. Boston: Routledge and Kegan Paul.

———. 1981. "Butch-Fem Relationships: Sexual Courage in the 1950s." *Heresies* 3(4): 21–24.

Newton, Esther. 1989. "The Mythic Mannish Lesbian: Radclyffe Hall and the New Woman." In *Hidden from History: Reclaiming the Gay and Lesbian Past,* edited by Martin Duberman, Martha Vicinus, and George Chauncey, Jr., 281–93. New York: New American Library.

Norton, Rictor. 2000, January 8. "Lesbian Pirates: Anne Bonny and Mary Read." *Lesbian History,* http://www.rictornorton.co.uk/pirates.htm.

Oboler, Regina Smith. 1980. "Is the Female Husband a Man? Woman/Woman Marriage among the Nandi of Kenya." *Ethnology* 19: 69–88.

Oldenberg, Veena Talwar. 1997. "Lifestyle as Resistance: The Case of the Courtesans of Lucknow." In *Lucknow: Memories of a City,* edited by Violette Graff, 136–54. Oxford: Oxford University Press.

Olyan, Saul M. 1994. "'And with a Male You Shall Not Lie the Lying Down of a Woman': On the Meaning and Significance of Leviticus 18:22 and 20:13." *Journal of the History of Sexuality* 5: 179–206.

Oram, Alison. 2007. *Her Husband Was a Woman! Women's Gender-Crossing in Modern British Popular Culture.* New York: Routledge.

Orgel, Stephen. 1992 "The Subtexts of *The Roaring Girl.*" In *Erotic Politics: Desire on the Renaissance Stage,* edited by Susan Zimmerman. New York: Routledge.

"Origin Tale (1931)." 2002. In *Gay, Lesbian, Bisexual, and Transgender Myths from the Arapaho to the Zuñi*, edited by Jim Elledge. New York: Peter Lang.

Palmberg, Mai. 1999. "Emerging Visibility of Gays and Lesbians in Southern Africa: Contrasting Contexts." In *The Global Emergence of Gay and Lesbian Politics: National Imprints of a Worldwide Movement*, edited by Barry D. Adam, Jan Willem Duyvendak, and André Krouwel, 266–92. Philadelphia: Temple University Press.

Park, Katharine. 1997. "The Rediscovery of the Clitoris: French Medicine and the Tribade." In *The Body in Parts*, edited by David Hillman and Carla Mazzio, 171–94. New York: Routledge.

Patai, Ralph. 1967. *The Hebrew Goddess*. Jersey City, NJ: Ktav.

Penrose, Walter. 2001. "Hidden in History: Female Homoeroticism and Women of a 'Third Nature' in the South Asian Past." *Journal of the History of Sexuality* 10: 3–39.

Petievich, Carla. 2002. "Doganas and Zanakhis: The Invention and Subsequent Erasure of Urdu Poetry's 'Lesbian' Voice." In *Queering India: Same-Sex Love and Eroticism in Indian Culture and Society*, edited by Ruth Vanita, 47–60. New York: Routledge.

Pflugfelder, Gary M. 2005. "'S' Is for Sister: Schoolgirl Intimacy and 'Same-Sex Love' in Early Twentieth-Century Japan." In *Gendering Modern Japanese History*, edited by Barbara Molony and Kathleen Uno, 133–90. Cambridge, MA: Harvard University Press.

———. 1999. *Cartographies of Desire: Male-Male Sexuality in Japanese Discourse, 1600–1950*. Berkeley: University of California Press.

Phillimore, Peter. 1991. "Unmarried Women of the Dhaula Dhar: Celibacy and Social Control in Northwest India." *Journal of Anthropological Research* 34: 331–50.

Plötz, Kirsten. 1999. *Einsame Freundinnen? Lesbisches Leben während der zwanziger Jahre in der Provinz*. Hamburg: MännerschwarmSkript Verlag.

Pöllauer, Gerhard. 2002. *Die verlorene Geschichte der Amazonen: Neueste Forschungserkenntnisse über das sagenumwobene Frauenvolk*. Klagenfurt: EBOOKS.

Pomeroy, Sarah B. 1975. *Goddesses, Whores, Wives, and Slaves: Women in Classical Antiquity*. New York: Schocken Books.

Povinelli, Elizabeth A., and George Chauncey. 1999. "Thinking Sex Transnationally: An Introduction." *GLQ: A Journal of Lesbian and Gay Studies* 5(4): 439–50.

Puff, Helmut. 2000. "Female Sodomy: The Trial of Katherina Hetzeldorfer (1477)." *Journal of Medieval and Early Modern Studies* 30: 41–61.

Rabinowitz, Nancy Sorkin. 2002. "Excavating Women's Homoeroticism in Ancient Greece: The Evidence from Attic Vase Painting." In *Among Women: From the Homosocial to the Homoerotic in the Ancient World*, edited by Nancy Sorkin Rabinowitz and Lisa Auanger, 106–66. Austin: University of Texas Press.

Ramet, Sabrina Petra, ed. 1996. *Gender Reversals and Gender Cultures: Anthropological and Historical Perspectives*. New York: Routledge.

Reddy, Gayatri. 2005. *With Respect to Sex: Negotiating Hijra Identity in South India*. Chicago: University of Chicago Press.

Rehak, Paul. 2002. "Imag(in)ing a Women's World in Bronze Age Greece: The Frescoes from Xeste 3 at Akrotiri, Thera." In *Among Women: From the Homosocial to the Homoerotic in the Ancient World*, edited by Nancy Sorkin Rabinowitz and Lisa Auanger, 34–59. Austin: University of Texas Press.

Reinfelder, Monika, ed. 1996. *Amazon to Zami: Towards A Global Lesbian Feminism*. London: Cassell.

Reynolds, Margaret, ed. 2000. *The Sappho Companion*. New York: Palgrave.

Rich, Adrienne. 1980. "Compulsory Heterosexuality and Lesbian Existence." *Signs: Journal of Women in Culture and Society* 5: 631–60.

Rich, Adrienne, Joan Nestle, Judy Tzu-Chun Wu, et al. 2003. "Adrienne Rich's 'Compulsory Heterosexuality and Lesbian Existence'—A Retrospective." *Journal of Women's History* 15(3): 9–89.

Richards, Jeffrey. 1990. *Sex, Dissidence and Damnation: Minority Groups in the Middle Ages*. London: Routledge.

Richardson, Mattie. 2002. "Historical Foundations: Dissemblance and the Pursuit of Heterosexuality and Erasure of 'Deviant' Sexuality." Paper presented at the Berkshire Conference on the History of Women, Storrs, CT.

Robertson, Jennifer. 2005. "Yoshiya Nobuko: Out and Outspoken in Practice and Prose." In *Same-Sex Cultures and Sexualities: An Anthropological Reader*, edited by Jennifer Robertson, 196–211. Malden, MA: Blackwell.

———. 1999. "Dying to Tell: Sexuality and Suicide in Imperial Japan." *Signs: Journal of Women in Culture and Society* 25(1): 1–35.

———. 1998. *Takarazuka: Sexual Politics and Popular Culture in Modern Japan*. Berkeley: University of California Press.

Robinson, David M. 2006. *Closeted Writing and Lesbian and Gay Literature*. Aldershot, UK: Ashgate.

———. 2001. "The Abominable Madame de Murat." *Journal of Homosexuality* 41(3–4): 53–67.

Rodriguez, Suzanne. 2002. *Wild Heart: A Life*. New York: HarperCollins.

Roscoe, Will. 1997. "Precursors of Islamic Homosexualities." In *Islamic Homosexualities: Culture, History, and Literature*, edited by Stephen O. Murray and Will Roscoe, 55–85. New York: New York University Press.

———. 1996. "How to Become a Berdache: Toward a Unified Analysis of Gender Diversity." In *Third Sex, Third Gender: Beyond Sexual Dimorphism in Culture and History*, edited by Gilbert Herdt, 329–72. New York: Zone Books.

Ross, Becki L. 1995. *The House That Jill Built: A Lesbian Nation in Formation*. Toronto: University of Toronto Press.

Roth, Norman. 1996. "A Research Note on Sexuality and Muslim Civilization." In *Handbook of Medieval Sexuality*, edited by Vern L. Bullough and James A. Brundage, 319–27. New York: Garland.

Ruan, Fang Fu. 1991. *Sex in China: Studies in Sexology in Ancient China*. New York: Plenum.

Ruan, Fang Fu, and Vern L. Bullough. 1992. "Lesbianism in China." *Archives of Sexual Behavior* 21: 217–26.

Ruether, Rosemary Radford. 2005. *Goddesses and the Divine Feminine: A Western Religious History*. Berkeley: University of California Press.

Rühling, Anna. 1980. "What Interest Does the Women's Movement Have in the Homosexual Question?" In *Lesbian-Feminism in Turn-of-the-Century Germany*, edited and translated by Lillian Faderman and Brigitte Eriksson, 81–91. Tallahassee, FL: Naiad.

Rupp, Leila J. 2001. "Romantic Friendship." In *Modern American Queer History*, edited by Allida M. Black, 13–23. Philadelphia: Temple University Press.

———. 1999. *A Desired Past: A Short History of Same-Sex Love in America*. Chicago: University of Chicago Press.

———. 1997. "Sexuality and Politics in the Early Twentieth Century: The Case of the International Women's Movement. *Feminist Studies* 23: 577–605.

———. 1989. "Feminism and the Sexual Revolution in the Early Twentieth Century: The Case of Doris Stevens." *Feminist Studies* 15(2): 289–309.

Russell, Jeffrey Burton. 1972. *Witchcraft in the Middle Ages*. Ithaca, NY: Cornell University Press.

San Francisco Lesbian and Gay History Project. 1989. "'She Even Chewed Tobacco': A Pictorial Narrative of Passing Women in America." In *Hidden from History: Reclaiming the Gay and Lesbian Past*, edited by Martin Duberman, Martha Vicinus, and George Chauncey, Jr., 183–94. New York: New American Library.

Sang, Tze-lan. 2003. *The Emerging Lesbian: Female Same-Sex Desire in Modern China*. Chicago: University of Chicago Press.

Sankar, Andrea. 1986. "Sisters and Brothers, Lovers and Enemies: Marriage Resistance in Southern Kwangtung." In *Anthropology and Homosexual Behavior*, edited by Evelyn Blackwood, 69–81. New York: Haworth.

Santos, Jesús Fernández. *Extramuros*. Translated by Helen R. Lane. New York: Columbia University Press.

Sappho. 1958. *Sappho: A New Translation*. Translated by Mary Barnard. Berkeley: University of California Press.

Sautman, Francesca Canadé. 1995. "Invisible Women: Lesbian Working-Class Culture in France, 1880–1930." In *Homosexuality in Modern France*, edited by Jeffrey Merick and Bryant T. Ragan, Jr., 177–201. New York: Oxford University Press.

Schader, Heike. 2004. *Virile, Vamps und wilde Veilchen: Sexualität, Begehren und Erotik in den Zeitschriften homosexueller Frauen im Berlin der 1920er Jahre.* Königstein/Taunus: Ulrike Helmer Verlag.

Schaeffer, Claude E. 1965. "The Kutenai Female Berdache: Courier, Guide, Prophetess, and Warrior." *Ethnohistory* 12: 193–236.

Schibanoff, Susan. 2001. "Hildegard of Bingen and Richardis of Stade: The Discourse of Desire." In *Same Sex Love and Desire among Women in the Middle Ages,* edited by Francesca Canadé Sautman and Pamela Sheingorn, 49–83. New York: Palgrave.

Schlierkamp, Petra. 1984. "Die Garçonne." In *Eldorado: Homosexuelle Frauen und Männer in Berlin 1850–1950,* 169–79. Berlin: Fröhlich & Kaufmann.

Schoppmann, Claudia. 1996. *Days of Masquerade: Life Stories of Lesbians during the Third Reich.* Translated by Allison Brown. New York: Columbia University Press.

Schuyf, Judith, and André Krouwel. 1999. "The Dutch Lesbian and Gay Movement: The Politics of Accommodation." In *The Global Emergence of Gay and Lesbian Politics: National Imprints of a Worldwide Movement,* edited by Barry D. Adam, Jan Willem Duyvendak, and André Krouwel, 158–83. Philadelphia: Temple University Press.

Sharma, Arvind. 1993. "Homosexuality and Hinduism." In *Homosexuality and World Religions,* edited by Arlene Swidler, 47–80. Valley Forge, PA: Trinity.

Sharma, Maya. 2007. "'She Has Come from the World of the Spirits . . .': Life Stories of Working-Class Lesbian Women in Northern India." In *Women's Sexualities and Masculinities in a Globalizing Asia,* edited by Saskia E. Wieringa, Evelyn Blackwood, and Abha Bhaiya, 243–64. New York: Palgrave Macmillan.

Shostak, Marjorie. 1981. *Nisa, the Life and Words of a !Kung Woman.* Cambridge, MA: Harvard University Press.

Silvera, Makeda. 1992. "Man Royals and Sodomites: Some Thoughts on the Invisibility of Afro-Caribbean Lesbians." *Feminist Studies* 18: 521–32.

Sinnott, Megan. 2007. "Gender Subjectivity: Dees and Toms in Thailand." In *Women's Sexualities and Masculinities in a Globalizing Asia,* edited by Saskia E. Wieringa, Evelyn Blackwood, and Abha Bhaiya, 119–38. New York: Palgrave Macmillan.

———. 2004. *Toms and Dees: Transgender Identity and Female Same-Sex Relationships in Thailand.* Honolulu: University of Hawaii Press.

Skinner, Marilyn B. 2002. "Aphrodite Garlanded: Erôs and Poetic Creativity in Sappho and Nossis." In *Among Women: From the Homosocial to the Homoerotic in the Ancient World,* edited by Nancy Sorkin Rabinowitz and Lisa Auanger, 60–81. Austin: University of Texas Press.

Slater, Philip. 1968. *The Glory of Hera: Greek Mythology and the Greek Family.* Boston: Beacon.

Smith, M. B. 1962. *Kinship and Community in Carriacou*. New Haven, CT: Yale University Press.

Smith-Rosenberg, Carroll. 1989. "Discourses of Sexuality and Subjectivity: The New Woman, 1870–1936." In *Hidden from History: Reclaiming the Gay and Lesbian Past*, edited by Martin Duberman, Martha Vicinus, and George Chauncey, Jr., 264–80. New York: New American Library.

———. 1976. "The Female World of Love and Ritual: Relations between Women in Nineteenth-Century America." *Signs: Journal of Women in Culture and Society* 1: 1–29.

Snyder, Jane McIntosh. 1997. *Lesbian Desire in the Lyrics of Sappho*. New York: Columbia University Press.

———. 1995. *Sappho*. New York: Chelsea House.

Sobol, Donald J. 1972. *The Amazons of Greek Mythology*. South Brunswick, NJ, and New York: A. S. Barnes.

Spencer, Colin. 1995. *Homosexuality in History*. New York: Harcourt Brace.

Stanley, Liz. 1992. "Romantic Friendship? Some Issues in Researching Lesbian History and Biography." *Women's History Review* 1: 193–216.

Stein, Arlene. 1997. *Sex and Sensibility: Stories of a Lesbian Generation*. Berkeley: University of California Press.

Stone, Merlin. 1976. *When God Was a Woman*. New York: Harcourt Brace Jovanovich.

Swarr, Amanda Lock, and Richa Nagar. 2004. "Dismantling Assumptions: Interrogating 'Lesbian' Struggles for Identity and Survival in India and South Africa." *Signs: Journal of Women in Culture and Society* 29: 491–516.

Sweet, Michael J., and Leonard Zwilling. 1993. "The First Medicalization: The Taxonomy and Etiology of Queerness in Classical Indian Medicine." *Journal of the History of Sexuality* 3: 590–607.

Talalay, Lauren E. 1994. "A Feminist Boomerang: The Great Goddess of Greek Prehistory." *Gender & History* 6(2): 165–83.

Tamagne, Florence. 2006. "The Homosexual Age, 1870–1940." In *Gay Life and Culture: A World History*, edited by Robert Aldrich, 167–95. London: Thames & Hudson.

———. 2004. *A History of Homosexuality in Europe: Berlin, London, Paris, 1919–1939*. Vol. 1. New York: Algora.

Tan, beng hui. 1999. "Women's Sexuality and the Discourse on Asian Values: Cross-Dressing in Malaysia." In *Female Desires: Same-Sex Relations and Transgender Practices across Cultures*, edited by Evelyn Blackwood and Saskia E. Wieringa, 281–307. New York: Columbia University Press.

Taylor, Verta, Katrina Kimport, and Ellen Ann Andersen. 2008. "Same-Sex Marriage as a Social Movement Tactic." Paper presented at the American Sociological Association meeting, Boston.

Taylor, Verta, and Leila J. Rupp. 1993. "Women's Culture and Lesbian Feminist Activism: A Reconsideration of Cultural Feminism." *Signs: Journal of Women in Culture and Society* 19: 32–61.

Terry, Jennifer. 1999. *An American Obsession: Science, Medicine, and Homosexuality in Modern Society*. Chicago: University of Chicago Press.

Thadani, Gita. 1996. *Sakhiyani: Lesbian Desire in Ancient and Modern India*. London: Cassell.

Thorpe, Roey. 1997. "The Changing Face of Lesbian Bars in Detroit, 1938–1965." In *Creating a Place for Ourselves: Lesbian, Gay, and Bisexual Community Histories*, edited by Brett Beemyn, 165–81. New York: Routledge.

Tietmeyer, Elisabeth. 1985. *Frauen Heiraten Frauen: Studien zur Gynaegamie in Afrika*. Hohenschäftlarn: Klaus Renner Verlag.

Topley, Marjorie. 1975. "Marriage Resistance in Rural Kwangtung." In *Women in Chinese Society*, edited by Margery Wolf and Roxane Witke, 67–88. Stanford, CA: Stanford University Press.

Tortorici, Zeb. 2007. "Masturbation, Salvation, and Desire: Connecting Sexuality and Religiosity in Colonial Mexico." *Journal of the History of Sexuality* 16: 355–72.

Traub, Valerie. 2007. "The Present Future of Lesbian Historiography." In *A Companion to Lesbian, Gay, Bisexual, Transgender, and Queer Studies*, edited by George Haggerty and Molly McGarry. Oxford, UK: Blackwell.

———. 2004. "Friendship's Loss: Alan Bray's Making of History." *GLQ: A Journal of Lesbian and Gay Studies* 10(3): 339–65.

———. 2002. *The Renaissance of Lesbianism in Early Modern England*. Cambridge: Cambridge University Press.

Trumbach, Randolph. 1993. "London's Sapphists: From Three Sexes to Four Genders in the Making of Modern Culture." In *Third Sex, Third Gender: Beyond Sexual Dimorphism in Culture and History*, edited by Gilbert Herdt, 111–36. New York: Zone Books.

"Über Lesben gestolpert." 2008, May–June. *Emma*, 40–41.

Vance, Carole S. 1989. "Social Construction Theory: Problems in the History of Sexuality." In *Homosexuality, Which Homosexuality? International Conference on Gay and Lesbian Studies*, edited by Denis Altman, Carole Vance, Martha Vicinus, et al., 13–34. Amsterdam: Dekker/Schorer.

Van der Meer, Theo. 1991. "Tribades on Trial: Female Same-Sex Offenders in Late Eighteenth-Century Amsterdam." *Journal of the History of Sexuality* 1(3): 424–45.

Vanita, Ruth. 2005a. "Born of Two Vaginas: Love and Reproduction between Co-wives in Some Medieval Indian Texts." *GLQ: A Journal of Lesbian and Gay Studies* 11(4): 547–77.

———. 2005b. *Love's Rite: Same-Sex Marriage in India and the West*. New York: Palgrave Macmillan.

———. 2004a. "CLAGS Reports." *Center for Lesbian and Gay Studies News* 14(2): 14.

———. 2004b. "'Married among Their Companions': Female Homoerotic Relations in Nineteenth-Century Urdu *Rekhti* Poetry in India." *Journal of Women's History* 16(1): 12–53.

———, ed. 2002. *Queering India: Same-Sex Love and Eroticism in Indian Culture and Society.* New York: Routledge.

———. 2001. "'At All Times Near': Love between Women in Two Medieval Indian Devotional Texts." In *Same Sex Love and Desire among Women in the Middle Ages*, edited by Francesca Canadé Sautman and Pamela Sheingorn, 233–50. New York: Palgrave.

———. 1996. *Sappho and the Virgin Mary: Same-Sex Love and the English Literary Imagination.* New York: Columbia University Press.

Vanita, Ruth, and Saleem Kidwai, eds. 2000. *Same-Sex Love in India: Readings from Literature and History.* New York: St. Martin's.

Van Over, Raymond. 1980. *Sun Songs: Creation Myths from Around the World.* New York: New American Library.

Vicinus, Martha. 2004. *Intimate Friends: Women Who Loved Women, 1778–1928.* Chicago: University of Chicago Press.

———. 1992. "'They Wonder to Which Sex I Belong': The Historical Roots of the Modern Lesbian Identity." *Feminist Studies* 18: 467–97.

———. 1984. "Distance and Desire: English Boarding-School Friendships." *Signs: Journal of Women in Culture and Society* 9: 600–622.

Vidal-Ortiz, Salvador. 2002. "Queering Sexuality and Doing Gender: Transgender Men's Identification with Gender and Sexuality." In *Gendered Sexualities*, edited by Patricia Gagné and Richard Tewksbury, 181–233. Amsterdam: JAI.

Vogel, Katharine. 1984. "Zum Selbstverständnis lesbischer Frauen in der Weimarer Republik." In *Eldorado: Homosexuelle Frauen und Männer in Berlin, 1850–1950*, 162–68. Berlin: Fröhlich & Kaufmann.

Wafer, Jim. 1997. "Muhammad and Male Homosexuality." In *Islamic Homosexualities: Culture, History, and Literature*, edited by Stephen O. Murray and Will Roscoe, 87–96. New York: New York University Press.

Waters, Sarah. 1998. *Tipping the Velvet.* New York: Riverhead Books.

Wawrytko, Sandra A. 1993. "Homosexuality and Chinese and Japanese Religions." In *Homosexuality and World Religions*, edited by Arlene Swidler, 199–230. Valley Forge, PA: Trinity.

Wekker, Gloria. 2006. *The Politics of Passion: Women's Sexual Culture in the Afro-Surinamese Diaspora.* New York: Columbia University Press.

———. 1999. "'What's Identity Got to Do with It?' Rethinking Identity in Light of the *Mati* Work in Suriname." In *Female Desires: Same-Sex Relations and Transgender Practices across Cultures*, edited by Evelyn Blackwood and Saskia E. Wieringa, 119–38. New York: Columbia University Press.

Westphal-Hellbusch, Sigrid. 1997. "Institutionalized Gender-Crossing in Southern Iraq." Translated by Bradley Rose. In *Islamic Homosexualities: Culture, History, and Literature*, edited by Stephen O. Murray and Will Roscoe, 233–43.
New York: New York University Press.

Whitaker, Brian. 2006. *Unspeakable Love: Gay and Lesbian Life in the Middle East*.
Berkeley: University of California Press.

Whitehead, Harriet. 1981. "The Bow and the Burden Strap: A New Look at Institutionalized Homosexuality in Native North America." In *Sexual Meanings:
The Cultural Construction of Gender and Sexuality*, edited by Sherry B. Ortner
and Harriet Whitehead, 80–115. Cambridge: Cambridge University Press.

Whitt, Jan. 2001. "A 'Labor from the Heart': Lesbian Magazines from 1947–
1994." *Journal of Lesbian Studies* 5(1–2): 229–50.

Whittier, Nancy. 1995. *Feminist Generations: The Persistence of the Radical Women's
Movement*. Philadelphia: Temple University Press.

Wickes, George. 1976. *The Amazon of Letters: The Life and Loves of Natalie Barney*. New York: Putnam's.

Wieringa, Saskia E. 2007. "Silence, Sin, and the System: Women's Same-Sex Practices in Japan." In *Women's Sexualities and Masculinities in a Globalizing Asia*,
edited by Saskia E. Wieringa, Evelyn Blackwood, and Abha Bhaiya, 23–45.
New York: Palgrave Macmillan.

———. 2005. "Women Marriages and Other Same-Sex Practices: Historical
Reflections on African Women's Same-Sex Relations." In *Tommy Boys, Lesbian
Men and Ancestral Wives: Female Same-Sex Practices in Africa*, edited by Ruth
Morgan and Saskia Wieringa, 281–307. Johannesburg: Jacana Media.

———. 1999. "Desiring Bodies or Defiant Cultures: Butch-Femme Lesbians
in Jakarta and Lima." In *Female Desires: Same-Sex Relations and Transgender
Practices across Cultures*, edited by Evelyn Blackwood and Saskia E. Wieringa,
206–31. New York: Columbia University Press.

Wieringa, Saskia E., and Evelyn Blackwood. 1999. Introduction to *Female Desires:
Same-Sex Relations and Transgender Practices across Cultures*, edited by Evelyn
Blackwood and Saskia E. Wieringa, 1–38. New York: Columbia University Press.

Wieringa, Saskia E., Evelyn Blackwood, and Abha Bhaiya, eds. 2007. *Women's
Sexualities and Masculinities in a Globalizing Asia*. New York: Palgrave
Macmillan.

Wiethaus, Ulrike. 2003. "Female Homoerotic Discourse and Religion in Medieval Germanic Culture." In *Gender and Difference in the Middle Ages*, edited by
Sharon Farmer and Carol Braun Pasternack, 288–321. Minneapolis: University of Minnesota Press.

Wijewardene, Shermal. 2007. "'But No One Has Explained to Me Who I Am
Now . . .': 'Trans' Self-Perceptions in Sri Lanka." In *Women's Sexualities and
Masculinities in a Globalizing Asia*, edited by Saskia E. Wieringa, Evelyn Black-
wood, and Abha Bhaiya, 101–16. New York: Palgrave.

Wilde, Lyn Webster. 1999. *On the Trail of the Women Warriors: The Amazons in Myth and History.* New York: St. Martin's.

Wilfong, Terry G. 2002. "'Friendship and Physical Desire': The Discourse of Female Homoeroticism in Fifth-Century CE Egypt." In *Among Women: From the Homosocial to the Homoerotic in the Ancient World*, edited by Nancy Sorkin Rabinowitz and Lisa Auanger, 304–29. Austin: University of Texas Press.

Wilhelm, Amara Das. 2007. "Tritiya-Prakriti: People of the Third Sex." Gay and Lesbian Vaishnava Association website, http://www.galva108.org/Tritiya_prakriti.html (accessed February 14, 2007).

Willett, Graham. 2000. *Living Out Loud: A History of Gay and Lesbian Activism in Australia.* St. Leonards: Allen & Unwin.

Williams, Walter L. 1986. *The Spirit and the Flesh: Sexual Diversity in American Indian Culture.* Boston: Beacon.

Winkler, John J. 1993. "Double Consciousness in Sappho's Lyrics." In *The Lesbian and Gay Studies Reader*, edited by Henry Abelove, Michèle Aina Barale, and David M. Halperin, 577–94. New York: Routledge.

Wu, Peichen. 2007. "Performing Gender along the Lesbian Continuum: The Politics of Sexual Identity in the Seitô Society." In *Women's Sexualities and Masculinities in a Globalizing Asia*, edited by Saskia E. Wieringa, Evelyn Blackwood, and Abha Bhaiya, 77–99. New York: Palgrave.

Zika, Charles. 2003. *Exorcising Our Demons: Magic, Witchcraft and Visual Culture in Early Modern Europe.* Leiden: Brill.

Zwilling, Leonard. 1992. "Homosexuality as Seen in Indian Buddhist Texts." In *Buddhism, Sexuality, and Gender*, edited by José Ignacio Cabezón, 203–14. Albany: State University of New York Press.

Index

Intersections:
Transdisciplinary Perspectives on Genders and Sexualities

GENERAL EDITORS: MICHAEL KIMMEL AND SUZANNA WALTERS

Sperm Counts: Overcome by Man's Most Precious Fluid
Lisa Jean Moore

Border Crossers: Mexican Immigrant Men and the Sexuality of Migration
Lionel Cantú, Jr.
Edited by Nancy A. Naples and Salvador Vidal-Ortiz

Moral Panics, Sex Panics: The Fear and the Fight over Sexual Rights
Edited by Gilbert Herdt

Out in the Country:
Youth, Media, and the Politics of Gay Visibility in Rural America
Mary L. Gray

Sapphistries: A Global History of Love between Women
Leila J. Rupp

About the Author

LEILA J. RUPP is Professor of Feminist Studies and Associate Dean of the Division of Social Sciences at the University of California, Santa Barbara. She is the author of *Mobilizing Women for War: German and American Propaganda, 1939–1945, Worlds of Women: The Making of an International Women's Movement,* and *A Desired Past: A Short History of Same-Sex Love in America*; and she is coauthor, with Verta Taylor, of *Survival in the Doldrums: The American Women's Rights Movement, 1945 to the 1960s* and *Drag Queens at the 801 Cabaret*. She is also coeditor of the seventh and eighth editions of *Feminist Frontiers*.